Markets for Federal Water

Subsidies, Property Rights, and the Bureau of Reclamation

Richard W. Wahl

Resources for the Future
Washington, D.C.

Printed in the United States of America

Published by Resources for the Future
1616 P Street, N.W., Washington, D.C. 20036

Books from Resources for the Future are distributed worldwide by The Johns Hopkins University Press.

Library of Congress Cataloging-in-Publication Data

Wahl, Richard W.
    Markets for federal water: subsidies, property rights, and the
Bureau of Reclamation / Richard W. Wahl.
        p.   cm.
    Bibliography: p.
    Includes index.
    ISBN 0-915707-48-9 (alk. paper)
    1. Water resources development—Government policy—West (U.S.)
2. Federal aid to water resources development—West (U.S.)
3. Irrigation—Government policy—West (U.S.)   4. Water transfer—
Government policy—West (U.S.)   5. Water rights—West (U.S.)
6. United States. Bureau of Reclamation.   I. Title.
HD1695.A17W34   1989
333.91′00973—dc20   89-32192
                                                                          CIP

This book is a product of the former Renewable Resources Division (now the Energy and Natural Resources Division) at Resources for the Future. The book was edited by Nancy A. Winchester and designed by Joan Engelhardt. The index was prepared by Margaret A. Lynch.

∞ The paper in this book meets the guidelines for permanence and durability of the Committee on Production Guidelines for Book Longevity of the Council on Library Resources.

Contents

List of Figures and Tables

Figures

Tables

Foreword

Lack of water was an obstacle to the initial settlement and development of the West. Rainfall was inadequate for dryland agriculture, and streamflows were erratic, providing little reliable flow in the absence of storage. By 1900 most of the West's easily irrigable lands were already developed, and even though development had focused on the most favorable sites, irrigation had been expensive and many irrigators and irrigation projects were hopelessly in debt. These conditions led many to conclude that greater federal support was needed to promote settlement of the West through irrigation. This support came initially through the Reclamation Act of 1902, which created the Reclamation Service—renamed the Bureau of Reclamation in 1923—to help family farms establish irrigation systems.

Today, nearly nine decades after passage of the original Reclamation Act, water scarcity remains a major obstacle to further development of the West. But, due in part to the efforts of the Bureau of Reclamation, current conditions are very different from those at the start of this century. About 40 million acres are now irrigated in the seventeen western states, with one-fourth of those acres receiving water from bureau projects. Irrigation accounts for nearly 80 percent of all freshwater withdrawn from western streams, lakes, and aquifers and for 90 percent of the region's consumptive use of water. All the good as well as many poor, dam and reservoir sites have already been developed, and the financial costs of developing new water supplies for offstream uses such as irrigation are high. Moreover, the environmental costs of building new dams and diverting more water are major obstacles to the construction of new water projects. Growing recognition of the high costs incurred as a result of decades of neglect of fish and wildlife habitat and other values of free-flowing streams is even raising concerns about water use on some of the bureau's existing projects. Large quantities of federally supplied water have been virtually locked in to relatively low-value uses with little, if any, incentive to conserve. Such projects increase the scarcity of water for other uses and can inhibit overall western development, which increasingly depends on the ability to reallocate supplies among competing uses in response to changing conditions.

The prospect of a second consecutive year of drought over much of the West (as well as some areas in the East) has helped focus public attention on the growing scarcity of western water and the anomaly of providing large quantities of highly subsidized irrigation water to farmers who may be growing surplus crops. The Bureau of Reclamation has become an agency under siege searching for a new direction to give it legitimacy under current conditions.

Markets for Federal Water: Subsidies, Property Rights, and the Bureau of Reclamation is an important and timely study that provides valuable insights into how the West might better manage and allocate its scarce water supplies and how the Bureau of Reclamation might once again play a constructive role in western development. Author Richard W. Wahl describes how the bureau developed from an agency initially intended to provide modest start-up subsidies for establishing small irrigated farms to one that is a lavish benefactor of some of the West's largest and wealthiest farms. More important, he offers timely suggestions for improving the efficiency of use of federally supplied water, and presents four case studies to illustrate the application and potential benefits of his proposals.

This book is enriched by Wahl's experiences and contacts over the past decade during which he has worked as an analyst focusing largely on water-related issues in the U.S. Department of the Interior's Office of Policy Analysis. This study reflects an insider's insights into the workings of the department and makes available for the first time data and information not previously published. Much of the writing of the book was done while Wahl was on leave from the department as a visiting fellow in the National Center for Food and Agricultural Policy at Resources for the Future.

The author has participated in government working groups charged with reviewing official policy positions on western water. He was a member of the working group that helped formulate *Water Efficiency: Opportunities for Action*, the 1987 report of the Western Governors' Association, which recommended measures to facilitate voluntary transfers of water. The Department of the Interior's official policy statement on water transfers (included as an appendix in this volume) released in December 1988 is a step in the direction Wahl advocates.

The efficient use and allocation of water and alternative means of meeting long-term water demands have been and continue to be an important area of interest at Resources for the Future. Richard Wahl's analysis of these issues in association with RFF predates his work here as a visiting fellow. With Robert K. Davis he coauthored a chapter, "Satisfying Southern California's Thirst for Water: Efficient Alternatives," in *Scarce Water and Institutional Change* (Kenneth D. Frederick, editor) published by RFF in 1986. *The Economic Value of Water* (1986) by Diana C. Gibbons and *Water for Western Agriculture* (1982), which I wrote with James C. Hanson, are other RFF publications that address some of these issues.

March 1989   KENNETH D. FREDERICK
                                    Senior Fellow
                                    Energy and Natural
                                        Resources Division
                                    Resources for the Future

Acknowledgments

Although it is impossible to trace all of the origins of one's efforts in putting together a book of this nature, I wish in particular to acknowledge the following contributions. The many hours spent discussing natural resources policy with Robert K. Davis, Robert H. Nelson, and Herbert H. Fullerton of the Office of Policy Analysis at the U.S. Department of the Interior were instrumental in developing my interest in the subject. Ideas on voluntary market transfers of water were further expanded through many meetings and conversations with Norman H. Starler and Kenneth G. Maxey of the Bureau of Reclamation, James J. Flannery of the Office of the Assistant Secretary for Land and Water Resources, and Richard R. Greenfield and Frank H. Osterhoudt of the Office of Policy Analysis.

Kenneth D. Frederick, director of the former Renewable Resources Division at Resources for the Future (RFF), encouraged me to produce a book manuscript on the subject. Richard L. Stroup, who was then director of the Office of Policy Analysis (on leave from Montana State University), also supported this idea. The National Center for Food and Agricultural Policy at RFF and its first director, Kenneth R. Farrell, made it possible for me to initiate this undertaking through the center's fellowship program, which was funded by the W. K. Kellogg Foundation. The Office of Policy Analysis granted me leave from the Department of the Interior to participate in the program. Special appreciation is also due Kenneth Frederick and John F. Ahearne, former vice president of RFF, for providing encouragement and assistance to continue the work under the auspices of RFF.

There are a number of individuals whose work at the Department of the Interior was worth including in the book. Some of their contributions are acknowledged at various points in the book, but the assistance of Kathleen Brennan and Benjamin M. Simon in calculating the irrigation subsidies (chapter 2), Diane M. Lim in compiling information on water rights on Bureau of Reclamation projects (chapter 6), and Richard C. Ready in analyzing the economic value of different Westlands settlement scenarios (appendix to chapter 4) merits special mention. Robert W. Johnson of the Bureau of Reclamation produced the paper on which chapter 8 is based (on the possibilities for voluntary market transfers of Central Arizona Project water) during his summer at the Office of Policy Analysis. Robert F. Stackhouse and Phillip T. Doe of the Bureau of Reclamation provided, respectively, information on water rates in the Central Valley Project and on acreage limitation. Appreciation is also due to the many employees of the Bureau of Reclamation whose efforts to improve the agency and to modernize its role have served to sharpen the views of the author and to strengthen the recommendations of this book.

I appreciate the comments of the anonymous reviewers, which did much to improve the presentation of material in the book, as well as the work of the editor, Nancy A. Winchester, and of managing editor Dorothy Sawicki and the publications staff at RFF.

Mary Ann Daly of the National Center for Food and Agricultural Policy, with assistance from Maybelle Frashure, always managed to type and revise sections of the original manuscript with remarkable speed and accuracy. Revisions for the final draft were produced by Anita Washington. Finally, I thank my wife, Claudia, who allowed me to divide our first conjugal years between attention to her and to the book.

RICHARD W. WAHL

Markets for Federal Water

With reference to irrigation, it is quite generally recognized that the cost has reached so high a level that the reclaimed land cannot compete for the settlers and that the settlers cannot repay the cost and compete with other farmers. The remedy proposed is not the obvious one of stopping reclamation until conditions are such that the lands can produce a return on the cost, or even of limiting it to lands that have peculiarly favorable conditions, either as to crops that can be grown or as to markets that render it capable of meeting competition. Rather it is proposed to subsidize irrigation reclamation to whatever extent may be necessary to enable the reclaimed lands to compete with other lands. That is the essence of the present Federal reclamation policy.

—*Ray P. Teele, 1927**

* Ray P. Teele, *The Economics of Land Reclamation in the United States* (New York, A.W. Shaw, 1927), pp. 54–55. Teele was a researcher employed by the U.S. Department of Agriculture and the Bureau of the Census.

Introduction

My purposes in writing this book were multiple, but related: to explore the origins of federal water development in the western United States; to summarize how the Bureau of Reclamation of the U.S. Department of the Interior arrived where it is today; and to describe why certain water subsidies were built into the program and how they have pyramided, leading to inefficient water use. One of the main arguments in the book is that federally subsidized water supplies have become property rights and that the most effective way to confront the issue of inefficient usage is to recognize those rights and to facilitate voluntary transfers of federally supplied water. In particular, the book contains recommendations for how Bureau of Reclamation policy and law could be modified to better define such rights in order to facilitate water transfers. Finally, it examines several cases where facilitating transfers might prove fruitful. In short, facilitating water trades is one major step that the Bureau of Reclamation can take to modernize its role.[1]

Part I: History and Evolution of Subsidies

The book begins with a discussion of the history of the reclamation movement before 1900. Chapters 1 and 2 examine the early debates over the proper federal role in developing irrigation in the western

---

[1] It should be noted that the conclusions and policy recommendations in this volume are those of the author and do not represent any official positions of the Department of the Interior.

United States. During much of the 1800s, federal construction of irrigation facilities was not regarded by Congress as a proper role of government. This attitude changed in the late nineteenth century, however, and the Bureau of Reclamation was founded in 1902 to construct irrigation facilities in the western states. Once the federal government provided subsidies to irrigation development, many opportunities arose to increase the level of subsidies through various means. This gave those farmers on project lands an advantage over private irrigation development. Although Congress sought to limit the amount of the subsidy accruing to any one individual receiving federally supplied water, it was difficult to impose effective limits.

Chapters 3 and 4 and the appendix to chapter 4 use contemporary cases to further illustrate the difficulty of administering the subsidy provisions of Reclamation law. Water rate-setting practices in the Central Valley Project in California, the implementation of provisions of the Reclamation Reform Act of 1982, and the settlement of financial terms stemming from a contract dispute with Westlands Water District are all examined in detail. These cases illustrate the importance of administrative practice, as well as legislation, in enlarging the amount of the reclamation subsidy (which now exceeds 85 percent of construction costs).

Part II: Policy Recommendations to Facilitate Water Marketing

The result of the substantial federal subsidies is that the low prices of federally supplied irrigation water do not reflect its true value. Thus, it is used inefficiently, for there is little incentive to conserve. While this inefficiency may not have posed a problem for the West during the early decades of this century, it has become increasingly serious because of the rising cost of new construction and because of the increasing competition for water for a variety of other uses—such as for growing urban populations and for recreation and wildlife.

Although raising the price of federal water has been suggested for many years as a means to promote efficient use, attempts to reduce the terms of the reclamation subsidy, such as the Reclamation Reform Act of 1982, have been largely unsuccessful. As the quotation at the beginning of this introduction suggests, these attempts have failed partly because they run counter to the long-standing trends of reclamation policy. The proposition put forth in part II of this book is that once water subsidies have been granted, they become, in effect, property rights of the beneficiaries. As such, they are vigorously defended by water users through efforts to influence Bureau of Reclamation policies, regulations, and contract terms, as well as through appeals to Congress.

This analysis leads to an alternative recommendation to promote more efficient use of federally supplied irrigation water. Rather than attempting to reduce the subsidies embodied in existing contracts, federal policymakers should seek to make the current property interests in federally supplied water more secure and to allow voluntary market trading of the resource among water users. Chapter 5 discusses several examples of trades of this type that have already taken place. However, bureau policy has generally not given the contracting entities sufficient control over their water to make transfers viable on a large scale.

Voluntary water transfers can take a variety of forms. In addition to permanent sales, they may be long-term leases, short-term leases, or leases contingent on drought conditions. They may be leases of contractual deliveries of Bureau of Reclamation water, rather than sales of actual water rights. In order to benefit the broadest possible segments of the public, voluntary transactions should be allowed both among contractors within federal projects and with water users outside of such projects. Chapter 6 explores provisions in Bureau of Reclamation policy, contracts, and law that must be complied with to implement market transfers of water. It also recommends changes in federal policy in these same three categories in order to more readily facilitate such transactions.

Part III: Case Studies of Potential Water Transfers

This section of the book examines four cases where voluntary water transfers might prove fruitful: (1) within California for those farmers in the Central Valley Project who are suffering from severe agricultural drainage problems, (2) within the Central Arizona Project, (3) in the Colorado River Basin for the federal resources utilized in operating the Yuma desalting plant, and (4) in interstate trading of water along the Colorado River. In each case, the economics of trading possibilities are examined in the context of the historical background of the project, as well as Bureau of Reclamation policies and legislation that would affect water trades.

Of these four future trading possibilities, interstate marketing would probably be the most difficult to implement and the longest in coming to fruition because states are accustomed to defending their allocations under the Colorado River Compact for in-state use. Indeed, the reader should not expect all of the potential trades discussed in this book to materialize: each depends on the willingness of existing water users to initiate or engage in the transactions. Rather, the purpose of these detailed examinations of possible transactions is to reach a better understanding of how reclamation policy would apply to these particular situations and to other trading possibilities as well. It is the detailed working out of arrangements best understood at the local and state levels that is the prime motivation for water transfer agreements.

Guidance to the Reader

This book is intended for a wide range of readers interested in water resources in the western United States. It is organized to permit selective reading and to highlight those sections containing specific recommendations. Therefore, readers who are most interested in the potential for water transfers may choose to skim the historical material in part I and go on to part II. Chapter 6 contains the major policy recommendations made in the book. They are in three categories: suggested changes in reclamation policy, contracts, and law. Additional recommendations for facilitating water transfers in some specific Bureau of Reclamation projects are found in each chapter in part III.

Of course, policy recommendations are often more effective if they take into account long-standing attitudes and expectations. The historical material in part I offers insight into why the recommendations were made and describes how existing subsidized water supplies have come to be de facto property rights. This attitude is held not only by water users but also by Congress and by the Bureau of Reclamation itself. The way in which the agency administers its water supply contracts provides ample evidence of this point. One interesting case is the settling of a water rate dispute with the largest reclamation district, Westlands Water District. This material is placed in the appendix to chapter 4 because it illustrates the main conclusion of chapter 4—that once subsidies are granted, they are extremely difficult to regulate or modify. Although the material in this appendix is not essential to an understanding of the main topics of the book, it will be of interest to anyone wanting to know how policies come to be administered to the advantage of water users.

Citations to U.S. statutes are provided for the major pieces of Reclamation law discussed in the text; the U.S. Code is also cited frequently. A three-volume set entitled *Federal Reclamation and Related Laws Annotated* (U.S. Department of the Interior, Office of the Solicitor, 1972) is a useful reference for Reclamation law through 1966.[2] The annotations include interpretations of the law made through various opinions of the department's solicitor. (The solicitor's

---

[2] A fourth volume continuing after 1966 is being prepared.

opinions are published in the *Decisions of the United States Department of the Interior* volumes.)

Recent Developments

This manuscript was begun in the fall of 1985, and a first draft was completed early in 1987. Of course, each year brings changes in Bureau of Reclamation policy and the status of Bureau of Reclamation projects (particularly those under construction), as well as in general economic conditions that bear on the analysis of the costs of projects in constant dollars. The year 1986 is used as a base year for all data and project developments unless otherwise noted. Where developments after 1986 are especially important or are crucial to an understanding of the subject, the material has been updated.

During the time that this manuscript was being prepared, the Western Governors' Association initiated a study of water efficiency (Western Governors' Association, 1986). Its report, *Western Water: Tuning the System,* focused on changes in state and federal policy and law that would facilitate voluntary transfers of water. On July 8, 1986, the association adopted a resolution summarizing the principal conclusions of its report. Among the recommendations for measures to be taken at the state level to improve water efficiency was the following:

> to facilitate voluntary transfers of rights to use water through state water banks, authorization to water districts to transfer water outside their boundaries, and other initiatives designed to facilitate market transactions in water.

The resolution further recommended that

> The [Western Governors' Association] . . . initiate a working group to include representatives of the Western Governors' Association, the Western States Water Council, and Department of the Interior to consult widely with western water interests to identify steps to facilitate voluntary water transfers and other needed changes and to develop recommendations for changes in law and practices at the federal, state, and local levels.

The working group was formed and produced a follow-on report, *Water Efficiency: Opportunities for Action* (Western Governors' Association, 1987). This report was adopted by the governors at their July 1987 meeting. It called for the Department of the Interior

> to develop and issue a policy statement facilitating voluntary transfers which involve water and/or facilities provided by the Bureau of Reclamation; to review other steps which it can take administratively to facilitate or remove impediments to transfers, conservation and salvage, and other means to enhance efficiency; and to prepare suggested

amendments to Reclamation law in order to resolve legal uncertainties that unnecessarily cloud certain voluntary water transfers. (p. v)

In recent years the Bureau of Reclamation has done some soul-searching, examining its past mission and current skills in relation to what more viable roles it could play today. This culminated with the publication of its *Assessment '87* report, which is an attempt to define for itself a redirected mission (U.S. Department of the Interior, Bureau of Reclamation, 1987). The thrust of this report is captured in the following excerpt from its findings and conclusions:

> The Bureau's primary role as the developer of large federally financed agricultural projects is drawing to a close. . . . The Bureau of Reclamation must change from an agency based on federally supported construction to one based on resource management. (p. 1)

Many of the recommendations in *Assessment '87* focus on various ways to facilitate more efficient management of the bureau's existing facilities and water supplies. Among the recommendations for new issues to be addressed by the bureau is the consideration of its role in facilitating voluntary water transfers. On December 16, 1988, the Department of the Interior took a major step in defining the Bureau of Reclamation's role in this area. In response to the July 1987 request of the Western Governors' Association, the department issued a set of principles designed to govern Bureau of Reclamation review of requests to transfer water. These principles, which are intended to define the department's administrative policies on water transfers within the provisions of existing law, indicate that the bureau will seek to facilitate transfer requests brought to it, provided the transfers do not injure third parties. The policy will allow water users to receive additional income from water transfers, provided federal contractual and legal commitments are fulfilled. (The full set of principles is reproduced as the appendix to this volume.)

Defining its role in the transfer process and implementing water transfers could well be one of the most important tasks confronting the Bureau of Reclamation over the years to come.

References

U.S. Department of the Interior, Bureau of Reclamation. 1987. *Assessment '87: A New Direction for the Bureau of Reclamation* (Washington, D.C.).

U.S. Department of the Interior, Office of the Solicitor. 1972. *Federal Reclamation and Related Laws Annotated* (Washington, D.C., Government Printing Office).

Western Governors' Association. 1986. *Western Water: Tuning the System* (Denver, Colo.).

_____. 1987. *Water Efficiency: Opportunities for Action.* (Denver, Colo.).

Part I

History and Evolution of Subsidies

1

History of Federal Involvement in the Reclamation Movement

Imagine what it would have been like to be an early explorer of the Colorado River region, such as John Wesley Powell. Observing the vast spaces, the deserts, and the river cutting its way from the Rocky Mountains to the Gulf of California, what visions might you have had of its future development? How would your visions compare with those of the one-armed major who guided his wooden dory through the rapids of the inner gorge of the Grand Canyon? How would they compare with the way the land and water resources in this region are used today?

Would you envision agricultural development only within the confines of the flat grassy valleys along the Colorado River and its tributaries? Or would you picture the water supply as sufficient to be diverted on a scale vast enough to make the deserts bloom? Would you want the federal government to steer this development, or would you trust the more haphazard and piecemeal results of leaving development to local and private interests? If you perceived a federal role, would it be limited to providing information on settlement opportunities or would it extend to providing loans, grants, and even construction of irrigation works? These are the questions that became central to the early debates over "reclamation" of the arid West.

Powell's expeditions and surveys, which began in 1867 and continued with his trips down the Colorado River in 1869 and 1871, motivated him to think about a plan for the western lands. His *Report on the Lands of the Arid Region of the United States,* published in 1879, embodies a set of proposals regarding irrigation. Powell's own views on these subjects changed somewhat over his lifetime, but he consistently emphasized several central points. For instance, he defined the arid West as that land receiving less than 20 inches of rainfall per year, which corresponds roughly to the lands west of the hundredth meridian (except for the areas of the Northwest with heavy rainfall). Most of this land, unlike the lands in the "subhumid" areas farther east, would need some form of irrigation to sustain settlement. Powell's scientific background allowed him and his associates to estimate river flows and to compute that, even if canals were put in place to divert and distribute the region's water, the acreage irrigated could be only a small portion of the vast space available (about 2.8 percent in Utah, for example).

From this, Powell reasoned that it was important that only the best areas be irrigated: those nearest streams, with the best soil conditions and to which water could most easily be diverted. Lands somewhat farther away should be reserved for pastureland (Powell envisioned settlements that combined irrigation and grazing). The boundaries of farm homesteads should be established not by rectilinear section lines, but in accord with the topography, so that each homestead had land fronting on the river as well as pastureland (Powell, [1879] 1962, pp. 34–36).

Powell did not believe that the selection of land for these purposes was best left to the early settlers. He believed that reservoirs on the larger streams would be advisable and was concerned that settlers would use so much land along smaller tributary streams that the acreage left to be served by the larger reservoirs would be insufficient to allow the reservoirs to pay for themselves. To ensure orderly settlement and to maximize the amount of land that could be irrigated, Powell believed that a government-sponsored survey should be launched to identify the lands capable of sustaining irrigation and to identify and retain the best reservoir sites in federal ownership. Powell's plan, typical of its time, reflected the Progressive faith in government action. In other words, Powell did not trust private development to identify the most desirable lands for irrigation and to develop them efficiently. He also feared that under private development monopoly interests would capture control of streams.

Powell believed that individual farmers would not be capable of constructing the larger reservoirs he envisioned: "Small streams can be taken out and distributed by individual enterprise, but cooperative labor or aggregated capital must be employed in taking out the larger streams" (Powell, [1879] 1962, p. 21). But he did not advocate federal construction of reservoirs (also see Davison, 1979, pp. 120–124; Stegner, 1982, pp. 350, 357, 366):

> A thousand millions of money must be used; who shall furnish it? Great and many industries are to be established; who shall control them?

Millions of men are to labor; who shall employ them? This is a great nation, the Government is powerful; shall it engage in this work? So dreamers may dream, and so ambition may dictate, but in the name of the men who labor I demand that the laborers shall employ themselves; that the enterprise shall be controlled by the men who have the genius to organize, and whose homes are in the lands developed, and that the money shall be furnished by the people; and I say to the Government: Hands off! Furnish the people with institutions of justice, and let them do the work for themselves. (Powell, [1879] 1962, p. 23)

On the basis of these views and his considerable experience with western land surveys, Powell eventually obtained federal authorization for an irrigation survey. But as we shall see, his success ultimately led to the undoing of many of his ideas.

Early Controversy Surrounding the Federal Government's Role in Irrigation Development

John Wesley Powell was involved in one of four general surveys of the western lands; the others were led by Clarence King, Frank Hayden, and George Wheeler. In 1880 Congress consolidated the four surveys into the U.S. Geological Survey, and Clarence King was appointed director. Powell became director of the Bureau of Ethnology at the Smithsonian Institution and then succeeded King as director of the U.S. Geological Survey in 1881. In this latter role, he managed to increase the budget for the western surveys, but the surveys came under increasing attack from Congress. In 1886 Congress held hearings on the proper role of government in the development of western lands, at which Powell emphasized the importance of surveys—especially topographic mapping—for irrigation. Criticism surfaced of even this limited government role. For example, Representative Hilary Herbert of Alabama insisted that "interested individuals and corporations" could undertake such surveys where they were needed (see Davison, 1979, p. 60; Stegner, 1982, pp. 290–292).

In fact, much of the settlement of the West was accomplished by private action. (Table 1-1 lists dates related to the history of the reclamation movement.) Even many of the principal irrigation developments were founded not by federal action, but by religious groups or other associations. For example, when the first group of Mormons arrived at Salt Lake Valley, Utah, in July 1847, they immediately set about diverting water to irrigation ditches and planting potatoes; by 1848 they had 5,000 acres of crops under irrigation (Golzé, 1952, p. 6).

Other western settlements that depended on irrigated farming, although not founded by an established religious institution, resulted

Table 1-1. Events Related to the Reclamation Movement, 1847 to 1902

1847	Mormons settle at Salt Lake City, Utah.
1870	The Union Colony of Colorado (the "Greeley Colony") is established.
1877	Desert Lands Act grants title to 640 acres of land (amended to 320 acres after 1890), provided that water is diverted to the land and the land is reclaimed.
1879	John Wesley Powell's *Report on the Lands of the Arid Region of the United States* is published.
1888	Congress appropriates funds for survey of lands to be reserved for reservoirs and withdrawal of potentially irrigable lands.
1890	Congress repeals withdrawal of potentially irrigable lands.
	William E. Smythe founds *Irrigation Age*.
1891	First Irrigation Congress, Salt Lake City, Utah, is held.[a]
1894	Carey Act grants each state up to 1 million acres of federal land in return for arranging for irrigation of the land.
	John Wesley Powell resigns as director of the U.S. Geological Survey.
1897	Captain Hiram Chittenden (U.S. Army Corps of Engineers) advocates federal construction of dams.
1901	Senator Francis G. Newlands introduces a reclamation bill.
1902	Theodore Roosevelt advocates federal reclamation in address to Congress.
	Reclamation Act becomes law.
	Frederick H. Newell is appointed first director of the Reclamation Service.

[a]Several subsequent irrigation congresses were held: 1893 (Los Angeles, Calif.), 1894 (Denver, Colo.), 1895 (Albuquerque, N. Mex.), 1896 (Phoenix, Ariz.), 1897 (Lincoln, Nebr.), and 1898 (Cheyenne, Wyo.).

from a missionary zeal on the part of interested backers. In 1868 Nathan Cook Meeker, an agricultural editor for the *New York Tribune* who had written some articles on the Oneida community, was sent by Horace Greeley to Utah to study the Mormon settlements. Blocked by heavy snows, Meeker journeyed only as far as Wyoming, and then went south to Colorado. During the summer of 1869, Greeley visited him in Colorado and was favorably impressed with the land's possibilities. On December 14, 1869, the *Tribune* published a proposal for establishing the Union Colony on the Cache La Poudre River north of Denver and solicited settlers (see Golzé, 1952, p. 10, and Davison, 1979, pp. 136–138). Enough responded that the settlement was established during the winter of 1870–1871 and became known as the Greeley Colony. Colonies were also established in California: the Anaheim Colony was founded by Germans from San Francisco, and the Riverside Colony was founded in 1871 as a cooperative venture. All of these settlements were successful enough to lead to permanent communities.

These were private efforts, and Congress saw no need for a public role in the irrigation development of the West during most of the

1800s. The first major federal action related to irrigation development in the western states occurred in 1877 and defined only a
limited federal role. In that year, the Desert Lands Act passed, which
granted title to 640 acres of land (reduced to 320 acres by an 1890
amendment) at $0.25 per acre (plus a $1.00 filing fee per tract),
provided that the settler diverted water to and reclaimed the land
within three years. Subsequently the land could be patented at $3.00
per acre.

Further federal direction of irrigation settlement occurred when
Powell's requests for federal surveys to identify irrigable lands eventually found support in Congress. In 1888 Senator William Stewart of
Nevada introduced a bill that provided $100,000 to the U.S. Geologi-
cal Survey for identifying "lands to be reserved for reservoirs." Some
140 reservoir sites were examined between 1888 and 1900, and 10
projects were estimated in detail (Golzé, 1952, pp. 21–23). Stewart
was concerned that speculators would purchase blocks of land to be
irrigated and monopolize their resale.[1] The bill also called for with-
drawing from homesteading the potentially irrigable lands connected with these reservoirs so that the reservoirs could be properly
designed, situated, and constructed. Although Powell did not originally advocate this latter provision, he did not vigorously oppose it,
probably because of his own disapproval of the practices of irrigation
companies, many of which lured settlers to their lands by advertising
but then failed to follow through on their claims.

As Powell's survey work progressed, he saw the result of the federal
withdrawal provision: settlers were beginning to occupy the lands
immediately adjacent to the lands withdrawn and to divert water to
these lands. This was contrary to his own plans under which the
irrigated lands would be nearest the river and the adjacent lands
would be used for pasture. It became clear to him that the actual
pattern of development occurring under federal withdrawals was
even worse than before the withdrawals. However, rather than aban-
doning his plans, he advocated more government management of
settlement, not less: Powell increased the size of the withdrawals of
irrigable lands.

Because Powell's irrigation survey was only partially complete,
settlers seeking to establish homesteads were confused about precisely which lands were, or would be, withdrawn. To make matters
worse, in 1889 the U.S. attorney general ruled that not only were

---

[1] This concern over how to prevent monopolization of benefits provided at government expense has been a continuing problem for the reclamation program, as wit-
nessed by the acreage limitation provisions of the Reclamation Act of 1902 and the
Reclamation Reform Act of 1982 (see chapter 4 in this volume).

those who settled on lands after they were surveyed and withdrawn not entitled to their lands, but also that any post-1888 homestead could be invalidated if Powell's survey subsequently indicated that the land should be withdrawn. As a result, early in 1890 the Land Office officially closed to entry nearly the entire public domain (see Golzé, 1952, pp. 21–22; Davison, 1979, pp. 92–95; Hibbard, 1924, pp. 430–431; Stegner in Powell, 1962, p. xxi; and Stegner, 1982, pp. 317–319), about 800 million acres (U.S. Department of Commerce, 1977, table 364, p. 225). With this ruling, Powell's survey was placed directly in the path of western settlement. The ensuing public uproar led to a series of congressional hearings, chaired by Senator Stewart of Nevada and held in the Midwest. As a result of these hearings, Congress in 1890 repealed the withdrawal of irrigable lands from entry but retained withdrawals of potential reservoir sites. This vote virtually ended Powell's hopes for imposing a federal plan of irrigation development on western settlement.

The hearings provided an early opportunity for the public to relay its views on western development directly to Congress and to press for federal assistance, yet the committee report concluded that no federal action was warranted beyond surveys for reservoir sites. In fact, the period from 1880 to 1890 had been something of a boom in private irrigation settlement. Companies sold stocks and bonds to finance projects in many parts of the West and lured settlers with pamphlets painting a rosy picture of farm life (Golzé, 1952, p. 11). The railroad companies also advertised to encourage western settlement (Robbins, 1976, pp. 326–327). However, dams and reservoirs were sometimes poorly built and failed to deliver the expected amount of water (there were, in fact, very few stream gauges in existence at this time that could have been used to more carefully plan water storage facilities). In some cases, settlers were enticed onto lands with heavy alkali concentrations, poor drainage, and short growing seasons (Robinson, 1979, p. 9).

Needless to say, a number of private ventures with weak foundations were overtaken by the vagaries of weather and climate and simply faded out of existence. One commentator sums up the situation as follows (Robinson, 1979):

> Irrigation companies were hastily formed. Many of the large canal projects were undertaken by promoters who obtained money from eastern investors. The basis for their operation was usually a preliminary survey and a claim to the water of a stream under the appropriation doctrine. Surveys were inadequately funded and there was little interest in accuracy since someone else's money was often at risk. In nearly every instance, engineers were pressured to reduce cost estimates so as

to encourage the sale of shares. Thus, in many cases projects began without sufficient capital, work was suspended before water was furnished, and the hopes and dreams of settlers depending on canals to mature crops were dashed. (p. 10)

Particularly devastating were the crop failures of the 1880s caused by low rainfall (see Robbins, 1976, p. 328). Nevertheless, a significant amount of acreage was successfully placed under irrigation. In fact, by 1890 the demand for information on irrigation development was sufficiently important that statistics were included in the census. As table 1-2 shows, 3.6 million acres were being irrigated in the seventeen western states in 1890 and double that by 1900.

It was, in fact, not from a ground swell of popular sentiment by western settlers but from a small number of irrigation enthusiasts, some of them almost fanatic, that the call for more extensive federal involvement in irrigation originated. Foremost among them was William E. Smythe, a staff member on the *Omaha Bee*. Undoubtedly influenced by the early irrigation settlements of the Mormons and the Greeley Colony, Smythe saw in the development of western irrigation

Table 1-2. Land Irrigated by Bureau of Reclamation Projects in the Seventeen Western States

(thousands of acres)

Year	Total acres irrigated	Number of acres irrigated by Bureau of Reclamation	Percent of acres irrigated by Bureau of Reclamation
1890	3,631	[a]	[a]
1900	7,528	[a]	[a]
1910	14,025	473	3.4
1920	18,593	2,205	11.9
1930	18,945	2,791	14.7
1940	20,395	3,391	16.6
1949	24,261	5,077[b]	20.9
1959	30,741	6,803	22.1
1969	34,804	8,576	24.6
1978	43,627	9,576	21.9

Sources: Total acreage irrigated for the years 1890 through 1940 is from Alfred R. Golzé, *Reclamation in the United States* (New York, McGraw-Hill, 1952), p. 14. Total irrigated acreage for subsequent years is from U.S. Department of Agriculture, *Agricultural Statistics* (Washington, D.C., 1983), table 553, p. 385. Acreage irrigated by the Bureau of Reclamation is from records of Contracts and Repayments Branch, Bureau of Reclamation, U.S. Department of the Interior, Washington, D.C.

[a]The Bureau of Reclamation program was established in 1902.

[b]For 1950.

settlements the possibility for bringing about a harmonious new society. He founded the *Irrigation Age* in 1890 and wrote of "the cross of a new Crusade," advocating a social revolution to be brought about by the development of small family farms (Davison, 1979, p. 139):

> No consideration of the subject can be appreciative when it starts with the narrow view that irrigation is merely an adjunct to agriculture. It is a social and industrial factor in a much broader sense. It not only makes it possible for a civilization to rise and flourish in the midst of desolate wastes; it shapes and colors that civilization after its own peculiar design. It is not merely the lifeblood of the field, but the source of institutions. . . . The essence of the industrial life which springs from irrigation is its democracy. (Smythe as quoted in Davison, 1979, p. 143)

The views of irrigation enthusiasts were also promoted through a series of irrigation congresses starting in 1891 (see table 1-1), conferences that attracted a number of western political leaders. It is notable that a major confrontation occurred at the International Irrigation Congress in 1893 between John Wesley Powell and the enthusiastic promoters of irrigation. In a speech delivered at the congress, Frederick H. Newell, who was an assistant to Powell at the U.S. Geological Survey, stated that the problems of irrigation in the western states stemmed from irrigation being overbuilt. Powell, in another speech, reiterated his scientific findings that water in western streams was insufficient for widespread development and that only a small percentage of the land could be irrigated. He acknowledged that his own plans to reserve certain lands for later irrigation settlement had failed.

Powell's cautious words were not popular and led to a barrage of criticism, and, in 1894, he resigned his office as director of the U.S. Geological Survey. To understand this criticism, one must appreciate the degree of enthusiasm for irrigation development at the time. Not only was there a widespread belief that a significant amount of the American desert could be "made to bloom," but other, more impossible views were put forth: that irrigation would reduce the hot winds of the desert, that irrigation of the western lands would make the climate itself less arid and would increase precipitation, and that irrigation would lead to a significant rise in the water tables of western lands on a wide scale (with a corresponding decrease in the well depth necessary to reach groundwater) (see Davison, 1979, pp. 167–175; Stegner, 1982, pp. 237–238, 298).

The various irrigation congresses and the writings of Smythe and other popularizers of irrigation did much to focus public and congressional attention on irrigation settlement. During this period, Senator Joseph M. Carey of Wyoming, chairman of the Senate Committee on Public Lands, introduced legislation to grant public lands to states to encourage irrigation development. The Carey Act of 1894 granted each state up to 1 million acres of federal land provided that the state arrange for its irrigation. States were to contract with private parties to construct irrigation works. In turn, these private firms would profit from the sale of water to settlers. However, few states took advantage of the Carey Act, possibly because many of the most favorable lands were already being settled. As of 1902, only Wyoming had gained title to lands under the act (11,321 acres), although six other states had taken some preliminary steps in this direction (Davison, 1979, p. 204; see also Golzé, 1952, pp. 16–19).

The Carey Act prompted further debate over the appropriate federal role in irrigation development. Representative Omer M. Kem of Nebraska supported federal construction of irrigation works, stating that they would "be self-supporting and not cost the government one cent" (Davison, 1979, p. 199). Senator Francis G. Newlands of Nevada expressed his view that the federal government should become involved in irrigation development. However, states near the West feared the competition from agricultural production that federal assistance would bring.

At the Irrigation Congress in Phoenix in 1896, George H. Maxwell of California opposed further grants of public land to the states for the purposes of fostering irrigation. Instead he advocated a federal irrigation policy and three years later established the National Irrigation Association to promote federal irrigation legislation (Robbins, 1976, p. 330). One further step toward federal construction of reservoir facilities was the publication in 1897 of a report by Captain Hiram Chittenden of the U.S. Army Corps of Engineers (see Robinson, 1979, p. 14). This report, spurred by Wyoming Senator Francis Warren's advocacy of federal appropriations for storage reservoirs, focused on sites for reservoirs for flood-control purposes in Wyoming and Colorado. The report also advocated federal construction and operation of reservoirs for irrigation purposes. In 1900, both the Republican and Democratic platforms favored federal assistance for irrigation (Robbins, 1976, p. 330).

Direct Federal Involvement—The Reclamation Act of 1902

In 1901 Senator Newlands introduced the first legislation providing for government construction of irrigation works. During the hearings on the bill, Frederick Newell, who was by that time the chief hydrologist at the U.S. Geological Survey and later named the first director of the Reclamation Service, testified that if 1 million acres of land were to receive surface irrigation water, another 2 million acres could be irrigated from groundwater pumped from wells and from seepage from irrigation canals and reservoirs. Newell further recommended that the government provide surface water for irrigation to 25 million acres in the West and that individuals and private corporations develop another 50 million acres. Newell also introduced the idea of using revenues from the sale of public lands to finance government construction. Others to testify in favor of government construction of projects included Dr. Elwood Mead, an expert on irrigation in the U.S. Department of Agriculture (later to become a commissioner of the Bureau of Reclamation) and George Maxwell, chairman of the executive committee of the National Irrigation Association.

The bill faced considerable opposition, though (see Golzé 1952, p. 25). Some argued that direct government construction of irrigation works was simply unconstitutional. Others argued that the bill would use public moneys belonging to all the people to benefit only a small section of the country and that it would lead to unfair competition among agricultural producers. (One counter to the argument that the Newlands bill would favor one section of the country was passage of the River and Harbor Act in 1899, which provided for federal construction favorable to the East and Midwest.) The debate pointed out that the bill provided for neither charging of interest on the federal expenditures nor a proper accounting of revenues and did not protect existing water rights.

Although the Newlands bill was not passed, it marked a major turning point in congressional views of the appropriate federal role in irrigation development. Among the factors accounting for the transition were the public enthusiasm for irrigation settlement and the general disappointment with the pace of settlement ensuing from the earlier Powell irrigation surveys and the Carey Act. In addition, the argument that the job was too large and too risky for individuals and cooperatives to undertake was gaining popularity. Nature had provided its own dramatic evidence for this view when, in 1891, the Colorado River changed its course and flooded the Imperial Valley in California. There was strong sentiment that major rivers needed to be controlled, but that on the scale necessary the job was beyond the means of individual irrigation companies.

It was Theodore Roosevelt who provided the decisive step in direct federal development of irrigation works. Although he was from the East, he had traveled in the West. When he came to Washington in the fall of 1901, he asked Gifford Pinchot and Newell to prepare portions of his first message to Congress (Robinson, 1979, p. 16). In his address, he advocated federal programs related to forestry and to water development. In particular he called for the federal construction of reservoirs and conveyance of water to provide lands for settlement:

> The forests alone cannot, however, fully regulate and conserve the water of the arid region. Great storage works are necessary to equalize the flow of streams and to save the flood waters. Their construction has been conclusively shown to be an undertaking too vast for private effort. Nor can it be best accomplished by the individual States acting alone.
>
> The Government should construct and maintain these reservoirs as it does other public works.
>
> The lands reclaimed by them should be reserved by the Government for actual settlers, and the cost of construction should so far as possible be repaid by the land reclaimed. (*Congressional Record,* 1901, p. 86)

With this lead from the executive branch, Senator Newlands introduced a modification of his bill, and many of the previous arguments extolling the benefits of irrigation settlements were revived:

> I believe the passage of this bill is in the interest of the man who earns his daily bread by his daily toil. It gives him a place where he can go and be free and independent; it gives him an opportunity to be an owner of the soil and to build a home. (Representative Oscar W. Underwood of Alabama in *Congressional Record,* 1902, p. 6672)

The principal backers of the irrigation movement at the time, including Maxwell and Mead, again rallied behind the bill.

The Newlands bill, called the Reclamation Act, passed in 1902 (32 Stat. 388; 43 U.S.C. 391). It established the Reclamation Fund from the sale of public land, the moneys of which were to be used for surveying, constructing, and maintaining irrigation works in the western states for delivering water both to land homesteaded from the public domain and to privately owned land. The fund was to operate as a revolving fund, with settlers making repayment, without interest, over a ten-year period. The act preserved the concept that the Secretary of the Interior could reserve from entry lands required for irrigation works. It further provided that the title to irrigation works would remain with the federal government even after project payments were made, until otherwise provided by Congress. It contained acreage limitation and residency provisions designed to prevent speculation in the land and monopolization of the water supply. Lands from the public domain that were provided irrigation water were to be settled under the homesteading laws in tracts of at least 40 but not more than 160 acres, in a size "reasonably required for the support of a family upon the lands." Privately developed land supplied with irrigation water from a federal project was subject to similar requirements: the landowner had to live on or "in the neighborhood of such land," and no individual landowner could receive water on more than 160 acres. The act also specified that water rights obtained for federal projects were not to interfere with state laws regarding the appropriation of water.

The Reclamation Act did not pass without opposition, mainly because, like the Newlands bill a year earlier, it was viewed as benefiting only a small portion of the population and promoting unfair competition in terms of crop production (see Hibbard, 1924, pp. 441–442; Robbins, 1976, p. 331). Senator Franklin Mondell of Wyoming countered that no cotton and little corn were grown on irrigated lands in the West or ever would be (Davison, 1979, p. 258).[2] There was also much concern that the principal beneficiaries of the bill would be western land speculators and railroad lines that had received land grants:

> This bill is the most insolent and impudent attempt at larceny that I have ever seen embodied in a legislative proposition. . . . They ask us . . . to give away an empire in order that their private property may be made valuable. (Representative William Hepburn of Iowa, *Congressional Record,* 1902, p. 6747)

> No wonder that these great railroad lines are here in mighty force to carry this measure through, for millions of acres of this land are still owned by the railroad companies. . . . And now they come and say, "You have given us this land; you have given us this subsidy of money; now put four, five, or six times the value into that land by taxing the people . . . ." (Representative Thomas Grosvenor of New York, *Congressional Record,* 1902, p. 6723)

The bill's promoters believed that the residency and acreage limitation provisions of the bill would prevent abuses. In the words of Senator Newlands,

> The purpose was to present a comprehensive plan . . . which would preserve this vast domain for home builders, and save it from concentrated monopolistic holding. We all wanted to preserve that domain in small tracts for actual settlers and home builders. We all wanted to prevent monopoly and concentration of ownership. (*Congressional Record,* 1902, pp. 6673–6674)

However, as the subsequent history of the reclamation program shows, it would prove much more problematic to enforce this vision of the program than these framers of the act foresaw (see chapter 4).

---

[2] Significant quantities of these crops have subsequently been grown on reclamation project lands.

Acreage Served by the Reclamation Program

The newly created Reclamation Service was placed under the U.S. Geological Survey and lost no time in proposing irrigation developments. Using the previous surveys of potential reservoir sites initiated by Powell, the service authorized four projects its first year and an additional sixteen by the end of 1905. Table 1-2 shows the total irrigated acreage in the seventeen western states for each decade starting with 1890, along with the acreage served by federal water supplies. As the table indicates, there were about 13.5 million acres of private irrigation development in 1910, the first year that information regarding federally supplied water was provided by the census. The percentage of irrigated acreage in the West that received some water from the Bureau of Reclamation rose to 21 percent of the total acreage in the West by 1949 and has remained approximately the same since that time. In 1978 the Bureau of Reclamation supplied irrigation water to about 9.6 million acres out of a total of 43.6 million irrigated acres in the seventeen western states. Not all of this is a "full" irrigation supply; much is in the form of a "supplemental" supply designed to augment local sources developed by irrigation districts or by individuals.

Table 1-3 shows the distribution of irrigated acreage among the seventeen western states in 1977 and indicates whether that acreage received a full irrigation supply from the bureau, a supplemental supply, or both. In two states, Idaho and Washington, more than 40 percent of the irrigated acreage receives some federally supplied water. In contrast, less than 10 percent of the acreage irrigated in Kansas, Nebraska, Oklahoma, and Texas receives federally supplied water.

Conclusions: The Increasing Federal Role in Irrigation Development

From the beginning of the reclamation movement, the appropriate role for the federal government in irrigation development in the arid western states was a subject of congressional debate. Up through the late 1880s, there was strong skepticism toward any federal assistance to irrigation, except possibly for preventing potential reservoir sites from being homesteaded. John Wesley Powell had hoped that by means of surveys, planning, and land withdrawals, the federal government could structure efficient private development of irrigation in the western states, but the pace of settlement simply was too rapid to accommodate his plan and Congress overturned it.

Table 1-3.   Land Irrigated by Bureau of Reclamation Projects, 1977
(thousands of acres)

State	Type of supply	Total acres irrigated	Number of acres irrigated by Bureau of Reclamation	Percent of acres irrigated by Bureau of Reclamation
Arizona	F	1,211	337	28
California	F/S	8,604	2,757	32
Colorado	F/S	3,458	866	25
Idaho	F/S	3,508	1,493	43
Kansas	F	2,686	60	2
Montana	F/S	2,086	349	17
Nebraska	F/S	5,698	471	8
Nevada	F/S	899	133	15
New Mexico	F	904	215	24
North Dakota	F	141	29	20
Oklahoma	F	602	44	7
Oregon	F/S	1,920	467	24
South Dakota	F/S	341	75	22
Texas	F/S	7,018	246	4
Utah	S	1,185	330	28
Washington	F/S	1,681	901	54
Wyoming	F/S	1,685	355	21
Subtotal		43,627	9,128	21
Other states		7,211	4[a]	0
Total		50,838	9,132	18

Note: Abbreviations: F, full irrigation supply; S, supplemental irrigation supply.
Sources: Bureau of Reclamation irrigated acreage is from U.S. Department of the Interior, Bureau of Reclamation, *Land and Water Resource Accomplishments: 1977* vol. 1 (1978), p. 10. Irrigated acreage by state is 1978 data from U.S. Department of Agriculture, *Agricultural Statistics* (Washington, D.C., 1983), table 552, p. 384, and table 553, p. 385.
[a]Hawaii.

Agricultural developments have always been subject to variations in weather, and dependence on irrigation supplies in the arid West only exacerbated these difficulties. Many of the speculative ventures of individuals and private irrigation companies failed, and the questionable practices of some irrigation companies in luring settlers to ill-planned developments prejudiced public opinion against purely private development. Dissatisfaction with the pace of irrigation settlement eventually led some leaders to propose federal construction of irrigation facilities. They argued that large-scale undertakings were simply too risky for smaller associations. Such arguments, of course, ignored the discipline that private capital markets and supply and demand impose on economic ventures. Without federal assistance, the factors of climate and hydrology, in combination with economic demand from developing western markets for agricultural production, would have sorted out which areas would have seen permanently established irrigated farming and which would not.

However, as the remainder of part I shows, once the concept of federal assistance was accepted, it was argued that additional assistance should be provided to those farmers on federal projects who were in difficulty. If nothing else, additional assistance came to be justified on the basis of protecting the federal financial investments and the commitments of purpose that had already been made. This led to substantial increases in the levels of federal expenditure and involvement, both through legislation and administrative practice.

References

Congressional Record. 57th Cong., 1st sess., 1901, vol. 35, pp. 81–92.

————. 57th Cong., 2d sess., 1902, vol. 35, pp. 6668–6708, 6722–6895.

Davison, Stanley R. 1979. *The Leadership of the Reclamation Movement, 1875–1902* (Originally Ph.D. dissertation, University of California, Berkeley, 1952; New York, Arno Press).

Golzé, Alfred R. 1952. *Reclamation in the United States* (New York, McGraw-Hill).

Hibbard, Benjamin H. 1924. *A History of the Public Land Policies* (New York, Macmillan).

Powell, John Wesley. [1879] 1962. *Report on the Lands of the Arid Region of the United States: With a More Detailed Account of the Lands of Utah.* Introduction by Wallace Stegner (Cambridge, Mass., Harvard University Press).

Robbins, Roy M. 1976. *Our Landed Heritage: The Public Domain, 1776–1970,* rev. ed. (Lincoln, University of Nebraska Press).

Robinson, Michael C. 1979. *Water for the West: The Bureau of Reclamation, 1902–1977* (Chicago, Public Works Historical Society).

Stegner, Wallace. 1982. *Beyond the Hundredth Meridian: John Wesley Powell and the Second Opening of the West,* rev. ed. (Lincoln, University of Nebraska Press).

U.S. Department of Commerce. 1977. *Statistical Abstract of the United States* (Washington, D.C., Government Printing Office).

2

Irrigation Subsidies in the Reclamation Program

Bureau of Reclamation publications frequently claim that the costs of the reimbursable functions of reclamation projects will be repaid to the United States:

> It has long been the philosophy of the Nation that all reclamation project costs for the purpose of irrigation, power, and municipal and industrial water supply should be repaid in full. (U.S. Department of the Interior, Bureau of Reclamation, 1972, p. ix)

In reality, the situation is far different. As discussed in this chapter, subsidies for water supply have been part of the reclamation program since its inception, and the extent of subsidy has generally increased over time.

Irrigation subsidies in Reclamation law take two forms: interest-free repayment and the basing of irrigators' repayment on the bureau's estimate of their "ability to pay." Revenues from federal hydropower are used to "repay" costs beyond the irrigators' "ability to pay." However, repayment by hydropower embodies a substantial subsidy as well, both because it is interest-free and because it occurs after forty or fifty years of irrigation repayment. If federal borrowing costs 4 percent annually, then repayment forty years later interest-free returns to the United States only 20.8 percent of the true cost of the loan. At a borrowing cost of 7 percent, only 6.7 percent is returned (also see Eckstein, 1961, pp. 228–234).

For municipal and industrial water supply, even though interest is charged, the Bureau of Reclamation routinely applies the project interest rate dating from the initial phase of project construction.

This often means that a low historical interest rate is used to finance successive stages of a project, even though federal borrowing rates are much higher at the time that the later stages are built. For example, as of 1986, only $1.6 billion out of an estimated total of $3.6 billion had been spent for the Central Arizona Project. However, the project interest rate of 3.342 percent was still being used as the basis for reimbursement of interest-bearing project functions. In addition, the Water Supply Act of 1958 (72 Stat. 320; 43 U.S.C. 390) provides that repayment for municipal and industrial water supply may be deferred for a period of up to ten years without accruing interest charges. On hydropower investment as well, the difference between government borrowing rates and initial project authorized interest rates has often provided a subsidy. For that portion of hydropower used for irrigation pumping, the cost is repaid interest-free.

The Gradual Enlargement of Irrigation Subsidies

The Reclamation Act of 1902 (32 Stat. 388; 43 U.S.C. 391) established the Reclamation Fund, which was to receive moneys from the sale of public lands in the western states. It was conceived of as a revolving fund, with expenditures for the construction of reclamation projects to be repaid within ten years or less (without interest) and then reused to build additional projects. However, the original idea was short-lived. Additional appropriations to the fund became so routine that the fund itself did not limit expenditures, and the concept of a revolving fund was eventually abandoned. Subsequent legislation also lessened the burden of repayment on water users by extending repayment periods, granting moratoriums on repayments, forgiving some charges, and shifting some of the irrigation costs to other project purposes such as hydropower.

The Reclamation Act of 1902 did not specifically exclude interest from the charges to be recovered for irrigation, but this has become standard bureau practice. The act stated that "charges shall be determined with a view of returning to the reclamation fund the estimated cost of construction of the project." The bureau's administrative interpretation not to charge interest was based on the fact that the act did not specifically mention interest charges and on the implicit approval of Congress, which did not object to bureau practice over the years. (Such an interpretation was given more force by the Reclamation Project Act of 1939, which is discussed later in this section. The sections of that act dealing with repayment for municipal water and power specify that interest charges are to be recovered; however, the sections on irrigation contain nothing about recovery of interest.)

The growth in the irrigation subsidy attributable to interest-free repayment is illustrated in table 2-1, which shows the percentage of subsidy for irrigation construction costs that is embodied in the major pieces of general reclamation legislation enacted between 1902 and 1939, as well as the effect of inflation since that time.[1] As the table indicates, interest-free repayment over ten years at the federal long-term borrowing rates of 1902 would have provided a subsidy of 14 percent of project construction costs. However, settlers had difficulty meeting repayment even under these terms. As a result, in 1914 Congress passed the Reclamation Extension Act (38 Stat. 686), which stretched the repayment period to twenty years. As indicated in table 2-1, this provision increased the interest subsidy to 42 percent of construction costs. The 1914 act also provided for a graduated repayment schedule. For new projects, a settler was to pay 5 percent of the construction charges for each of the first five years and 7 percent annually starting in the sixth year until all costs were repaid. Relief was also provided for settlers on existing projects. Repayment was extended to twenty years from the date of the act on a graduated scale based on the remaining construction charges: 2 percent for the first four years, 4 percent for the next two years, and 6 percent for the next fourteen years. However, the act levied a 1 percent penalty on all payments more than three months late and provided that no water should be delivered to lands for which payments were more than one year in arrears. Provisions for a graduated repayment schedule, as well as other subsequent provisions that were not uniformly applicable to all projects, are not reflected in table 2-1.

Still, repayment continued to be a problem. In 1921, "in view of the financial stringency and the low price of agricultural products," the Secretary of the Interior was authorized to continue water deliveries to settlers for that year even if the settlers were more than one year behind in repayment (42 Stat. 4). Similar legislative deferrals were granted in 1922 (42 Stat. 489) and 1923 (42 Stat. 1324): upon a showing of hardship, both capital and operation and maintenance charges could be deferred for the two-year period. Although the capital charges deferred were to carry an interest charge of 6 percent during the period of deferral, the accumulated repayment could be amortized over the remaining repayment period, thereby further reducing the burden of repayment. A 1924 act (43 Stat. 116) provided similar deferrals through 1927. Then, in 1926 the secretary was

---

[1] For another quantitative account of the evolution of the reclamation subsidy for irrigation, see Rucker and Fishback (1983). See also Golzé (1952, pp.26–30, 243–247) and LeVeen and Goldman (1978).

Table 2-1. Interest Subsidy for Irrigation Capital Costs Embodied in General Reclamation Law

Year	Prevailing federal borrowing rate[c] (percent)	Repayment period (years)	Interest subsidy[a,b] (percent)		Legislation
			Assuming no development period	Assuming ten-year development period[d]	
1902	2.7	10	14	—	Reclamation Act
1914	3.3	20	42	—	Reclamation Extension Act
1926	4.0	40	51	—	Omnibus Adjustment Act
1939	2.4	40	36	50	Reclamation Project Act[e]
1950	2.3	40	35	48	
1955	2.8	40	40	54	
1960	4.0	40	51	67	
1965	4.3	40	53	69	
1970	7.3	40	67	84	
1975	8.0	40	70	86	
1978	8.4	40	71	87	
1979	9.4	40	74	89	
1980	11.5	40	79	93	
1981	13.9	40	82	95	
1982	13.0	40	81	94	
1983	11.1	40	78	92	
1984	12.4	40	80	93	
1985	10.6	40	77	92	

Notes: Dashes mean not applicable.

Specific project-authorizing acts may set repayment periods other than those listed here. The table does not reflect granting of deferred repayment (see text). Subsidy shown is for a project first placed in service in the year indicated. There would be an additional interest subsidy during the period of construction up to the in-service date.

[a]Value of interest-free repayment is calculated as the present worth of equal annual payments over the repayment period discounted at the prevailing federal borrowing rate. Subsidy to irrigators could exceed the amount shown if, under "ability-to-pay" criteria, repayment is made by other water users (see note e).

[b]Assumes payments are due at the end of each contract year.

[c]Long-term government borrowing rate (bonds with ten years to maturity).

[d]It is assumed that no payments are made during the development period, which is also interest-free.

[e]The Reclamation Project Act of 1939 provided for a payment-free development period of up to ten years and also allowed costs to be shared with other water users.

given the authority to defer repayment of operation and maintenance charges for another five years and to defer the repayment of construction charges on whatever schedule he found necessary (44 Stat. 479). In either case, the amount deferred carried an interest charge of 6 percent. The impact of these various deferrals is not reflected in table 2-1; however, all told this legislation would have allowed qualifying settlers to defer operation and maintenance charges from 1922 through 1931 and to defer capital charges for at least as long, provided interest charges were added to the amount deferred.

Yet another set of repayment modifications was authorized by the "Fact Finders Act" of 1924 (43 Stat. 672). This act was based on the recommendations of a committee of special advisers known as the Fact Finders, which had been appointed in 1923 by the Secretary of the Interior in light of the widespread concerns regarding the problems with repayment on reclamation projects. The act allowed the secretary to assess different charges against different classes of land in the same project in order to "equitably apportion" repayment according to the productive value of the different land classes. It further established repayment as 5 percent of the average gross income per acre, although this latter provision was repealed in 1926.

The Omnibus Adjustment Act of 1926 (44 Stat. 636) allowed the Secretary of the Interior to double the interest-free repayment period for irrigation construction costs to forty years, which, as table 2-1 indicates, increased the subsidy to more than 50 percent of costs given the 4 percent rate of government borrowing prevailing at the time. It also embodied a different type of forgiveness of charges—removal of certain "unproductive" lands from the burden of repayment. Problems with inadequate drainage of irrigated lands were frequent, and the Omnibus Adjustment Act, which ran to more than twenty pages, forgave payment on such lands in nineteen projects. Typical of the rationales provided in the act for forgiving repayment are the following:

> six thousand eight hundred and ninety-seven acres permanently unproductive because of topography steep and rough, . . .
>
> ten thousand five hundred acres temporarily unproductive for lack of fertility in the soil, seepage, and excessive alkali salts, . . .
>
> six thousand eight hundred and ninety-five acres . . . awaiting further developments, temporarily unproductive, . . .
>
> two thousand nine hundred and ninety acres water-logged.

Payments still owed on lands classified as either temporarily or permanently unproductive were simply removed from the books rather than shifted to the remaining lands of the projects, as would have been necessary under privately financed development. Furthermore, any payments previously made on lands declared unproductive were credited toward the remaining obligation on the productive lands. Reclamation engineers and settlers had simply been too optimistic about the pace of settlement of lands and the lands' long-term irrigability.

Further deferrals of repayment on reclamation projects were granted during the depression years. In 1932, repayment of construction charges for all reclamation projects was suspended for one year, and the payment for 1932 was reduced to 50 percent of the regular charge (47 Stat. 75).[2] In 1933, the remaining 50 percent of charges for 1932 was deferred, as well as all construction charges for 1933 (47 Stat. 1427). This deferral was later extended to include charges for 1934 (48 Stat. 501), 1935 (49 Stat. 337), and 50 percent of the charges for 1936 (49 Stat. 1207). In combination with deferrals granted by legislation during the 1920s, this additional legislation qualified some settlers for deferment from 1921 through mid-1936. The effect of these deferrals varied from one irrigation district to another and is not reflected in table 2-1.

Even with all these extensions and deferrals, repayment was still a problem. In 1937 Congress authorized the Secretary of the Interior to create the Repayment Commission to examine the conditions on projects (Golzé, 1952, p. 30). The commission reported to Congress that the repayment of construction charges within the fixed statutory limits was too great a burden for many water users and that there was need for further economic relief on reclamation projects. The commission's report led to the passage of the Reclamation Project Act of 1939 (53 Stat. 1187; 43 U.S.C. 485), which provided for additional deferrals and further reduction of the repayment burden. Repayment could be deferred for up to ten years after project facilities were placed in service. This provision came to be used to allow all future projects a ten-year "development period" during which no payments had to be made. At the 2.4 percent rate of government borrowing at the time, a ten-year deferral increased the interest subsidy from 36 percent to 50 percent (refer to table 2-1). At a 4 percent rate of interest, the interest subsidy is 51 percent without the development period and 67 percent with it. In addition, the Reclamation Project Act increased the possibilities for subsidizing irrigation by allowing costs exceeding the

---

[2] The Leavitt Act of 1932 (47 Stat. 564; 25 U.S.C. 386a) deferred the collection of construction charges assessed against American Indian lands for any federal irrigation project. This provision has been interpreted as permanent forgiveness of construction charges, provided the lands remain in Indian hands.

irrigators' "ability to pay" to be paid by other water users (such as users of hydroelectric power), a factor that varies from one project to another and that is not reflected in the table.

Since 1939, inflation has raised the level of the interest subsidy for newly constructed projects (or new construction in established projects). The effect is especially noticeable for the 1970s, when interest rates began to climb above the 4 percent level. Comparing the years 1939 and 1979, for instance, the interest subsidy increased from 36 percent to 74 percent assuming no development period and from 50 percent to 89 percent assuming a ten-year development period. At interest rates above 10.6 percent, which prevailed from 1980 through 1985, the interest subsidy exceeded 90 percent of construction costs. The elevated levels of inflation prevailing during the 1970s and early 1980s were, of course, unforeseen at the time that the 1939 act was framed, which means that the subsidy now far exceeds the level implicit in that legislation at the time of enactment.

In summary, various pieces of general reclamation legislation have lengthened the interest-free repayment period for irrigation, thereby increasing the value of the interest subsidy. The effect of the interest subsidy in the Reclamation Act of 1902 was to forgive about 14 percent of construction costs, but by 1939 this level had reached 50 percent. In addition, the gradual rise in nominal interest rates has greatly increased the value of the subsidy since 1960, reaching levels as high as 95 percent. The various deferrals granted by additional reclamation legislation also resulted in extensions of the repayment period, thereby further increasing the effective subsidy beyond the levels shown in table 2-1.

Estimates of the Interest and "Ability-to-Pay" Subsidies

In addition to the interest subsidy reflected in table 2-1, the Reclamation Project Act of 1939 provided an additional subsidy: irrigation costs above the irrigators' estimated "ability to pay" could be shifted to other project beneficiaries, such as consumers of the project's hydroelectric power. (As discussed below, the bureau's estimated "ability to pay" is less than the water users' actual ability to pay, thereby conferring an additional subsidy through administrative means.) Various estimates have been made of the combined effect of the interest and "ability-to-pay" factors on the subsidy to irrigation. One such study on composite federal cost-sharing (including both capital and operation and maintenance costs) was conducted by the U.S. Water Resources Council in 1975 (see table 2-2). This study was based on repayment schedules for existing projects and a 6 percent rate of

Table 2-2. Federal Subsidy of Capital and Operation and Maintenance Costs (Combined) on Water Resources Projects (Water Resources Council Study, 1975)

Project purpose	Bureau of Reclamation (percent)	U.S. Army Corps of Engineers (percent)	Soil Conservation Service (percent)
Agricultural water supply— irrigation	82	81	46
Municipal and industrial water supply	29	46	0
Hydroelectric power	35	39	—
Recreation	85	83	38
Drainage	—	65	42
Urban flood damage reduction	n.a.	83	n.a.
Rural flood damage reduction	82	92	53
Navigation	93	93	—
Composite for all project purposes	63	80	51

Notes: Costs include capital and operation and maintenance costs, using a 6 percent discount rate.

Dashes mean not applicable; n.a. means not available.

Source: U.S. Water Resources Council, *Options for Cost Sharing, Part 5a: Implementation and OM&R Cost Sharing for Federal and Federally Assisted Water and Related Land Programs* (Washington, D.C., 1975), p. 41.

interest. As table 2-2 indicates, the percent of subsidy provided to irrigation water supply ranges from a high of 82 percent for Bureau of Reclamation projects to a low of 46 percent for Soil Conservation Service projects.[3]

Another study, based on the repayment of capital costs only, was conducted for a sample of reclamation projects by the Department of the Interior in its draft environmental impact statement on acreage limitation (U.S. Department of the Interior, Bureau of Reclamation, 1981). This study focused on eighteen representative irrigation projects. Table 2-3 shows that the absolute value of the construction cost subsidy ranges from a low of $58 per acre on the Moon Lake Project in Utah to a high of $1,787 per acre on the Wellton-Mohawk Irrigation District in Arizona (both in 1978 dollars). In percentage terms, from

---

[3] By comparison, the subsidies afforded to municipal and industrial water supply by using below-market rates of interest and deferral of repayment are 29 percent for Bureau of Reclamation projects and 46 percent for U.S. Army Corps of Engineers projects. The subsidies for hydropower production are 35 percent on Bureau of Reclamation projects and 39 percent on U.S. Army Corps of Engineers projects.

Table 2-3. Irrigation Construction Cost Subsidy on Eighteen Sample Districts (Department of the Interior Study, 1981)

Irrigation district	Subsidy as of 1978 Percent[a]	Subsidy as of 1978 Dollars/acre	Number of irrigable acres in district in 1977[b]
East Columbia Basin, Wash.	96.7	1,619	134,501[c]
Farwell, Nebr.	92.9	1,446	50,051
Malta, Mont.	92.2	812	42,432
Glenn-Colusa, Calif.	90.7	101	152,258-S[d]
Lugert-Altus, Okla.	89.6	675	47,123
Black Canyon #2, Idaho	89.0	762	53,200
Wellton-Mohawk, Ariz.	88.9	1,787	65,849
Grand Valley, Colo.	85.1	1,623	23,341
San Luis Unit, Calif.[e]	84.7	1,422	571,888[c,f]
Truckee-Carson, Nev.	83.4	931	73,002
Oroville-Tonasket, Wash.	81.9	417	9,493
Cachuma Project, Calif.[e]	81.4	1,378	38,151-S[d]
Goshen, Wyo.	74.0	416	52,484
Imperial, Calif.	73.5	149	519,506
Lower Yellowstone #1, Mont.	72.6	507	34,451
Coachella Valley, Calif.	69.5	1,000	78,530[c]
Elephant Butte, N. Mex.	63.6	363	102,082
Moon Lake, Utah	56.9	58	75,256-S[d]

Note: The subsidy is calculated as the present worth of irrigation construction costs less the present worth of past and expected future repayments by irrigators, discounted using ten-year government borrowing rates extending over the repayment period of each district. Percent interest rates used are as follows:

1902–1907: 2.72	1948–1957: 2.33
1908–1917: 3.26	1958–1967: 3.77
1918–1927: 4.04	1968–1977: 5.80
1928–1937: 3.42	1978: base year
1938–1947: 2.59	1979 and beyond: 8.48

For additional details concerning the method of calculation and its rationale, see source.

Source: U.S. Department of the Interior, Bureau of Reclamation, *Acreage Limitation: Draft Environmental Impact Statement, Westwide Report Appendix* (Denver, Colo., Water and Power Resources Service, 1981), pp. F-6–F-19.

[a]Percentage of full construction costs not repaid by irrigators.

[b]Irrigable area for service in 1977 (see note c).

[c]District had substantial additional project acreage not for service in 1977.

[d]S indicates supplemental irrigation service (project water supplements a supply from nonproject sources).

[e]Data provided cover more than one district: San Luis Unit includes Westlands Water District; Cachuma Project includes Goleta County Irrigation District.

[f]Irrigable acres in 1978.

56.9 percent to 96.7 percent of the full irrigation construction costs are subsidized. On twelve of the eighteen projects, the subsidy exceeds 80 percent of construction costs. A higher level of subsidy than revealed by the Water Resources Council study would be expected, since the Department of the Interior study excludes operation and maintenance costs, which, for the most part, are 100 percent reimbursable for irrigation.[4]

In 1981 the U.S. General Accounting Office (GAO) published a study indicating the percentage of construction costs that would be paid by the federal government on six irrigation projects (U.S. General Accounting Office, 1981). On the projects studied, the percentage of subsidy ranges from 92.2 percent to 97.8 percent (see table 2-4). The higher rates of subsidy obtained in this study, compared to the Department of the Interior and Water Resources Council studies, are attributable to (1) the discount rate used (7.5 percent versus the 6 percent rate used in the Water Resources Council study and most of the historical government long-term borrowing rates used in the Department of the Interior study); (2) the fact that the GAO study used recent and ongoing projects, which are more costly than the average project reflected in the other two studies; and (3) the likelihood of a higher level of the "ability-to-pay" subsidy. The combined effect of interest and "ability-to-pay" factors has been that federal subsidies for the capital cost of specific irrigation water supply projects range from 57 percent to more than 90 percent.

In 1987 some new data were assembled by the Bureau of Reclamation that allow for a more complete estimate of the subsidy in the overall irrigation program. In response to a request from Congressman George Miller of California, the bureau assembled year-by-year construction costs and repayment amounts for irrigation on all projects. In those cases where a future repayment schedule was unavailable, the bureau assumed repayment within forty years. Since repayment periods are often extended, this assumption is probably optimistic.

Based on these data, the estimated subsidy in 1986 dollars for irrigation construction costs from 1902 to 1986 ranges from $19.0 billion to $19.7 billion (see table 2-5), depending on which of two historical series of federal borrowing rates is used. In either case about 86 percent of total construction costs are subsidized, which is consistent with the estimates reported in the Water Resources Council and Department of the Interior studies discussed previously.[5] In

---

[4] One major exception in which operation and maintenance costs have not been paid is the Central Valley Project in California (see chapter 3).

[5] Note that these estimates represent the opportunity cost of the federal investment

Table 2-4. Irrigation Construction Cost Subsidy on Six Projects
(GAO Study, 1981)

Project	Construction costs eventually to be repaid (millions of dollars)	Present value[a] (millions of dollars)	Subsidy[b] (percent)
Auburn-Folsom, Calif.	724.5	39.8	94.5
Dallas Creek, Colo.	16.2	1.3	92.2
Fryingpan-Arkansas, Colo.	88.0	4.4	95.0
North Loop, Nebr.	131.6	2.9	97.8
Oroville-Tonasket, Wash.	38.9	3.0	92.3
Pollock-Herreid, S. Dak.	34.6	1.3	96.4

Source: U.S. General Accounting Office, *Federal Charges for Irrigation Projects Reviewed Do Not Cover Costs,* Report No. PAD-81-07 (Washington, D.C., March 3, 1981).
[a]The discount rate used was 7.5 percent.
[b]Present value as a percentage of construction costs.

these calculations, the outstanding unpaid balance was refinanced every ten years, reflecting, for example, the substantial increase in interest rates during the 1970s. In 1985 about 9.9 million acres were irrigated with water supplied by the Bureau of Reclamation (including 5.7 million acres provided with a supplemental water supply), meaning that the average subsidy ranged from $1,920 to $1,990 per acre. These per-acre values are higher than those in table 2-3 for several reasons: (1) the accumulation of interest on the unpaid balance during the eight years from 1978 to 1986 (which would increase the estimate by approximately 111 percent if there were no additional costs or repayments during the intervening period); (2) the fact that the estimates are based on the acres actually irrigated, rather than the larger number of "irrigable" acres capable of being served by the projects (over the past few years irrigable acreage has exceeded irrigated acreage by about 21 percent); and (3) the large expenditures on some projects during the 1978–1986 period.[6]

in 1986 dollars. The total irrigation investment to 1986 in "as-spent" dollars is $5.4 billion. The subsidy in as-spent dollars would be about 86 percent of this amount, or $4.6 billion.

[6] The subsidy values provided by the Bureau of Reclamation to Congressman Miller based on the same information were $9.8 billion for the program through 1986, or $995 per acre and $54 per acre per year. These lower values were the result of several factors: the failure to incorporate the unpaid balance as of 1986 (less expected future payments); the use of historical rather than then-current yield rates during the period from 1945 to 1980, which were considerably below the cost of government borrowing; and the use of inconsistent compounding methods to calculate the total subsidy to date.

Table 2-5. Irrigation Construction Cost Subsidy on All Projects

	Series I	Series II
Construction cost, present worth[a] (billions of dollars)	22.2	22.9
Past repayments, present worth (billions of dollars)	2.3	2.3
Expected future repayments, present worth (billions of dollars)	0.9	0.9
Construction cost subsidy[b] (billions of dollars)	19.0	19.7
Percent subsidy	85.6	85.9
Irrigable acreage in 1985 (millions of acres)	9.9	9.9
Construction cost subsidy per acre (dollars/acre)	1,920	1,990

Note: Percent interest rates used to calculate present worth are as follows:

	Series I	Series II
1902–1907	1.96	2.72
1908–1917	2.33	3.26
1918–1927	3.01	4.04
1928–1937	3.42	3.42
1938–1947	2.53	2.59
1948–1957	2.33	2.33
1958–1967	3.77	3.77
1968–1977	5.80	
1978–1982	8.42	
1983–1985	12.18	
1986	base year	
1987 and beyond	8.875	

Series I interest rates prior to 1962 are based on the average yields of long-term government bonds as reported in Sidney Homer, *A History of Interest Rates* (New Brunswick, N.J., Rutgers University Press, 1963), tables 46 and 48. Series II rates are ten-year government borrowing rates from *Economic Report of the President* and *U.S. Federal Reserve Bulletin* (also see U.S. Department of the Interior, Bureau of Reclamation, *Acreage Limitation: Draft Environmental Impact Statement, Westwide Report Appendix,* Denver, Colo., Waters and Power Resources Service, 1981, pp. F-6–F-19). The two series are identical after 1968.

Source: Recent data from the Bureau of Reclamation, U.S. Department of the Interior, Washington, D.C.

[a]Present worth of construction costs from 1902 to 1986, expressed in 1986 dollars.

[b]Present worth of construction costs less present worth of past and expected future repayments.

This brief history of the evolution of the reclamation subsidy is revealing. What began as a proposal for modest federal assistance in settling the arid West, providing a revolving fund to which costs would be repaid within ten years, evolved into a program that provided major subsidies to irrigation water users—sometimes more than 90 percent of construction costs. Several factors led to enlargement of the subsidy. (1) Congress did an inadequate job in specifying a program that would be viable. (2) The Bureau of Reclamation developed projects in locations where soil conditions were not conducive to long-term irrigation. (3) The hardships that settlers had to endure, whether from inexperience, drought, or poor project design, undoubtedly aroused the sympathies of members of Congress as well as Bureau of Reclamation personnel administering the program. (4) Once federal dollars had been committed to specific irrigation projects, the federal government was vulnerable to arguments that additional financial concessions were necessary to make continued farming viable on project lands. (5) Inflation considerably enhanced the value of interest-free repayment. (6) Once the precedent of the interest subsidy had been established, there was little inclination on the part of Congress to modify it.

Ex Post Evaluation of Irrigators' "Ability to Pay" and of Project Economic Benefits

Two questions naturally arise regarding federal subsidies of the capital costs of irrigation development on federal projects: (1) What amount could irrigators actually pay toward project costs, as opposed to what they do pay? (2) Are these subsidies justified by the projects' economic benefits?

Since 1939 the amount that irrigators repay has been based on their "ability to pay." The Bureau of Reclamation estimates this amount by developing farm budgets typical of the farm enterprises expected on projects. The net income of a typical farm is estimated by taking the expected crop revenues less expenses for seed, equipment, land (exclusive of water costs), and hired labor and an imputed cost for family farm labor. "Ability to pay" is taken as a percentage of net income (usually 75 percent and sometimes 100 percent), and this amount is used in establishing the district's water rate.

How accurate is this method in determining ability to pay? One way to answer this question is to examine what price irrigators actually pay for land with a federal water supply when the land is resold. The difference in land values with and without a federal water supply is a functioning market test of irrigators' actual willingness to pay (and ability to pay) for project water. Column 1 of table 2-6 indicates in present worth terms what irrigators pay in water charges to the federal government. Column 2 indicates the approximate benefits of the project, measured as willingness to pay for irrigation water. Column 2 is the amount that subsequent irrigators paid for the federal water supply when the land was resold (the difference in land values between irrigated and nonirrigated land obtained from land appraisals plus the present worth of water charges paid to the govern-

40

Table 2-6. Comparison of Irrigators' "Ability to Pay" and Willingness to Pay for Project Water

District	Repayment for construction[a] (dollars/acre) (1)	Willingness to pay[b] (dollars/acre) (2)	Ratio (2)÷(1) (3)	Full financial cost[c] (dollars/acre) (4)	Ratio (2)÷(4) (5)	First construction (year) (6)	Water deliveries (acre-feet/acre) (7)
Glenn-Colusa, Calif.	10	510	51.0	111	4.6	1938	1.59
Moon Lake, Utah	44	444	10.1	101	4.4	1936	1.13
Elephant Butte, N. Mex.	208	1,233	5.9	571	2.2	1914	2.27
Truckee-Carson, Nev.	186	1,576	8.5	1,117	1.4	1904	3.80
Goshen, Wyo.	146	791	5.4	561	1.4	1926	2.03
Cachuma, Calif.	315	2,315	7.3	1,693	1.4	1949	1.40
Lower Yellowstone No. 1, Mont.	191	741	3.9	698	1.1	1905	2.13
Grand Valley, Colo.	285	1,585	5.6	1,908	0.8	1911	5.38
Wellton-Mohawk, Ariz.	223	1,578	7.1	2,010	0.8	1950	6.91
Imperial, Calif.	54	154	2.9	203	0.8	1933	5.73
San Luis Unit, Calif.	258	1,208	4.7	1,600	0.7	1961	2.74
Coachella, Calif.	439	989	2.3	1,439	0.7	1936	6.21
Lugert-Altus, Okla.	78	513	6.6	753	0.7	1941	0.55
Black Canyon No. 2, Idaho	94	494	5.3	856	0.6	1937	4.13
East Columbia Basin, Wash.	55	705	12.8	1,674	0.4	1933	4.25
Malta, Mont.	69	344	5.0	881	0.4	1906	0.86
Oroville-Tonasket, Wash.	92	142	1.5	509	0.3	1964	4.46
Farwell, Nebr.	110	210	1.9	1,555	0.1	1958	1.12

Note: Data current as of 1978 and expressed in 1978 dollars.
Source: Columns 1, 4, 6, and 7 are based on records from the Bureau of Reclamation, U.S. Department of the Interior, Washington, D.C. Column 2 is based on *Acreage Limitation: Draft Environmental Impact Statement, Westwide Report Appendix*, U.S. Department of the Interior, Bureau of Reclamation (Denver, Colo., Water and Power Resources Service, 1981), p. F-9.

[a]Present value of past and future repayments (for construction only) using long-term government borrowing rates.
[b]Difference in land value with and without the project water supply plus present value of repayment for construction (column 1). Difference in land value is from *Acreage Limitation: Draft Environmental Impact Statement, Westwide Report Appendix*, p. F-9.
[c]Full financial cost is the sum of repayment to date plus unpaid full cost, each expressed in present worth terms.

ment). A comparison of columns 1 and 2 indicates that for all of the eighteen districts in the table, the actual willingness to pay for project water exceeds the amount paid to the government. The ratios in column 3 show that the willingness to pay ranges from 1.5 to 51 times the repayment to the federal government.

In fact, as column 5 shows, in seven of the eighteen cases, the irrigator's demonstrated willingness to pay for water exceeds the full financial cost allocated to irrigation (including past and future interest charges). On these seven projects, willingness to pay ranges from 1.1 to 4.6 times full cost, indicating that these projects might well have been viable under private development even without the various water subsidies provided by the federal government. This does not necessarily mean that such high levels of willingness to pay were present when those projects were first established. There may have been several years of uncertainty as to whether project farming would be successful and whether viable communities and markets would be established. Nor does it necessarily mean that there should be some attempt on existing projects to raise water rates in order to allow the federal government to recover a greater percentage of its original investment. Especially on older projects, many of the lands have been resold, so that the present owner has already paid the values resulting from the subsidized water rates (column 2) to the original landowner. But column 3 reveals that the federal procedures for estimating ability to pay have been tilted heavily in favor of the landowners.

Table 2-6 also provides a means for performing an approximate ex post benefit–cost test on these eighteen projects. Column 5 is the ratio of the private market benefits of the project (as measured by increase in land values owing to the project water supply) to the full irrigation costs of the project.[7] Therefore, seven of the eighteen projects have benefits exceeding costs. On the other eleven, the full cost of the project exceeds the willingness to pay, with the market value of irrigation benefits ranging to as low as 10 percent of project construction costs. It is possible, of course, that some of these eleven projects could recover their full financial cost (with interest) if all the water used in irrigation were not restricted to irrigation.

Other Bureau of Reclamation Claims Regarding Repayment

In addition to the general statement quoted at the beginning of this chapter that the reimbursable costs of reclamation projects are re-

---

[7] This ratio may differ from the ratio of social benefits to social cost in cases of externalities or other market failures.

paid, the Bureau of Reclamation has put forth other questionable statistics regarding repayment on its projects. Because these statistics are reported so widely and so frequently, some discussion of them is warranted.

The bureau claims that 84 percent of its project costs will be repaid. The basis of this claim is the following. Between 1902 and 1980, the Bureau of Reclamation spent about $10.5 billion on construction for all purposes, including irrigation, municipal and industrial water supply, hydropower, recreation, and fish and wildlife. Of this amount, $8.8 billion (84 percent) has been repaid to date or is under contract to be repaid (about $2 billion had been repaid as of 1980). The remaining $1.7 billion is nonreimbursable. The 84 percent figure ignores the interest cost of borrowing, such as the interest subsidy provided to irrigation and the below-market rate of interest provided to municipal and industrial water supply and hydropower. If $100 is repaid fifty years later without interest, the bureau's calculation counts this as 100 percent repayment. Accordingly, the calculation regards the irrigation function as 100 percent repayable. However, when the timing of investment and repayment is taken into account, irrigation repays on average only about 14 percent of its cost and, in some cases, less than 10 percent. In addition, some irrigation costs on projects with "unproductive" lands have simply been removed from the books. The data most directly comparable to the 84 percent Bureau of Reclamation value are those in table 2-2, developed by the Water Resources Council. The 84 percent figure is for repayment across all project functions. The last row of table 2-2 indicates that across all project purposes, the reclamation program can be expected to recover about 37 percent of its costs when the cost of borrowing is taken into account.

Another claim is that the bureau's projects more than pay for themselves in the form of the federal tax revenues generated or the tax revenues accruing to state and local governments. Brochures distributed by the bureau typically state that "the Reclamation program stimulates economic activity that brings over $3 billion in revenues to the federal Treasury each year." Furthermore, "when state and local tax revenues (about $1.4 billion a year) are considered, the return in government revenues is more than four dollars for every dollar appropriated for the annual Bureau of Reclamation budget." These estimates are based on a methodology developed for the bureau by the Denver Research Institute in 1972. They attempt to trace the economic activity associated with reclamation projects, such as the value added in food processing. The problem—long recognized by the benefit–cost procedures applicable to the bureau's projects—is that the secondary regional benefits generated by a project do not necessarily increase the net production of the nation as a whole. If the same federal funds had been spent elsewhere in the economy, say to support an industrial park or office complex, then similar secondary impacts would have been generated with similar tax revenues to the United States. In fact, if such alternative investment projects returned more direct benefits than a water resources project with a benefit–cost ratio of less than one (which is what would be expected if the alternatives were economically viable), then greater secondary benefits and tax revenues could be expected. Alternatively, if the federal tax revenues had not been spent on subsidized projects but had been left in the hands of individuals and businesses, then the private investment generated would have produced secondary impacts and associated tax revenues. The most that can be said in favor of such estimates of secondary economic effects and the tax revenues associated with them is that they are an estimate of the impacts on the regional economy—an effect that could have been realized in another economic sector or in another geographic area.

Other Sources of Federal Subsidies for Irrigation

There are other major sources of subsidies on Bureau of Reclamation projects, although they do not apply programwide, namely, the subsidies in the salinity control and dam safety programs. The Colorado River Basin Salinity Control Act of 1974 (88 Stat. 266; 43 U.S.C. 1571) provides that 25 percent of the costs of the program are to be repaid without interest over fifty years from moneys in the Colorado River Basin funds for the Lower Basin and the Upper Basin. (Contributions are made to the fund, principally from power revenues, and no more than 15 percent of the reimbursable amount will be paid by the Upper Basin, with the remainder to be paid by the Lower Basin.) The total expenditures for the salinity control program have been estimated to range from $1.5 billion to $4.0 billion (U.S. Department of the Interior, Bureau of Reclamation, 1983, p. xiii). Using the repayment terms of the act and a 9 percent rate of interest, repayment is less than 6 percent of total costs. Part of this amount can be regarded as an additional subsidy to irrigation in the Colorado River Basin for two principal reasons. First, about 37 percent of the salinity concentration in the Colorado River is attributed to irrigation (U.S. Department of the Interior, Bureau of Reclamation, 1983, p. 4). Federal expenditures for treating salinity are, therefore, a cost that individual irrigation districts do not have to pay. Second, because irrigation is one of the primary uses of Colorado River water, irrigation is a significant beneficiary of the salinity control program, especially in the Lower Basin.

The Reclamation Safety of Dams Act, passed in 1978 (92 Stat. 2471; 43 U.S.C. 506), was motivated in part by the failure of Teton Dam in Idaho in 1976. It provides for the Bureau of Reclamation to perform work to preserve the structural safety of bureau dams classified into one of two categories: (1) those being modified because of "new hydrologic or seismic data or changes in state-of-the-art criteria deemed necessary for safety purposes" and (2) those being modified owing to "age and normal deterioration of the structure or from nonperformance of reasonable and normal maintenance of the structure by the operating entity." In the first case, the costs are nonreimbursable; that is, there is a 100 percent subsidy for dam safety modifications in this category. In the second case, costs "will be allocated to the purposes for which the structure was authorized initially to be constructed and will be reimbursable as provided by existing law." The second provision means that, as dams age, they can be replaced with the same subsidy terms used for their original construction, such as the interest subsidy for irrigation. Work falling into the first category clearly receives a much greater degree of subsidy than the second, and it is a question of judgment as to how costs should be allocated between the two categories. The 1978 act authorized a total of $100 million for expenditures falling into either category.

In 1984 the Reclamation Safety of Dams Act Amendments (92 Stat. 1981; 43 U.S.C. 506) raised the cost ceiling by $650 million because the Bureau's 1984 list of dam safety modifications had a total estimated cost of $705 million (see U.S. General Accounting Office, 1986, pp. 21–24). The 1984 act also increased the level of nonfederal cost sharing from 0 percent to 15 percent for modifications in the first category—those deriving from new hydrologic or seismic data or changes in state-of-the-art safety criteria. The repayment period for irrigation was set at fifty years and at a level "capable of being repaid by the irrigation water users." Assuming a long-term government borrowing rate of 9 percent, interest-free repayment of 15 percent of costs over fifty years would provide a subsidy of 97 percent for the dam safety costs in this category that are allocated to irrigation.

Conclusions: Effects of the Irrigation Subsidy

Irrigation subsidies have generally been extended in favor of the water users through a variety of means, such as extension of the repayment period, deferment of repayment, and forgiveness of repayment on problem lands. Thus, a public program of irrigation stands in sharp contrast to privately developed irrigation. As discussed in chapter 1, many private irrigation companies simply failed, reflecting the uneconomical nature of the enterprise, poor management, or, in some cases, the false expectations established by promoters. In contrast, the federal government tends to maintain irrigation development, however uneconomical, by modifying the repayment burden.

This does not mean that the lives of farmers on reclamation projects have been any easier than the lives of farmers elsewhere. In fact, because of the arid conditions under which many projects have been developed, farming on reclamation projects has been difficult. In the absence of federal subsidies for water supply, farmers would bring lands into production up to the point where private marginal returns equaled marginal costs (including returns to land and labor). Those lands where marginal costs exceeded marginal returns could not be cultivated on a long-term basis. The provision of federal subsidies increases the amount of land that will yield sufficient private returns in comparison with private costs. The provision of subsidies merely changes the quantity of arid land on which farming can be economical, but farming on the most marginal lands may be just as difficult.

Therefore, the principal effects of the irrigation subsidy have been locational. In general, it can be said that federal water subsidies have resulted in more irrigation development in the western states at the expense of bringing additional land into production in the Midwest and South. For example, cotton grown on reclamation projects in California with subsidized water competes with privately developed cotton grown in the South. Of course, this locational effect was one of the principal goals of establishing the original Reclamation Act— that is, to encourage the settlement of the arid West through the provision of water to lands that could be homesteaded.

From the standpoint of national economic development, these extensive water subsidies have led to inefficient use of land and water resources as well as capital, labor, and materials. Since the 1950s, reclamation projects have been subject to benefit–cost analyses. In principle, if projects were designed and constructed so that incremental benefits were greater than costs, then there would be no distortions of resource use. As has been shown, however, many projects have been located where benefits fail to exceed costs (refer to table 2-6). Consequently, dams have been placed where the rivers, in the absence of the irrigation subsidy, would have been left in their natural state. Furthermore, low-cost water has provided little incentive for careful use of the resource. This means that water has been diverted to uses other than those that would produce the greatest economic benefits and has, for the most part, continued to be used for the original purposes.

Significant amounts of hydropower on reclamation projects are dedicated to the pumping of irrigation project water supply. Hydropower is provided at a very low charge because of the interest-free subsidy for irrigation pumping. This means that reliable and relatively inexpensive hydropower has been diverted from other productive uses to provide for irrigation. In some cases, the Bureau of Reclamation has found it necessary to participate in the construction of thermal power plants to provide necessary power for project pumping. In general, in the absence of the irrigation subsidy, many of the natural and human resources dedicated to these water diversions and power plants would have been devoted to other, more productive uses.

References

Eckstein, Otto. 1961. *Water-Resource Development: The Economics of Project Evaluation* (Cambridge, Mass., Harvard University Press).

Golzé, Alfred R. 1952. *Reclamation in the United States* (New York, McGraw-Hill).

LeVeen, Phillip, and George E. Goldman. 1978. "Reclamation Policy and the Water Subsidy: An Analysis of the Distributional Consequences of Emerging Policy Choices," *American Journal of Agricultural Economics* vol. 60, no. 5 (December), pp. 929–934.

Rucker, Randal R., and Price V. Fishback. 1983. "The Federal Reclamation Program: An Analysis of Rent-Seeking Behavior," in Terry L. Anderson, ed., *Water Rights: Scarce Resource Allocation, Bureaucracy, and the Environment* (Cambridge, Mass., Ballinger).

U.S. Department of the Interior, Bureau of Reclamation. 1972. *Repayment of Reclamation Projects* (Washington, D.C., Government Printing Office).

———. 1981. *Acreage Limitation: Draft Environmental Impact Statement, Westwide Report Appendix* (Denver, Colo., Water and Power Resources Service).

———. 1983. *Colorado River Water Quality Improvement Program* (Denver, Colorado River Water Quality Office).

U.S. General Accounting Office. 1981. *Federal Charges for Irrigation Projects Reviewed Do Not Cover Costs,* Report No. PAD-81-07 (March 3).

———. 1986. *Implementation of the Bureau of Reclamation's Safety of Dams Program,* Report No. RCED-86-139BR (April 25).

U.S. Water Resources Council. 1975. *Options for Cost Sharing, Part 5a: Implementation and OM&R Cost Sharing for Federal and Federally Assisted Water and Related Land Programs.*

3

Administrative Extension of Subsidies:
The Central Valley Project

Federal legislation gradually increased the subsidy for irrigation construction costs on both new and existing federal projects by lengthening the interest-free repayment period, deferring repayment during hardship years, and limiting repayment to the water users' estimated "ability to pay." Furthermore, subsidy levels increased above those originally envisioned by Congress as general inflation led to higher interest rates, thereby increasing the value of the interest-free subsidy. Subsidies on existing projects also grew beyond those authorized by reclamation legislation through administrative measures taken by the Bureau of Reclamation—for example, the establishment of long-term contracts with fixed rates that made no allowance for inflation adjustments for increased operating costs. The most prominent case of this type is the Central Valley Project (CVP) in California, where fixed-rate contracts have led to a situation in which the federal government receives neither yearly capital repayment nor sufficient repayment to cover annual operating costs, despite water users' ample ability to pay. In other words, the federal government is operating the irrigation portion of the project at an annual loss. This situation may well continue until a majority of the contracts expire in the mid-1990s. The story of how it came about and the difficulty of resolving it is important because the Central Valley Project is among the largest federal reclamation financial investments in the country. The project's story also illustrates how difficult it is to alter de facto entitlements to water supplies once they become established, no matter how disadvantageous the financial terms are to the United States.

Development of the Federal Central Valley Project and Conflict with the State Water Project

The Central Valley in California contains two major river systems: the Sacramento River flowing from the north and the San Joaquin River flowing from the south, both joining at the Sacramento–San Joaquin Delta (called the Delta) and emptying into Suisun Bay (figure 3-1). During the early part of the twentieth century, many of the large wheat farms and cattle ranches of the Central Valley were subdivided into smaller family units, many less than fifty acres in size. The dry period of 1928–1935 led to increased pumping of groundwater. The high cost of sinking deeper wells and the increased pumping costs sent many of these small farms into bankruptcy. As a result, there was a general appeal to the state of California to provide a water supply plan for the valley (see Kahrl, 1978, pp. 47–48).

Several years earlier, in 1919, Robert B. Marshall had quit his job as a geographer for the U.S. Geological Survey to promote just such a plan. Marshall's plan consisted of storage facilities in the northern Sacramento River valley, with one canal system on the east side of the Sacramento and San Joaquin rivers and another on the west side. Inspired by Marshall and the success of the Los Angeles Aqueduct to Owens Valley, the state mandated a more thorough study of the plan in 1921. One of the principal arguments against Marshall's proposal, however, was that riparian water rights holders would be able to successfully block such a project. This obstacle was removed by legislation in 1928 that limited riparian owners to a reasonable use of water, similar to the requirement for holders of appropriative rights.[1]

The Central Valley Project was authorized by the California legislature as a state project. Approved by the governor on August 5, 1933, it immediately became the subject of a state referendum petition requiring that it be approved by the electorate. The election was held in December 1933, and the project was approved. State officials then turned to the problem of how to finance it. The state legislature had authorized the sale of public bonds for this purpose, but, in the midst of the depression, these were found to be unmarketable. Requests for

---

[1] Most of the surface water rights held in the western states are "appropriative" water rights. Such rights are obtained by the first user of the water and are measured by the amount of water put to "beneficial" use. Appropriative rights can usually be purchased for new developments and can be transferred to new locations under processes established by each state. Some western water rights were granted under the riparian system used in the eastern United States. Riparian rights are attached to the land that is adjacent to a stream. They do not require the owner to maintain reasonable, beneficial use, and they cannot be sold for use elsewhere.

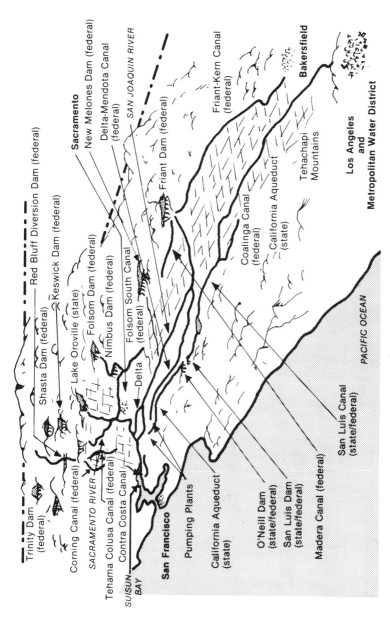

Figure 3-1. Central Valley Project and State Water Project. *Source:* Adapted from map of the Central Valley Project, Bureau of Reclamation, Washington, D.C.

federal grants and loans were submitted but were turned down. State officials then asked the federal government to undertake construction of the project.

The U.S. Congress authorized construction of the initial Central Valley Project facilities in the River and Harbor Act of August 30, 1935 (49 Stat. 1028, 1038). This act authorized the U.S. Army Corps of Engineers to construct the Shasta, Keswick, and Friant dams, the Tracy pumping plant, the Delta-Mendota and Friant-Kern canals, and the Contra Costa Canal and related facilities (see figure 3-1). On September 10, 1935, the president signed an executive order that transferred $20 million in Emergency Relief Act funds to the Department of the Interior for construction of the initial features of the project. That same year, the Bureau of Reclamation submitted to Congress a feasibility report favorable to the project, and in 1937 Congress shifted authority for construction of all CVP facilities from the Corps of Engineers to the Bureau of Reclamation (50 Stat. 84).

By 1944 Shasta Dam was producing the project's first power, and seven years later it was delivering the first irrigation water. Since that time, Congress has authorized the construction and operation of several additional units and facilities: the Folsom, Nimbus, and Sly Park dams and related facilities on the American River in 1949 (63 Stat. 852); the Red Bluff Diversion Dam, Corning Canal, and Tehama-Colusa Canal in the Sacramento Valley in 1950 (64 Stat. 1036); the Trinity River Division in 1955 (69 Stat. 719); the San Luis Unit in 1960 (74 Stat. 156); the New Melones, Hidden, and Buchanan projects in 1962 (76 Stat. 1191); the Auburn-Folsom South Unit in 1965 (79 Stat. 615); the San Felipe Division in 1967 (81 Stat. 1873); the Black Butte Project in 1970 (84 Stat. 1097); and the Allen Camp Unit in 1976 (90 Stat. 1328). Each time a new unit or facility was added, the entire CVP was included in the reauthorization legislation to preserve the concept established by Congress of an "operationally and financially integrated project." This phrase was later used as the rationale for pooling facility costs in establishing water rates for the project (for example, see U.S. Department of the Interior, Bureau of Reclamation, 1971, p. 30). Pooling of costs, in turn, became the principal rationale for lack of contractor-by-contractor accountability for project repayment and the justification for other financial practices that proved disadvantageous to the United States.

It had at first been envisioned that California would operate and control the project once federal construction was completed. However, a considerable struggle for control developed when the original facilities were under construction. Much of this centered around the acreage limitation provisions of federal law (refer to chapters 1 and 4), since state administration of the project would carry none of the restrictions of federal law. Those farming interests that opposed the 160-acre ownership limitation on federal project lands in California had three major strategies: (1) to assert state control over the project, (2) to obtain a legislative exemption for the project, and (3) to supplant Bureau of Reclamation control in certain parts of the valley by securing construction of water supply systems by the U.S. Army Corps of Engineers. These forces were successful only in this last strategy (Kahrl, 1978, pp. 50–51). State purchase of the project received some consideration in 1945 when the Secretary of the Interior suggested a purchase price of $357 million. In fact, in 1952 the state appropriated $10 million for studying this proposal. But by then, the Bureau of Reclamation's new appraisal of the project's cost had doubled, and the interest in state takeover subsided (Kahrl, 1978, pp. 49–50).[2]

Those interests opposed to federal acreage limitations subsequently adopted a fourth strategy: state construction of additional water facilities. In 1945 the legislature created the State Water Resources Control Board and directed it to study state water needs. The resultant 1951 report, prepared under the direction of Arthur Edmunston, called for the construction of a dam at Oroville to divert water from the Feather River; augmentation of the Sacramento River during dry periods; and delivery systems from the Delta to supply water to the San Francisco Bay area, the farmers of the San Joaquin Valley, and the urban areas of the southern California coastal plain. As figure 3-1 reveals, this is largely the project that is in place today. It was financed through the State Water Resources Development Bond Act in 1959 (also known as the Burns-Porter Act).

History of Water Rate-Setting Practices in the Central Valley Project

Figure 3-1 shows the basic components of the Central Valley Project that are relevant to water rate-setting policy. Most of the federal storage reservoirs are on the upper tributaries of the Sacramento and San Joaquin rivers. The principal transport of water by the project is from north to south, from that part of California with the most rainfall to the more arid sections. Whereas this southward transport can be accomplished via the Sacramento River north of the Delta,

---

[2] However, see a recent report regarding state operation of the federal project: *Reconnaissance Report: State Operation and Management of the Central Valley Project* (Sacramento, California Department of Water Resources, 1982).

canals and pumping plants must be used to transport water to service areas south of the Delta. From the Tracy Pumping Plant on the Delta, water is lifted into the federal Delta-Mendota Canal. The Harvey O. Banks pumping plant (state) lifts water from the Delta at about the same location to flow southward through the California Aqueduct of the State Water Project. The aqueduct is farther to the west and at a higher elevation than the Delta-Mendota Canal. Pumping lifts are also required at various points along the length of each canal. The two canals have one principal point of interconnection at the San Luis Dam and O'Neill Forebay and Afterbay facilities. Both canals continue to flow southward from this point. At the O'Neill Forebay, water can be dropped from the California Aqueduct (state) to the federal Delta-Mendota Canal or pumped up in the reverse order between the canals. South of the O'Neill Forebay, the more westward of the canals is called the San Luis Canal in the federal project and the California Aqueduct in the State Water Project. This canal is a joint federal–state facility to the point where the federal service area ends. At that point it becomes solely a state facility, the California Aqueduct. The aqueduct carries water southward to service areas in southern California. A final set of pumps lifts water from the state project over the Tehachapi Mountains into Los Angeles.

Two types of contracts with water districts are allowable under the bureau's principal contracting authority, the Reclamation Project Act of 1939 (53 Stat. 1187; 43 U.S.C. 390). Under "repayment contracts," capital costs are amortized over the repayment period in annual installments. This fixed annual charge is not dependent on the exact amount of water delivered each year. Under "water service contracts," a combined capital and operation and maintenance charge is levied for each acre-foot of water delivered to the district. In both types of contracts, capital repayment for irrigation is usually amortized over a forty- or fifty-year repayment period on an interest-free basis and may be further adjusted downward based on the water users' ability to pay.[3]

Because of the financially integrated nature of the CVP, water service contracts were used and were written for terms of forty years. Irrigation capital costs that were beyond the irrigators' ability to pay were to be recovered from sales of hydropower and municipal and industrial water. Water rates were established for each service area based on the rates included in the applicable feasibility report. Water rates for irrigation ranged from $2.00 per acre-foot in the Sacramento

---

[3] For additional discussion of the Reclamation Project Act of 1939 and interest-free repayment, see chapter 2.

Valley (near the major sources of supply) to $3.50 per acre-foot in the San Joaquin Valley (where pumping was required to lift water out of the Delta) and $7.50 per acre-foot for the San Luis Unit (where additional pumping was required). None of these CVP contracts included provisions for revising rates to accommodate increasing costs.

By the mid-1960s, an examination of the repayment status of the project indicated that the water rates that had been established were too low and that the fixed-rate contracts would not produce sufficient revenue to recover both increasing annual operating costs and added capital investment costs. Under the "average cost-of-service approach" used in the project, the costs of the new facilities (which can often be more expensive per acre-foot than existing facilities) would normally be averaged into the rates for existing supplies. However, this could not be done because of the existing fixed-rate contracts. Put another way, in recent years, the average cost-of-service approach has sought to shift some of the costs of added facilities to existing customers; however, this is frustrated because existing customers have water rates that at present cannot be raised.

Steps were taken to modify the rate-setting policy for new contracts in order to provide for rate adjustments during the contract term. Under the bureau's 1970 proposal, the rate structure was to include separate components for annual operating costs and capital investment costs. The annual operating cost component was to be adjusted at five-year intervals, and the capital component was to be adjusted in the twentieth and thirtieth years of each new forty-year water service contract, with reevaluations of the irrigators' "ability to pay" in the twentieth and thirtieth years. The 1970 proposal was never formally approved, however, and no new irrigation contracts were executed before additional revisions were proposed in 1974.

The 1974 "cost-of-service" approach based water rates on various components of the cost of providing water service to each contractor.[4] The interest-free capital cost and the operation and maintenance cost of providing various project services or components (such as storage, conveyance, conveyance pumping, and canalside relift pumping) were to be calculated for each district. For example, water users who drew water directly from the Sacramento River were to pay for use of storage facilities but not conveyance facilities or conveyance pumping. Water users south of the Delta who received water pumped into

---

[4]The 1974 concept is essentially the "component" rate-setting concept that is currently used in establishing CVP rates. Note that "cost of service" as used by the bureau is not actual cost of service since the bureau's rates for irrigation exclude interest charges.

the Delta-Mendota Canal were to pay for storage, conveyance, and conveyance pumping. Water charges would continue to be set on a pooled, average-cost basis in some respects: all users of CVP storage facilities would pay the same storage charge, and any user of CVP conveyance facilities would pay the same rate as any other, regardless of the fact that the different conveyance facilities in the project differed in length, construction cost, and operation and maintenance cost.[5] However, charges for conveyance pumping and canalside relift pumping would differ for each contractor based on the amount of electrical energy required. Of course, the total water rates for each district would continue to be set as the lesser of the "cost of service" or the irrigators' "ability to pay." To avoid the problems associated with fixed rates, all new contracts executed from 1974 through 1978 included some form of provision for water rate adjustments. Beginning in 1979, all new irrigation water service contracts included a provision for adjustments at five-year intervals. This rate-setting policy applied immediately only to new contracts and was not intended to modify any of the contract rates already established until they expired.

On May 19, 1977, the Secretary of the Interior requested that the department's Office of Inspector General (then the Office of Audit and Investigation) audit the financial condition of the Central Valley Project. In January 1978 and September 1979, the office issued audit reports criticizing several of the water marketing, financial, and rate-setting practices used by the Bureau of Reclamation in operating the project. The January 1978 report dealt primarily with the irrigation and power functions of the project (U.S. Department of the Interior, Office of the Inspector General, 1978). The auditors felt that improvements were needed to put irrigation water sales on a more businesslike basis. Specifically, the inspector general raised concerns about the fixed-rate, long-term contracts, about the potential limits on individual contractor irrigation water rates because of "ability-to-pay" provisions, and about the propriety of extending the end of the required repayment period each time a new CVP facility was placed in service—the "rolling repayment" concept. Under the rolling repayment concept, a new fifty-year repayment period for all CVP irrigation costs was established each time a new facility was added to the project. This policy was justified by the bureau on the basis of the "financially integrated" concept established by Congress.

In September 1979, the inspector general issued a follow-up audit

---

[5] In the State Water Project, however, water rates differ by the length of canal used (see California Department of Water Resources, 1986).

report on the project's municipal and industrial water activities (U.S. Department of the Interior, Office of the Inspector General, 1979).[6] Many of the comments were also pertinent to irrigation. In addition to commenting on the fixed-rate contracts and the use of the rolling repayment concept, this report recommended that a clear rate-setting policy be established based on pooled cost, unit cost, service area cost, or some other basis. Even though most of the existing CVP irrigation water service contracts do not expire until after 1990, the auditors felt that immediate action should be taken to develop a water rate policy that established a uniform and consistent rate structure and incorporated sound business practices. Establishing such a policy would allow water users and the bureau to plan ahead to the dates when new rates would take effect.

The Bureau of Reclamation concurred with several of the points raised by the inspector general in the 1979 report and agreed that it was important to establish a basic rate-setting policy that could be applied immediately to new and amended contracts and contracts with rate review and adjustment provisions. Accordingly, the bureau presented a new CVP rate-setting policy for public review and comment in January 1981. This policy was similar to the 1974 proposal but included the provision (dating from 1979) that rates were subject to adjustment every five years. The proposal elicited a wide range of responses from CVP water users as well as from various governmental entities, special interest groups, and the general public, but the 1981 proposal was never formally adopted.

One reason was passage of the Reclamation Reform Act of 1982, which included requirements for charging "full cost" on lands in excess of new 960-acre limitations on the size of a farming operation. The "full cost" charge was to be on a district-by-district basis.[7] No prior CVP rate-setting proposal had developed district-by-district accounts because operation and maintenance and capital accounts were pooled projectwide. The development of accounts for each district was a massive undertaking, and it was not until April 1984 that a revised irrigation rate-setting proposal was released for public review and comment (U.S. Department of the Interior, Bureau of Reclama-

---

[6] The municipal and industrial account of the project (capital, interest at the project's authorized rate, and operation and maintenance) has been in deficit since before 1955. The cumulative municipal and industrial deficit grew from $17 million in 1981 to $30 million in 1985 and $37 million in 1986.

[7] As explained in chapter 4, "full cost" as defined by the act is less than the actual full cost of the water on existing projects because it does not incorporate past interest charges.

tion, 1984). This proposal again adopted the component rate-setting concept; however, rates would be adjustable annually instead of every five years. More important, the use of rolling repayment would be discontinued: a final repayment date of 2030 was established for the project (fifty years from the 1980 in-service date of the most recent addition to the project, the New Melones Dam). Furthermore, when contracts were renewed at the end of their current expiration dates, each contractor would be liable for repaying by 2030 his allocated capital cost (on the interest-free basis provided in Reclamation law) and any operation and maintenance deficit attributable to his water deliveries.

The 1985 "cost-of-service" rates for capital repayment were $2.13 per acre-foot for storage and $1.94 per acre-foot for conveyance. Operation and maintenance costs for these same two service components were $1.19 and $2.70 per acre-foot, respectively. Among those districts using conveyance pumping, capital repayment rates ranged from $0.52 to $1.23 per acre-foot and operation and maintenance costs from $0.55 to $3.19 per acre-foot. Only a limited number of contractors use direct pumping, for which capital costs ranged from $0.76 to $3.29 per acre-foot and operation and maintenance costs from $0.05 to $1.96 per acre-foot. The resulting total "cost-of-service" water rates for each district (including adjustments for past deficits and payments) ranged from $1.31 to $21.25 per acre-foot. Contract rates would continue to be limited to a ceiling of the contractor's estimated "ability to pay," but this was expected to be a constraint for only a limited number of districts in the northern part of the Central Valley Project, where growing seasons were shorter.

Analysis of CVP Repayment

The following analysis is based on the 1984 proposal as well as on some of the modifications made during 1985 and 1986 in response to public comments. Table 3-1 shows the 1986 repayment status of the forty-one largest CVP contracts (those with deliveries of 25,000 acre-feet or more). These contracts account for about 80 percent of 1986 projected water deliveries for irrigation (3.28 million acre-feet out of the 4.02 million acre-feet). For each contract the table shows the projected water deliveries, the long-term contract rates, the 1986 operation and maintenance expenses, and the resulting operating surplus or deficit, on both a per-acre-foot basis and a total contract basis. As the table shows, only six of these contracts were making any repayment to capital as of 1986: two of the three blocks of water allocated to Westlands Water District and the contracts with Glenn-Colusa Irrigation District, the Sutter Municipal Water Company, the Kanawha Water District, and the Panoche Water District. The contracts shown in the table result in an expected annual operating deficit of $4.1 million, which, when combined with the contract losses from other districts, yields a total expected operating loss of $5.0 million.[8]

Table 3-2 shows net repayment for the Central Valley Project on annual and cumulative bases since the beginning of the project. Under Bureau of Reclamation accounting produces, annual CVP revenues are credited first to annual operation and maintenance expenses and then to capital. The payment remaining for capital varies considerably from year to year because of annual variation in water deliveries and operating costs. However, a trend in repayment is clearly evident. The project had an annual operating deficit in six of the thirty-three years of operation prior to 1982 and has experienced annual operating losses in three out of the four years from 1982 through 1985. Cumulative net payments credited toward capital in the irrigation account have gradually declined from a high of $51 million in 1981 to $38 million in 1985. In the bureau's CVP accounts, previous payments toward capital are used to finance operation and maintenance costs in subsequent years. This means that as of 1985, thirty-seven years after project repayment began, less than 4 percent of capital costs ($38 million out of $950 million) had been repaid.[9] Furthermore, the repayment status of the project will worsen for a number of years as operation and maintenance costs escalate while contract rates stay fixed. The last column of table 3-1 shows the earliest adjustment dates (the expiration date in most cases) for the major CVP contracts. Most are not adjustable until some time between 1991 and 1996; several are not adjustable until 2003 or 2004; and the San Luis Unit contracts with the Westlands Water District (CVP's largest contract), the San Luis Water District, and the Panoche Water District do not expire until 2008.

Figure 3-2 shows the bureau's projected capital repayment under the "component" rate-setting policy proposal. Total capital repay-

---

[8] The actual operating losses for 1986 differed from the values in the table because actual water deliveries varied from projected deliveries. However, projected deliveries were used to better represent the average deliveries expected over the remaining life of the existing contracts.

[9] This calculation is based on interest-free repayment as provided in Reclamation law. When interest charges are taken into account, only about 3 percent of capital costs were repaid over the same period (see table 3-3).

Table 3-1. Operating Deficits in California's Central Valley Project Based on Projected Water Deliveries for 1986

District/contract	Projected water deliveries[a] (acre-feet)	Contract rate (dollars/acre-foot)	O&M cost (dollars/acre-foot)	Surplus (deficit) (dollars/acre-foot)	Total annual surplus (deficit) (dollars)	Adjustment date
Westlands WD/San Luis Canal[b]	900,000	8.00	9.19	(1.19)	(1,071,000)	2008
Westlands WD/San Luis Canal[b]	195,000	16.07	9.19	6.88	1,341,600	adj[c]
Arvin-Edison WSD/Class II	142,827	1.50	3.49	(1.99)	(284,226)	1995
Lower Tule River ID/Class II	114,240	1.50	3.49	(1.99)	(227,338)	1992
Delano-Earlimart ID	108,800	3.50	7.01	(3.51)	(381,888)	1992
Glenn-Colusa ID	105,000	2.00	1.80	0.20	21,000	2004
South San Joaquin MUD	97,000	3.50	7.01	(3.51)	(340,470)	1990
Sutter MWC	95,000	2.00	1.80	0.20	19,000	2004
Madera ID/Class II	89,280	1.50	3.49	(1.99)	(177,667)	1992
Madera ID	85,000	3.50	7.01	(3.51)	(298,350)	1992
San Luis WD/San Luis Canal	79,500	8.00	10.13	(2.13)	(169,335)	2008
Chowchilla WD/Class II	76,800	1.50	3.49	(1.99)	(152,832)	1991
Tulare ID/Class II	67,680	1.50	3.49	(1.99)	(134,683)	1991
Lower Tule River ID	61,200	3.50	7.01	(3.51)	(214,812)	1992
Westside WD	55,400	2.75	5.18	(2.43)	(134,622)	1995
Chowchilla WD	55,000	3.50	7.01	(3.51)	(193,050)	1991
Shafter-Wasco ID	50,000	3.50	7.01	(3.51)	(175,500)	1995
Westlands WD/Delta-Mendota Canal	50,000	11.49	6.85	4.64	232,000	adj[c]
West Stanislaus ID	50,000	3.50	6.85	(3.35)	(167,500)	1994
Panoche WD/Delta-Mendota Canal	49,900	3.50	6.85	(3.35)	(167,165)	1996
Orland-Artois WD	48,300	2.75	5.15	(2.40)	(115,920)	1995
Colusa County WD	46,500	3.50	5.88	(2.38)	(110,670)	1995
San Luis WD/Delta-Mendota Canal	45,000	3.50	6.85	(3.35)	(150,750)	2008

						adj[c]
Kanawha WD	45,000	10.95	5.21	5.74	258,300	1995
Panoche WD/San Luis Canal	44,000	8.00	7.56	0.44	19,360	2008
Kern-Tulare ID	40,000	7.10	7.49	(0.39)	(15,600)	1995
Arvin-Édison WSD	40,000	3.50	7.01	(3.51)	(140,400)	1995
Orange Cove ID	39,200	3.50	7.01	(3.51)	(137,592)	1989
Fresno ID/Class II	36,000	1.50	3.49	(1.99)	(71,640)	1995
Delano-Earlimart ID/Class II	35,760	1.50	3.49	(1.99)	(71,162)	1992
James ID	35,300	3.50	6.85	(3.35)	(118,255)	2003
Hospital WD	34,105	3.50	6.85	(3.35)	(114,252)	1994
Lindmore ID	33,000	3.50	7.01	(0.39)	(115,830)	1990
Lower Tule River ID	31,102	7.10	7.49	(0.39)	(12,130)	1995
Pixley ID	31,102	7.10	7.49	(0.39)	(12,130)	1995
Tulare ID	30,000	3.50	7.01	(3.51)	(105,300)	1991
Linday-Stratmore ID	30,000	3.50	7.01	(3.51)	(105,300)	1989
Terra Bella ID	29,000	3.50	7.01	(3.51)	(101,790)	1991
Corning WD	25,300	3.50	6.34	(2.84)	(71,852)	1995
Banta Carbona ID	25,000	3.50	6.85	(3.35)	(83,750)	1995
Broadview WD	25,000	3.50	6.85	(3.35)	(83,750)	1995
Subtotal	3,276,296				(4,137,250)	
Other districts	743,754				(909,425)	
Total	4,020,050				(5,046,675)	

Note: Abbreviations: WD, Water District; ID, Irrigation District; MUD, Municipal Utility District; MWC, Municipal Water Company; WSD, Water Storage District. Class II water is water in excess of storage capacity, available during high water years. No storage costs are assessed on class II water.

Sources: Projected annual deliveries are from U.S. Department of the Interior, Bureau of Reclamation, *CVP Ratesetting Policy Proposal* (Sacramento, Calif., April 1984). Contract rates, adjustment dates, and 1986 operation and maintenance costs are from records of Bureau of Reclamation, U.S. Department of the Interior, Sacramento, Calif.

[a] Although annual water deliveries vary from year to year, projected annual deliveries better represent the expected long-term average deliveries.

[b] For an explanation of the two sets of rates for water from the San Luis Canal for Westlands Water District and the controversy surrounding the district's contract, see the appendix to chapter 4.

[c] "adj" means that the contract rate is currently adjustable on an annual basis.

Table 3-2. Revenues, Operating Costs, and Net Repayment for California's Central Valley Project

(in thousands)

Year	Water deliveries (acre-feet)	Revenues (dollars)	Operation and maintenance (dollars)	Annual net repay-ment[a] (deficit) (dollars)	Cumulative net payment[a] (deficit) (dollars)
1949	196	309	74	235	235
1950	371	566	930	(363)	(128)
1951	337	527	1,128	(601)	(729)
1952	510	986	1,589	(603)	(1,332)
1953	904	2,013	1,030	984	(348)
1954	1,103	2,652	2,015	637	288
1955	1,156	2,881	2,227	653	942
1956	1,261	3,095	2,823	272	1,214
1957	1,462	3,644	2,586	1,057	2,271
1958	1,346	3,330	2,830	500	2,771
1959	1,748	4,769	3,322	1,446	4,218
1960	1,085	3,671	3,230	441	4,659
1961	974	3,394	3,632	(238)	4,421
1962	1,470	3,717	3,401	316	4,737
1963	1,817	4,856	3,928	927	5,664
1964	1,772	5,190	1,576	3,614	9,279
1965	2,041	5,164	3,990	1,174	10,453
1966	2,121	6,062	5,073	989	11,442
1967	1,653	4,323	3,409	914	12,356
1968	2,742	7,907	4,386	3,522	15,878
1969	1,774	5,803	7,460	(1,657)	14,221
1970	3,273	10,493	8,373	2,121	16,342
1971	2,336	9,187	8,237	950	17,291
1972	2,872	11,554	8,976	2,579	19,870
1973	2,886	11,686	9,303	2,383	22,253
1974	3,759	14,575	9,356	5,219	27,472
1975	4,041	16,703	11,133	5,570	33,041
1976[b]	4,758	22,141	15,136	7,005	40,047
1977	1,419	5,691	10,367	(4,676)	35,371
1978	3,355	14,080	13,477	604	35,974
1979	4,402	23,784	15,791	7,993	43,968
1980	4,573	20,071	17,353	2,718	46,686
1981	3,889	20,783	16,453	4,329	51,015
1982	4,583	18,909	20,511	(1,601)	49,414
1983	4,453	17,807	23,048	(5,241)	44,173
1984	4,892	23,344	20,594	2,750	46,923
1985	4,016	20,121	28,983	(8,862)	38,061
Total	87,350	335,790	297,729	38,061	
Present worth				135,436	

Source: Records of Bureau of Reclamation, U.S. Department of the Interior, Sacramento, Calif.

[a]Excludes charges for capital repayment (values shown are revenues less operation and maintenance charges).

[b]Includes transition quarter.

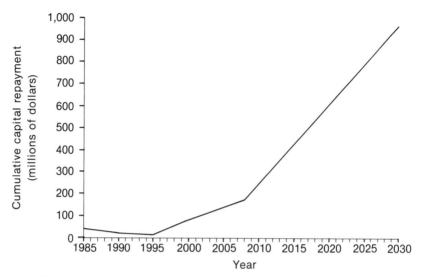

Figure 3-2. Projected repayment of capital costs for irrigation in California's Central Valley Project—component rate-setting method.
Source: Records of Bureau of Reclamation, U.S. Department of the Interior, Sacramento, Calif. Based on current contract rates and expiration dates.

ment will continue to decline because of operating deficits until the 1991–1993 period, when a number of contracts expire. The other major kinks in the curve occur in 1995, when a large number of additional contracts expire, and in 2008, when the Westlands and San Luis contracts expire. The increasing operating deficits indicated by the figure may be offset to some extent by the requirements of the Reclamation Reform Act: new or amended contracts and individual electors must pay water rates that cover operation and maintenance costs. There are various incentives in the act for farming operations to amend before April 1987 (for a more complete discussion, see chapter 4). At one extreme, if all contractors were to amend their contracts by April 1987, then the cumulative net repayment to capital would not decline after that date. Just what percentage of contractors would amend is not known, but the expected pattern of capital repayment would be quite similar to that shown in the figure.

How does this expected capital repayment compare with the repayment that would have occurred under the normal forty- or fifty-year repayment provisions of Reclamation law? Table 3-3 compares, on a present worth basis, the value of expected repayment (extending 82 years from 1949 to 2030) with repayment occurring within forty or fifty years of plant in-service dates. Under forty-year repayment

Table 3-3. Value of Repayment of Capital Costs, Central Valley Project, California

	Present worth (millions of dollars)	Percent of total present worth
Capital costs		
Total CVP capital expenditures of $954 million (1948–1983)	3,766	100
Revenues credited to repaying capital costs		
Expected CVP repayment		
1942–1985	135	3
1986–2030	68	2
Total	203	5
Hypothetical repayment		
Forty years after in-service dates	1,567	42
Fifty years after in-service dates	1,288	34

Note: Historical interest rates used were taken as the yields on government bonds of ten-year maturity at the beginning of each period. For the period beginning in year t, the yield is taken as the average of yields for the three years $t-1$, t, and $t+1$. Percent interest rates used are as follows:

1948–1957	2.33
1958–1967	3.77
1968–1977	5.80
1978–1982	8.42
1983–1985	12.18
1986	base year
1987–2030	9.00

Sources: Total capital expenditures are from records of Bureau of Reclamation, U.S. Department of the Interior, Sacramento, Calif. Expected CVP repayment is from records of past payments and projections of future payments based on the proposed CVP rate policy. Hypothetical repayment is calculated based on historical cost records.

terms, 42 percent of CVP capital costs would have been repaid in present worth terms ($1.57 billion out of $3.77 billion). Under fifty-year repayment terms, only 34 percent, or $1.29 billion, would have been repaid. These values can be compared with the expected present worth of repayment under the current rate-setting proposals for the project—$203 million, or approximately 5 percent of CVP construction costs (that is, about $3.56 billion of construction costs will be a federal subsidy).[10] In other words, the expected repayment will return only about 13–16 percent of the costs normally repayable under Reclamation law. This increased subsidy in the project has resulted

[10] For an alternative estimate of the subsidy, see LeVeen and King (1985).

from administrative practices such as fixed-rate contracts that provide subsidies over and above those embodied in general Reclamation
law. These practices will defer about 75 percent of capital repayment
until after 2010, some sixty years beyond the date that project repayment began.

Recent Influences on CVP Rate-Setting

During the public comment period on the bureau's 1984 proposal, the
Central Valley Project Water Association (an association of CVP
contractors) recommended that the rate-setting policy be changed. It
requested the bureau to adopt a "postage-stamp" approach to pricing,
under which all water users would be charged the same water rates,
rather than basing charges on just those service components used by
a particular contractor (storage, conveyance, conveyance pumping,
and so on). The water users evidently felt that adopting a postage-
stamp approach would do more to preserve the financially integrated
nature of the project and to forestall any attempts on the part of the
federal government to place the repayment burden for future CVP
additions on specific groups of water users. In response to the association's request, the bureau formulated a "modified postage stamp"
proposal, which pooled conveyance and conveyance pumping and the
net payment positions (surplus or deficit) of all contractors. The
consequences of this would have been to shift repayment of some
project costs to different groups of contractors. Among users of conveyance facilities, costs would have shifted from those water users with
high conveyance pumping costs to those with little or no conveyance
pumping costs. For example, about $64 million in repayment ($8.0
million in present worth) would have shifted from the Westlands
Water District, which has some of the highest conveyance pumping
costs in the project, to other districts. The pooling of contractor deficits would effectively have shifted repayment from those contractors
with adjustment dates far in the future to those with earlier adjustment dates. For example, pooling of net payment positions would have
shifted an additional $53 million ($1.3 million in present worth) from
Westlands to other districts, because Westlands receives a major
block of water (900,000 acre-feet) that will not be adjustable until
2008.[11] Consequently, other water districts would have begun paying
for capital repayment accruing to Westlands long before 2008.

---

[11] This calculation takes into account that Westlands would pay "cost-of-service"
rates for some of the water it receives from the San Luis Canal and for the water from
the Delta-Mendota Canal (see the three Westlands entries in table 3-1).

There was some question as to whether the pooling of contractor deficits would allow the bureau to use a consistent set of calculations for its water rates and for the determination of "full cost" charges under the Reclamation Reform Act.[12] As noted above, the definition of "full cost" appears to imply that district-by-district accounting should be used in the calculations. In addition, the definition of "full cost" in the act requires the bureau to include any operation and maintenance deficits funded, which normally occur on a district-by-district basis. Therefore, the bureau rejected the modified postage stamp approach and recommended instead a "component" rate-setting option with the pooling of net payment positions. This would still have been advantageous to contractors with low current rates (relative to the "cost of service") and later expiration dates. The bureau was preparing to publish this proposal for a final round of public comments prior to adoption when Congress intervened. Public Law 99-546 (100 Stat. 3050; 43 U.S.C. 422a), enacted in October 1986, requires that each new or amended contract in the Central Valley Project include provisions to recover "any annual deficit (outstanding or hereafter arising)" incurred by a CVP water contractor from that contractor. Furthermore, interest is to be charged on any such deficit that arises after October 1, 1985. The interest rate is set to reflect government borrowing rates rather than the project authorized interest rates. These interest charges are not payable until after a district's current contract expires or is amended. The Bureau of Reclamation determined that, provided the provisions of the law are not altered or successfully challenged before being implemented, P.L. 99-546 rules out the pooling of individual contractor deficits. Accordingly, in May 1987, the bureau issued for public review a rate-setting proposal with individual contractor deficits, patterned after its 1984 proposal. This rate-setting policy was ultimately adopted in May 1988.

Conclusions: The Consequences of Public Versus Private Development

The federal government's role in the Central Valley Project is something of a historical accident: the project was converted from a state project to a federal one as the result of the depression. The Bureau of Reclamation established low water rates with no cost adjustments partly to ensure that the water supplies it had developed could be

---

[12] For the definition of "full cost" charges under the Reclamation Reform Act and illustrative values, see chapter 4.

placed under contract. No systematic means was used to ensure that these rates would repay the cost of the project. This was possible partly because the bureau could rationalize that the project was incomplete (to be built in several stages) and, therefore, that no final payout date could be established. No attempt has been made by the Bureau of Reclamation to renegotiate or invalidate the contracts that now accrue operation and maintenance deficits in spite of the requirements of the Reclamation Project Act of 1939 that water service contracts have "such rates as in the Secretary's judgment will produce revenues at least sufficient to cover an appropriate share of the annual operation and maintenance cost and an appropriate share of such fixed charges as the Secretary deems proper."

In addition, the bureau adopted average cost pricing based on the authorizing language established by Congress that the project should be "financially integrated." As a result, the costs of increasingly expensive project additions have been averaged in with the costs of older facilities. Therefore, the cost of water to water users for additional supplies is far less than the long-run marginal cost of providing new supplies.

The history of the Central Valley Project and water rate-setting reveals that the federal subsidy for irrigation has been significantly increased through administrative means. Whereas the interest-free subsidy embodied in Reclamation law amounts to $2.20 billion–$2.48 billion of the project's $3.77 billion cost (in 1986 dollars), administrative measures will increase this subsidy to about $3.56 billion. Clearly, once the provision of water supplies and the establishment of water prices are moved from the private sector to the federal government, there is no longer an effective set of checks and balances to provide more efficient water rates. A private water company simply could not operate on the same terms as the bureau: it would fall far behind on its payments to bondholders and have to declare bankruptcy. The result—reorganization or the establishment of a new water supplier—would lead to a system of prices that would recover costs. However, since the Central Valley Project is constituted as a federal project, the bankruptcy of the project is not seen as separate from the financial status of the U.S. Treasury, with its vast financial resources. Alternatively, if the project had been constituted as a public utility, its regulating commission would long ago have required a revision of water rates to guarantee an adequate rate of return to shareholders. But when operated as a federal endeavor, rate-setting is no longer bound by the normal stricture of adequate financial returns. The interest-free repayment provisions of Reclamation law have allowed continued deferral of repayment with no interest penalty.

The pressure exerted by water users to influence rate-setting practices in their favor is brought about most directly at the regional level
of the Bureau of Reclamation. In the early contracting years, water
users were successful in demanding the certainty of long-term fixed
rates before they contracted for water. In 1984 water users succeeded
in getting the bureau to consider pooling the net payment positions of
contractors, to the advantage of certain contractor groups (in this
case, the difference in the value of revenues to the federal government
was minimal). In contrast to rate-setting by the normal public utility,
it took direct intervention by Congress through the Reclamation
Reform Act of 1982 and P.L. 99-546 in 1986 to force enhanced federal
revenue recovery on existing contracts. These two pieces of legislation
also virtually forced the Bureau of Reclamation to turn to a rate-
setting structure that required accounting for deficits contractor by
contractor, rather than pooling such deficits projectwide. So far, water
user groups have been unsuccessful in getting Congress to repeal the
key enforcement provisions of the Reclamation Reform Act, but, as
discussed in the next chapter, they did succeed in getting the Department of the Interior to support repeal and to write rules weakening
the enforcement of the act. In addition, several districts filed a lawsuit
alleging that certain key provisions of the Reclamation Reform Act
were unconstitutional on the grounds that they effectively revised the
repayment terms established by existing contracts. To date these
challenges have been unsuccessful. Because revenue recovery in the
Central Valley Project is ultimately decided in the political arena,
rather than on the basis of profitability, there remains the possibility
that these recent pieces of legislation will be revised by Congress,
successfully challenged in court, or interpreted and implemented by
the bureau in such a way as to have a mitigated effect on the prices
paid by water districts.

References

California Department of Water Resources. 1982. *Reconnaissance Report:
    State Operation and Management of the Central Valley Project* (Sacra-
    mento, Calif.).
_____. 1986. *Management of the State Water Project*. Bulletin 132-86 (Sacra-
    mento, Calif.).
Kahrl, William L., ed. 1978. *The California Water Atlas* (Sacramento, Cali-
    fornia Office of Planning and Research and California Department of
    Water Resources).
LeVeen, E. Phillip, and Laura B. King. 1985. *Turning Off the Tap on Federal
    Water Subsidies, Volume 1, The Central Valley Project: The $3.5 Billion*

Giveaway (San Francisco, Calif., Natural Resources Defense Council, Inc., and the California Rural Legal Assistance Foundation).

U.S. Department of the Interior, Bureau of Reclamation. 1971. *Central Valley Project, California: A Financial Analysis of the Authorized Central Valley Project–Past, Present, Future* (Sacramento, Calif.)

———. 1984. *CVP Ratesetting Policy Proposal* (Sacramento, Calif.)

U.S. Department of the Interior, Office of the Inspector General. 1978. *Review of the Central Valley Project, Bureau of Reclamation* (Washington, D.C.).

———. 1979. *Review of Municipal and Industrial Water Activities, Central Valley Project, Bureau of Reclamation* (Washington, D.C.).

4

Attempts to Limit the Reclamation Subsidy: The Reclamation Reform Act of 1982

The idea of promoting social justice and the general welfare by dividing up the large estates of wealthy landowners to provide small family farms and homesites for the landless classes is central to the twentieth-century history of China, Mexico, and other countries. However, such land reform is unlikely to be associated with the United States. Yet, in the 1960s, reform proposals were strongly advocated by certain agrarian interests in the western United States and were actually considered as serious options by the Department of the Interior under Secretary Cecil Andrus. These interests seized upon the acreage limitation and residency provisions applicable to land within federal irrigation projects as a vehicle for social reform. As with other land reform movements, the goal was to break up large landholdings in order to provide ownership opportunities to those who had previously been laborers on the farms.

This movement was spurred largely by a few energetic individuals, including George Ballis, the director of National Land for People; Mary Lois Frampton, legal counsel to National Land for People (Frampton, 1979); and Ben Yellin, a medical doctor in the Imperial Irrigation District in southern California. Yellin's medical practice brought him into close contact with many farm workers. He believed that to improve working conditions and the health of his patients, land reform was necessary. Ballis and National Land for People complained that the Bureau of Reclamation was not enforcing the 160-acre limitation against large landowners and that it was impossible for those wanting to establish small farms to do so. They contended that one of the primary goals of the Reclamation Act of 1902 was thus being thwarted.

The framers of the 1902 Reclamation Act were concerned that the benefits of the irrigation subsidy would become concentrated in the hands of land speculators or existing private owners with large land-holdings. Accordingly, the act required owners of land receiving sub-sidized water to be residents and limited the size of ownerships:

> No right to the use of water for land in private ownership shall be sold for a tract exceeding 160 acres to any one landowner, and no such sale shall be made to any landowner unless he be an actual bona fide resident on such land, or occupant thereof residing in the neighborhood of said land, and no such right shall permanently attach until all payments therefore are made.

However, as discussed below, the bureau enforced neither the resi-dency nor the acreage-limitation requirement consistently.

In 1976 National Land for People filed a lawsuit against the De-partment of the Interior to force it to establish uniform rules for administering the residency requirement and the 160-acre owner-ship limitation of the Reclamation Act. Of course, to the framers of the act, the 160-acre limitation on ownership of reclamation project land was not a means to effect land reform as much as to limit the distribu-tion of federally provided benefits and promote the development of small family farms. Lack of enforcement of the 160-acre limitation, especially in those areas where large landholdings were already an established practice, meant that renewed enforcement would alter established patterns of land management and would threaten the accumulated financial interests of larger farming operations.[1]

How such forces as the limitation of the federal water subsidy, the promotion of land reform, and the protection of established economic and property interests interact will help shape the reclamation pro-gram in the years to come. On the one hand, failure to effectively restrict the amount of federal subsidy accruing to any one beneficiary will undermine one of the principal rationales for the program, namely, that benefits accrue to small family farms rather than large farms or corporate interests. On the other hand, developments over the past decade highlight just how difficult it is to alter de facto property interests once they have been established by public action, whether legislative or administrative, especially when these inter-ests involve assets of considerable financial value.

---

[1] For economic analyses of the acreage limitation controversy written around this time, see Martin (1978), LeVeen and Goldman (1978), Hall and LeVeen (1978), and Seckler and Young (1978). Also see Sax (1965).

Acreage Limitation and Residency Under the 1902 Act

In placing acreage limitations on landownership, the Reclamation Act of 1902 followed the pattern established by the Homestead Act of 1862 (12 Stat. 392; 43 U.S.C. 161) and the Desert Land Act of 1877 (19 Stat. 377; 43 U.S.C. 321).[2] The Reclamation Act did not limit the size of private landholdings within reclamation projects, but merely the size of any landholding that was entitled to receive federally supplied water. While this method of specifying the acreage limitation was seen as an equitable distribution of the resource actually subsidized—water, not land—such formulation complicated enforcement for decades. Since larger landholdings were still allowable within the boundaries of the irrigated lands of reclamation projects, the bureau needed to keep track of which acreage actually received water.

Furthermore, in areas of private landownership (in contrast with homesteads from the public domain), many landholdings larger than 160 acres had been legitimately established prior to the construction of a bureau project, and the landowners subsequently wanted to qualify for delivery of federal project water to all of their land. How to bring these lands into conformance with the Reclamation Act led to considerable controversy. The Omnibus Adjustment Act of 1926 (44 Stat. 636) attempted to strike a compromise. It required that lands previously held in excess of the acreage limitation be placed under a "recordable contract," which mandated the eventual sale of "excess lands" at a price that did not allow the value of the irrigation subsidy to accrue to the original landowner. Specifically, section 46 of the act required that

> [Any] contract [for the delivery of water] with irrigation districts . . . shall further provide that all irrigable land held in private ownership by any one owner in excess of one hundred and sixty irrigable acres shall be appraised in a manner to be prescribed by the Secretary of the Interior and the sale prices thereof fixed by the Secretary on the basis of its actual bona fide value at the date of appraisal without reference to the proposed construction of the irrigation works; and that no such excess land so held shall receive water from any project or division if the owners thereof shall refuse to execute valid

[2] The Homestead Act of 1862 allowed a settler to select 160 acres of land from the public domain and to acquire title to it after residing on the land for five years (later amended to fourteen months) and after establishing cultivation. The Desert Land Act of 1877 applied to eleven states in the far West and granted title to 640 acres of land (reduced to 320 acres by an amendment in 1890) (26 Stat. 391), provided a settler diverted water to and reclaimed the land within three years.

recordable contracts for the sale of such land under terms and conditions satisfactory to the Secretary of the Interior.

The usual term for recordable contracts was ten years. In other words, the law provided those owners with larger landholdings a grace period to bring their ownership into compliance with acreage limitation. While the Omnibus Adjustment Act was the first example of legislation designed to ensure enforcement of the acreage limitation provisions of the Reclamation Act of 1902, it was also an open acknowledgment that prior practice was not in strict conformance with the law.[3]

Because of the considerable advantage of receiving low-cost, federally supplied water, it is not surprising that the ownership limitations of the 1902 act were tested by several other means: multiple ownerships within one family, deeding to children of land that was still being farmed by the parents, and establishment of farming operations with the ownership distributed among several landowners, each owning 160 acres or less. The Reclamation Act of 1902 did not specify the allowable extent of land ownerships by several members of the same family, nor did it explicitly limit the establishment of farming operations in which a single operator leased land from several owners. In several instances, the Department of the Interior took steps to define more precisely the nature of allowable practices. For example, in 1945 Interior Solicitor Fowler Harper issued an opinion that 320 acres of irrigable land could be held as joint property by husband and wife. In 1948 Commissioner of Reclamation Michael W. Straus ruled that a landowner could deed his excess acreage to a child or other party and could arrange to operate the property jointly with his own land as one unit, provided that he divest himself of ownership in good faith and that the child receive the full benefit of operation of his own acreage. Straus also maintained that several farmers each holding 160 acres could farm their lands jointly as a unit under mutual agreement. Such actions again acknowledged established practices.

The enforcement of acreage limitation varied a great deal from one Bureau of Reclamation region to another. Evidence of the results is contained in a 1979 land tenure survey conducted by the Economics, Statistics, and Cooperative Service of the U.S. Department of Agriculture.[4] The survey personnel contacted 15,200 individual land-

---

[3] As was the case with legislation lengthening the period for repayment of construction costs (discussed in chapter 2), reclamation legislation was often designed to legalize activity that had already become commonplace.

[4] Subsequent information obtained by the Bureau of Reclamation pursuant to its

Table 4-1. Size Distribution of Land Ownerships on Reclamation
Projects in 1979

Size of ownership (acres)	Owners		Irrigable acres		
	Number	Cumulative percent	Total	Mean	Cumulative percent
1–160	114,467	90.9	4,572,638	40	52.1
161–320	8,518	97.6	1,838,941	216	73.0
321–640	2,018	99.2	890,916	441	83.2
641–960	435	99.6	332,392	765	87.0
961–1,280	180	99.7	200,567	1,115	89.2
1,281–1,920	195	99.9	317,236	1,630	92.9
1,921 +	149	100.0	629,341	4,220	100.0
Total	125,962		8,782,031	70	

Note: Owners are those who own land either solely or in combination with others. The amount of land per owner in this table is each owner's prorated share of land held in joint or multiple ownerships. Thus, for example, an incorporation of four people owning 640 acres would be listed in the table as four owners in the 1- to 160-acre-size class, each with 160 acres. Multiple ownerships of more than ten owners were treated as single owners.

Source: U.S. Department of the Interior, Bureau of Reclamation, *Acreage Limitation: Draft Environmental Impact Statement, Westwide Report Appendix* (Denver, Colo., Water and Power Resources Service, 1981), p. 3-11.

owners and farm operators on Bureau of Reclamation projects, more than 93 percent of whom responded. The survey was intended to provide estimates of the pattern of landholdings on all reclamation projects. It indicated that in 1978 more than 8.4 million acres of land lay within established project service areas. This land was held by ar estimated 126,000 owners and was assembled into about 47,000 farming operations, reflecting the importance of leased land in farming operations. In fact, almost one-third of all farming operations contained leased land, and about 37 percent of irrigated land on reclamation projects was leased rather than farmed by the owner (U.S. Department of the Interior, Bureau of Reclamation, 1981, p. 3-13). Table 4-1 shows the size distribution of land ownerships, and table 4-2 gives the size distribution of farm operations, consisting of owned and leased land. As table 4-1 indicates, more than 90 percent of the estimated 126,000 landownerships westwide were smaller than 160 acres, and the average size of a landownership on a federal project was 70 acres. Only 0.4 percent of the ownerships exceeded 960 acres,

authority under the Reclamation Reform Act of 1982 confirms the conclusions drawn from the 1979 survey.

Table 4-2. Size Distribution of Farm Operations on Reclamation Projects in 1979

Size of farm operations (acres)	Farm operations		Irrigable acres		
	Number	Cumulative percent	Total	Mean	Cumulative percent
1–160	35,498	74.5	1,948,320	55	23.0
161–320	5,810	86.7	1,343,859	231	39.0
321–640	4,494	96.1	2,013,683	448	62.8
641–960	607	97.4	487,420	803	68.6
961–1,280	399	98.3	433,463	1,086	73.7
1,281–1,920	396	99.1	605,275	1,530	80.8
1,921+	435	100.0	1,618,630	3,721	100.0
Total	47,639		8,450,650[a]	177	

Source: U.S. Department of the Interior, Bureau of Reclamation, *Acreage Limitation: Draft Environmental Impact Statement, Westwide Report Appendix* (Denver, Colo., Water and Power Resources Service, 1981), p. 3-14.

[a]This number is about 4 percent less than the estimate from table 4-1, which is well within the margin of statistical error inherent in both estimates.

yet these accounted for 13 percent of the total acreage. Table 4-2 indicates that 97.4 percent of the farming operations, consisting of owned and leased land, were smaller than 960 acres, but the remaining 2.6 percent accounted for 26.3 percent of the total acreage. The average size of a farming operation was 177 acres.

Table 4-3 indicates the amount of excess land (land in ownerships larger than 160 acres) by state, showing that by far the largest percentage, 89.3 percent, lies in California. This is accounted for in part by the large percentage of all reclamation project land to be found in California (42.7 percent) and by the patterns of ownership that existed in California before the construction of reclamation projects: the large Spanish land grants obtained by early settlers and the large corporate landholdings in some areas of the state.

Westlands Water District is an area of some 600,000 acres in California's San Joaquin Valley that receives water from the bureau's Central Valley Project. In its 1976 lawsuit, National Land for People objected to the fact that excess land in Westlands was being sold in large blocks, making it impossible for small farmers to enter the market for land and thereby frustrating the intent of Reclamation law to provide land for small family farms. The group specifically requested that land be sold "(a) in lots of not more than one hundred sixty acres per buyer, (b) to residents of the land or those living in the neighborhood, and (c) at prices which reflect the value of the land

Table 4-3.   **Western States Ranked by Excess Land According to Limitations in Reclamation Act of 1902 (1979 data)**

State	Number of districts	Excess land Irrigable acres	Excess land Percent	Total reclamation land Irrigable acres[a]	Total reclamation land Percent
California	136	997,773	89.3	4,506,863	42.7
New Mexico	8	30,838	2.8	278,814	2.6
Texas	4	15,572	1.4	115,064	1.1
Nebraska	20	14,723	1.3	498,747	4.7
Montana	23	13,659	1.2	342,735	3.2
Wyoming	26	9,530	0.9	354,313	3.4
Arizona	8	8,564	0.8	412,797	3.9
Washington	31	6,484	0.6	909,209	8.6
Idaho	83	6,370	0.6	1,668,519	15.8
Oregon	44	6,128	0.5	478,469	4.5
South Dakota	4	2,936	0.3	81,030	0.8
Oklahoma	1	1,342	0.1	47,123	0.4
North Dakota	6	1,246	0.1	31,729	0.3
Utah	14	893	0.1	434,114	4.1
Colorado	11	672	0.1	249,441	2.4
Kansas	5	299	0.0	72,598	0.7
Nevada	1	0	0.0	73,002	0.7
Total	425	1,117,029	100.0	10,554,567	100.0

Source: U.S. Department of the Interior, Bureau of Reclamation, *Acreage Limitation: Draft Environmental Impact Statement, Westwide Report Appendix* (Denver, Colo. Water and Power Resources Service, 1981), p. 3-13.

[a]Based on a Crop Census definition that includes land in industrial and residential uses and other land not under cultivation. The area under cultivation that corresponds with irrigable acreage as defined in tables 4-1 and 4-2 is 8.8 million acres.

without the federally subsidized irrigation" (U.S. Department of the Interior, Bureau of Reclamation, 1981, p. 1-2). In August 1976 the court ruled in favor of National Land for People and issued an injunction against further excess land sales in Westlands until rules and regulations were written by the Department of the Interior and offered for public review and comment (National Land for People, Inc., v. Andrus, 417 F. Supp. 449 (D. D.C. 1976)).

As a result, on August 25, 1977, the Department of the Interior issued proposed rules that would apply to all reclamation project lands in the seventeen western states (refer to table 4-4 for dates relevant to the implementation of acreage limitation). Publication of final rules was halted by an injunction obtained by the Westlands Water District; the counties of Fresno (one of the three counties in which the district is located), Kings, Kern, and Imperial; the Lower

Table 4-4. Important Dates Regarding Implementation of Acreage Limitation on Reclamation Project Lands

1902	Reclamation Act establishes 160-acre ownership limitation.
1926	Omnibus Adjustment Act requires excess landholdings to be placed under "recordable contracts."
1945	Interior Solicitor Harper confirms that husband and wife may own 320 acres jointly.
1948	Commissioner Michael W. Straus approves trusts for children and the joint farming of land held by several owners.
1976	National Land for People files suit for enforcement of acreage limitation.
August 25, 1977	Department of the Interior publishes proposed rules to implement acreage limitation.
November 10, 1977	*County of Fresno et al. v. Andrus* (Westlands Water District; counties of Fresno, Kings, Kern, and Imperial; and others file suit against proposed rules).
December 7, 1977	Rules enjoined by U.S. District Court in Fresno, Calif., requiring environmental impact statement to be written.
January 8, 1981	Department of the Interior publishes draft environmental impact statement on proposed rules.
January 14, 1981	Department of the Interior publishes proposed rules and opens ninety-day comment period.
February 19, 1981	Secretary of the Interior James Watt indefinitely suspends the comment period on the proposed rules and the draft environmental impact statement.
July 21, 1981	Comment period resumed and extended to December 31, 1981.
December 8, 1981	Secretary of the Interior James Watt presents House testimony (December 10 in Senate).
December 31, 1981	Comment period extended to March 5, 1982.
March 15, 1982	House Report on Acreage Limitation Bill (H.R. 5539).
April 29, 1982	Senate Report on Acreage Limitation Bill (S. 1867).
May 6, 1982	House passes Acreage Limitation Bill (H.R. 5539).
July 16, 1982	Senate passes Acreage Limitation Bill.
September 22, 1982	Conference report on Acreage Limitation Bill.
October 12, 1982	President Ronald Reagan signs the Reclamation Reform Act, superseding rule-making under prior law.
May 3, 1983	Department of the Interior publishes draft rules to implement the Reclamation Reform Act of 1982.
December 6, 1983	Department of the Interior publishes final rules to implement the Reclamation Reform Act of 1982 (except rules to implement Section 203(b)—the hammer clause—which would take full effect on April 12, 1987).
November 7, 1987	Department of the Interior publishes revised proposed rules for acreage limitation, including provisions to implement Section 203(b).
April 13, 1988	Department of the Interior publishes final rules.

Tulare River Irrigation District; the California Farm Bureau Federation; and the American Farm Bureau Federation (County of Fresno et al. v. Andrus, No. F-77-202-Civ. (E.D. Cal., Dec. 7, 1977)). In their lawsuit, these agricultural interests claimed that the Department of the Interior had failed to comply with the National Environmental Policy Act. As a result, rule-making was suspended until an environmental impact statement (EIS) could be prepared.

It took nearly three years, until late 1980, for the department to prepare its draft EIS. On December 1, 1980, fourteen members of the House of Representatives requested that Secretary Cecil Andrus not release the EIS "in order to give the incoming administration an opportunity to review the data which have been gathered as well as the conclusions reached." Nevertheless, Andrus approved the draft EIS, which was filed on January 7, 1981, less than two weeks before President Jimmy Carter left office.

Legislative Proposals Leading to the Reclamation Reform Act of 1982

While the Department of the Interior was proceeding with rule-making and completion of the final EIS, those water users who would be most affected by regulations enforcing acreage limitation were seeking new legislation. Bills modifying Reclamation law were introduced in both the Ninety-fifth and Ninety-sixth Congresses. Notable among these was H.R. 6520 (U.S. Congress, House of Representatives, Committee on Interior and Insular Affairs, 1980; also see table 4-5). However, new legislation was not enacted until the Ninety-seventh Congress. Meanwhile, in order to give Congress time to act and himself time to consider the issues involved, Secretary James Watt slowed down the rule-making process: during his first weeks in office, he suspended the ninety-day comment period after it had been open scarcely four weeks (see table 4-4). Under pressure from the court order to issue regulations, he reopened the comment period in July 1981. However, the closing date was later extended from December 31, 1981, to March 15, 1982. Taking into account all the suspensions and postponements, the final date for comments was fourteen months after the proposed rules had been published (see table 4-4).

During this period of slowed rule-making, congressional interests were getting closer to writing a bill that could secure passage. On July 24, 1981, a new acreage limitation bill (H.R. 4265) was introduced in the House. Watt first issued the position his department would take on acreage limitation during testimony before the House Committee on Interior and Insular Affairs (referred to hereafter as

Table 4-5. Comparison of Significant Provisions of Acreage Limitation Legislation

Provision	Reclamation Act (1902)	Andrus's proposed rules (August 1977)	House committee bill H.R. 6520 (July 1980)	Watt's proposal (1981)	House bill H.R. 5539 (March 1982)	Senate bill S. 1867 (April 1982)	Reclamation Reform Act (October 1982)
Residency required	Yes	Yes, within 50 miles	No	No	No	No	No
"Prior law" option	—	No	No	No	Yes	No	Yes, with hammer
Acreage limitation on ownership and leasing	160 acres owned, silent on leasing	160 acres owned, lease up to 320 acres more; up to 640 acres owned in family ownerships, lease up to 320 acres more (total of 960)	960 acres owned, "full cost" on leasing over 960	960 acres owned, "full cost" on leasing over 960	960 acres owned, "full cost" on leasing over 960	1,600 acres owned plus 1,600 acres leased; if more than 3,200 acres, "full cost" on all acres over 1,600	960 acres owned, "full cost" on leasing over 960
Westwide application	Silent	Westwide	Silent	Westwide	District	Silent	Westwide
Equivalency	No	Only if previously authorized	Yes	Yes	Yes	Yes	Yes
Corporate entitlement	Silent	Family corporations if eligible to receive water prior to Jan. 1, 1978; other corporations phased out in 5 years	Same as individual if 18 or fewer members and received water prior to Oct. 1, 1981; "full cost" for water if first	Same as individual	Same as individual if 18 or fewer members and received water prior to Oct. 1, 1981; "full cost" for all water if first	Same as individual if 25 or fewer members; 640 acres owned if more than 25 individuals	Same as individual if 25 or fewer members and received water prior to Oct. 1, 1981; "full cost" for all water over

			received water after that date; no ownership if more than 18 individuals	received water after that date; no ownership if more than 18 individuals		320 acres; "full cost" for all water if first received after that date; 640 acres owned if more than 25 members
Interest charges under "full cost"	—[a]	Future interest only; current yield rates	Future interest only; current yield rates	Future interest only; historical yield rates; 5% minimum	Future interest only; current coupon rates	Future interest only; historical yield rates; 7.5% minimum
Interest rate applicable in 1982	—	13.5%	13.5%	Variable, at least 5%	9.38%	Variable, at least 7.5%
Special O&M cost provisions	—	—	None	None	None	Yes
Exemptions Corps projects exempted	No	Yes (intended)	Yes (intended)	Yes (intended)	Yes (intended)	Yes
Early payout allowed	Silent	Yes	No	No	No	No
Trusts	Silent; solicitor's opinions contained 7 conditions	Fiduciary capacity	Deferred to House and Senate	Fiduciary capacity	Fiduciary capacity	Fiduciary capacity

Note: Dashes mean not applicable.

[a] Acreage limit on leasing rather than full cost pricing. However, full cost pricing was considered as an option in the draft environmental impact statement written on Andrus's rules. The option defined full cost as including past as well as future interest.

the House Interior Committee) on December 8, 1981. In the course of his testimony, Watt further goaded Congress to action by threatening to issue strict regulations implementing the Reclamation Act of 1902 unless Congress enacted new legislation during its current session. The committee reported out an acreage limitation bill (H.R. 5539) to the House in March 1982 (U.S. Congress, House of Representatives, Committee on Interior and Insular Affairs, 1982).

The Senate was working on a parallel track (S. 1867; U.S. Congress, Senate, Committee on Energy and Natural Resources, 1982), but the bills adopted by the House and the Senate in 1982 differed in their approaches to acreage limitation, and these approaches varied from the rules proposed by Secretary Andrus and the legislation recommended by Secretary Watt. An examination of these differences provides some insight into the controversy surrounding acreage limitation and into how the legislation would be implemented. Table 4-5 compares the most significant provisions of the 1902 act, Secretary Andrus's proposed rules in 1977, the bill reported to the House in 1980 by the House Interior Committee, Secretary Watt's legislative proposals, the House and Senate bills, and the Reclamation Reform Act, which was signed into law on October 12, 1982 (96 Stat. 1263; 43 U.S.C. 390).

Residency

The Reclamation Act of 1902 required that a recipient of water on reclamation project land be a "resident" or "occupant," "residing in the neighborhood" of the land. However, the Bureau of Reclamation never specified precisely how this requirement was to apply, and absentee ownership came to be tolerated. Even so, the 1979 survey by the Department of Agriculture indicated that about 80 percent of landowners and 95 percent of farm operators lived within 15 miles of their land (U.S. Department of the Interior, Bureau of Reclamation, 1981, p. 3-15). Secretary Andrus's proposed rules would have enforced residency by requiring a landowner to live within 50 miles of his irrigated land. However, as table 4-5 shows, Congress was intent on abolishing the residency requirement. Secretary Watt was also convinced that a residency requirement was no longer useful. As a result of the Reclamation Reform Act, landowners, lessees, and farm operators no longer have to live on or near farms on reclamation projects. In recognizing existing practice, this change in Reclamation law also removed one of the original rationales for the reclamation program— to provide settlers with small family farms. Farmland on reclamation projects can now be owned by a distant urban dweller and leased merely as a business proposition.

Option to Remain Under Prior Law

Those water users who would be most affected by limitations on leased land argued that any new restrictions would be an unconstitutional taking of their current property interests and that therefore they should have the right to remain under prior law. In recognition of this claim, the major acreage limitation bill approved by the House allowed a two-track approach: districts could remain under prior law, or they could receive an expanded acreage limitation under new law. Secretary Andrus's rules, of course, did not contemplate a two-track approach because they were designed to implement prior law. Secretary Watt also advocated a single set of revised acreage limitation provisions and opposed the two-track approach. The Reclamation Reform Act (RRA), as enacted, retains a two-track approach in modified form. Existing irrigation districts and farmers have a choice: either they can continue to farm under the terms of Reclamation law in existence prior to the RRA (but amended by repeal of the residency requirement and by certain other changes) or they can elect to receive the expanded ownership entitlements of the new act. This choice can be made either at the district level or by individual farmers. If a district amends its contract to conform to the new acreage limitations, then the decision is binding on all of its members. However, even if a district decides not to amend, farmers may individually elect to do so. The RRA itself provided an incentive to accept the new legislative provisions within four and one-half years (by April 12, 1987) by means of the so-called hammer clause: farmers who did not choose the new limitations became subject to a more stringent set of requirements after April 12, 1987. Examined below are the provisions applying to the two groups: those amending their contracts and those remaining under prior law.

Provisions Applying to Amended Contracts and Individual Electors

Limitations on Ownership and Leasing.   The Reclamation Act of 1902 limited ownership to 160 acres, with subsequent Department of the Interior rulings allowing 320 acres for husband and wife. The act placed no explicit acreage limits on leasing. However, during the development of Andrus's rules and new legislative proposals in the late 1970s and early 1980s, there was a great deal of discussion as to whether the framers of the original act foresaw the extent to which leasing would be used to provide for farming operations greatly exceeding the ownership limits and whether such leasing was consistent with the intent of the 1902 act to promote small family farms and to limit the concentration of the benefits of irrigation water provided largely at federal expense. Secretary Andrus's proposed rules permitted the inclusion of leased land in a farming operation up to a total farm operation size of 480 acres for an individual. Husband and wife could own 320 acres, and family ownerships that included children could total 640 acres. Leasing was permitted by husband and wife (and in family ownerships) up to a total farm size of 960 acres. These values were based in part on studies of the economics of farm size conducted by the Department of Agriculture during the course of the draft EIS. These studies showed that over a wide range of farm types and climatic conditions, most of the economies of scale were attained in a farm of 600 acres or less.[5] Therefore, a 960-acre limitation would not restrict the efficiency of farming but would limit the amount of subsidy available to any one family.

Bills adopted by the House set forth a substantially larger limitation on ownership than Secretary Andrus's rules—960 acres. The bills did not call for any absolute, statutory limitation on leased land. Rather, a substitute concept—"full cost" pricing—was introduced as a means to control the distribution of the subsidy. Under "full cost" pricing, the subsidized rate specified in a district's contract would apply for all water delivered up to 960 acres. However, a "full-cost" rate would apply for any water delivered to leased land in excess of 960 acres. The intent was either to force divestiture of leased land over 960 acres or to remove the future interest subsidy from water delivered to these lands. This was in contrast to Andrus's proposal, which was only to limit farm size, regardless of whether the land was owned or leased (Andrus's proposed rules contained no "full cost" provisions). Watt essentially endorsed the House proposals. The Senate adopted even more liberal ownership and leasing limitations: 1,600 acres could be owned with an additional 1,600 acres leased. If the total acreage in a farming operation exceeded 3,200 acres, then "full cost" had to be paid on all but the first 1,600 acres of the farming operation.

The provisions of the House bill prevailed in the Reclamation Reform Act: districts and individuals can elect to expand the ownership limitation from 160 acres under prior law (320 acres for husband and wife) to 960 acres. Separate 960-acre entitlements cannot be held by a spouse or by dependent children because RRA limitations apply to an individual and include his or her spouse and other dependents as defined in the tax code of the Internal Revenue Service. "Full cost"

[5] For other studies of the economies of scale in farming that yield comparable results, see Martin (1978).

pricing applies to those lands leased by a farming operation that exceeds the 960-acre limit.

The bill had to address some additional questions of ownership and leasing. How would the provisions apply if a farmer owned or leased land in more than one district? Should owners of less productive lands be allowed a larger limitation? Should corporations be afforded the same privileges as an individual? These issues, which had become known respectively as "westwide application," "equivalency," and "corporate ownership" are discussed in turn.

Westwide Application.   The Reclamation Reform Act clearly intended to affect leasing of land and individual owners with land in several districts, as made clear by its definition of landholding:

> [the] total irrigable acreage of one or more tracts of land situated in *one or more districts owned or operated under a lease* which is served with irrigation water pursuant to a contract with the Secretary [emphasis added].

The acreage of land owned or leased by an individual in different districts must be totaled to determine the size of the landholding. The original 1902 act made no distinction between district and westwide entitlements because, under its residency requirement, ownership in one district was all that could legitimately be realized. Secretary Watt also advocated a limitation applied westwide rather than district by district. It is notable that the Conference Committee bill included a westwide limitation, given that only a district-by-district limitation had been included in the final House bill and that the Senate bill was silent on this provision.

Equivalency.   All of the congressional proposals shown in table 4-5 were flexible in their acreage limitations on less productive land. Under the RRA, districts may request an equivalency determination. The bureau then determines the equivalent of 960 acres of land of class I productive potential for land of lower land classes. As a result, operations larger than 960 acres are allowable on some lands.

Corporate Ownership.   It was also debated whether special limitations should apply to corporate ownership, especially in light of the intent of the 1902 act to promote opportunities for family farming. Indeed, some questioned whether corporations should be entitled to any subsidized irrigation water. The 1979 land tenure survey indicated that about 9 percent of all land owned in reclamation projects was under some form of nonfamily partnership or corporate ownership. About 7 percent of total land owned was held by corporate ownerships involving ten or more individuals. In terms of land in farming operations, about 18 percent (approximately 1.5 million acres) was managed by some form of nonfamily corporate ownership, with about 14 percent of the total land operated by corporations with ten or more individuals (U.S. Department of the Interior, Bureau of Reclamation, 1981, pp. D-2, D-3, and D-7).

Secretary Watt believed that a corporation should be treated the same as an individual. The House bill adopted that limitation, provided the corporation had eighteen or fewer individuals and was already receiving water. However, the House felt that newly formed corporations should not be entitled to subsidized water and should have to pay "full cost" for all of their water. Further, larger corporations (those with more than eighteen shareholders) were not granted any ownership entitlement. The Senate bill had somewhat more liberal restrictions: it treated a corporation of up to twenty-five members the same as an individual, and larger corporations could own up to 640 acres. The RRA basically adopted the corporate entitlements of the Senate bill but added the House bill restriction requiring prior receipt of water. Furthermore, a more stringent cost recovery provision applies to corporations: they are to be charged "full cost" for all water delivered to land in excess of 320 acres.

The RRA "Full Cost" Formula.   Since RRA "full cost" was established by a legislative compromise, its precise terms were the subject of negotiation. In fact, "full cost" as defined by the RRA is not the full financial cost of providing the irrigation water supply. This is because under the RRA "full cost" pricing formula, interest is charged only prospectively from 1982, not retrospectively. Interest charges accruing between the time of project construction and the date of the act are, in effect, forgiven. More specifically, in calculating RRA "full cost," payments to date are subtracted from the cost allocated to irrigation, and the result is amortized with interest over the remaining contract term or repayment period provided by Reclamation law.[6]

Another point of negotiation in Congress was the interest rate to be included in the formula. As table 4-5 shows, the interest rates applicable for 1982 ranged from 5 percent to 13.5 percent under the various legislative proposals. This is because in some proposals historical rates were used instead of the higher costs of government borrowing in 1982; coupon rates on all outstanding U.S. obligations were used rather than the higher market yield rates on bonds issued in 1982; or

---

[6] On the other hand, the RRA "full cost" definition removes the "ability-to-pay" subsidy that is usually paid from hydropower revenues (see chapter 2). The RRA "full cost" formula is based on the total cost allocable to irrigation rather than on a district's remaining repayment obligation.

minimum applicable rates were incorporated. The actual cost of long-term government borrowing in 1982 would be reflected most accurately by the then-current yield rate (13.5 percent), which was the provision incorporated into Watt's legislative proposal and the House Interior Committee bill. The rates adopted in the RRA were lower, since they were based on the weighted average of government borrowing rates prevailing during the years of project construction. The fourth column of numbers in table 4-6 shows the interest rates applicable on a sample of districts.

Table 4-6 also shows the result of applying the RRA "full cost" formula to these districts, compared with the actual full financial cost of the project irrigation water supply. Actual full financial cost ranges from $5.30 per acre to $1,043.20 per acre, whereas RRA "full cost" charges range from $1.90 per acre to $902.70 per acre. In percentage terms, the RRA "full cost" charges range from 3 percent to 87 percent of the corresponding full financial costs. The principal reason for the difference is the forgiveness of past interest. In summary, the "full cost" pricing formula is the result of a political compromise: some of the large farming interests in California estimated that they could break even on land to which the RRA "full cost" formula would apply.

As of June 1987 (two months after new penalties applied to nonamending districts; see discussion of "hammer" provisions below), five of the districts shown in table 4-6 had amended their contracts to become subject to the new provisions of the RRA. Seven of the eighteen districts had chosen to remain under prior law (although individual farmers in these districts have the option to become individual electors). The remaining six districts shown in the table are exempt from "full cost" charges because they have completed contract repayment or because of court decisions (the Imperial court case is discussed under the subsection "Exemptions from Acreage Limitation").

Special Provisions on Payment of Operation and Maintenance Costs. The RRA also requires amending districts (and individual electors) to pay water rates that at least cover operation and maintenance (O&M) costs on their first 960 acres. This provision was directed largely at districts in the Central Valley Project in California, where water rates are fixed per acre-foot in forty-year contracts.[7] As discussed in chapter 3, although the rates were intended to cover both O&M and capital costs, they currently fail to do so in many districts.

[7] This provision does not affect most other districts, where, pursuant to Bureau of Reclamation contracts, O&M charges must be paid annually in advance of the irrigation season.

Districtwide amendment would require that all farming operations, even those below 960 or 160 acres in size, pay higher water rates to cover O&M costs. The practical consequence is that, in the Central Valley Project, individual election rather than districtwide amendment is likely to be the form of amendment most used.

In summary, under the RRA there are two potential costs of obtaining an expanded ownership entitlement compared with the 1902 Reclamation Act: full O&M costs must be paid for all water, and "full cost" must be paid for water delivered to land in excess of 960 acres in larger farming operations. These costs were the impetus for the Reclamation Reform Act provisions allowing districts to choose the prior law option.

Districts Wishing to Remain Under Prior Law

Under the prior law option, the 160-acre ownership limitation still applies, but farming operations are not subject to any limit on the amount of land they can lease, to "full cost" pricing, or to the O&M cost provisions. One might well wonder why, aside from an operator's desire to have outright ownership of all lands in a farming operation, farms would choose the expanded ownership provisions. The answer lies in the "hammer clause" of the RRA and the requirements imposed on districts wishing to receive the benefits of additional federal expenditures.

The Hammer Provision (Section 203(b)).   Section 203(b) of the RRA states that any district not amending its contract before April 12, 1987, must pay "full cost" for any land leased in excess of 160 acres. This "hammer"—a much more stringent 160-acre, rather than 960-acre, entitlement to water at the subsidized rates of prior law—is clearly an incentive for amendment by the April 1987 deadline. Section 203(b) demonstrates congressional intent to eventually place all districts under the O&M and "full cost" pricing provisions of the RRA, while providing a four-and-one-half-year grace period for the transition to take place. A hammer provision was not included in either the House or the Senate bill, but was adopted by the Conference Committee as a last-minute compromise to avoid the threat of a filibuster by Senator Howard Metzenbaum of Ohio.

Supplemental or Additional Benefits.   Districts can be forced under the expanded ownership provisions of the RRA (with the associated requirements on "full cost" pricing and full O&M costs) if they request and receive further federal financial assistance. Specifically, districts that enter into a new or amendatory contract (after the date

Table 4-6. Actual Full Financial Cost and "Full Cost" as Defined Under the Reclamation Reform Act for Selected Irrigation Districts (excluding operation and maintenance costs)

Irrigation district: project	Actual full financial cost (dollars/acre)[a]	RRA "full cost" (dollars/acre)[b]	RRA "full cost" as percent of actual full cost	Interest rate for "full cost" (percent)[c]	RRA status[d]
Pacific Northwest region					
Oroville-Tonasket: Chief Joseph Dam	1,043.20[e,f]	902.70	87	11.2	Prior law
Black Canyon #2: Boise	68.90	14.61[g] / 15.95[h]	21[g] / 23[h]	7.5[g] / 7.5[h]	Prior law
East Columbia Basin: Columbia Basin	168.18[e,ij]	61.90[i]	37	7.9	Prior law
Mid-Pacific region					
Cachuma: Cachuma	128.20	39.19	31	7.5	Prior law
Truckee-Carson: Newlands	82.80	62.31	75	7.5	District amended
Glenn-Colusa: Central Valley	9.20	5.99	65	8.0	Prior law
San Luis Unit: Central Valley	53.65[k,l]	29.70[k,m]	55	8.0	Prior law
Lower Colorado region					
Coachella Valley: Boulder Canyon	99.40	7.71[n] / 10.45–11.72[o]	8[n] / 11–12[o]	11.5[n] / 11.5[o]	District amended
Wellton-Mohawk: Gila	170.50	31.37	18	7.5	Prior law
Imperial Valley: Boulder Canyon	14.20	Exempt	—	—	Exempted by courts

(continued)

Table 4-6 *(continued)*

Irrigation district: project	Actual full financial cost (dollars/acre)[a]	RRA "full cost" (dollars/acre)[b]	RRA "full cost" as percent of actual full cost	Interest rate for "full cost" (percent)[c]	RRA status[d]
Upper Colorado region					
Moon Lake: Moon Lake	5.30	Exempt	—	—	Received payout exemption
Grand Valley: Grand Valley	145.50	Exempt	—	—	Received payout exemption
Southwest region					
Elephant Butte: Rio Grande	32.10	Exempt	—	—	Received payout exemption
Lugert-Altus: W. C. Austin	61.00	1.90	3	7.5	District amended
Upper Missouri region					
Malta: Milk River	72.50	2.80	4	7.5	District amended
Lower Yellowstone #1: Lower Yellowstone	44.80	Exempt	—	—	Received payout exemption
Lower Missouri region					
Farwell Pick-Sloan Missouri	133.30	52.35	39	7.5	District amended
Goshen: North Platte	38.20	Exempt	—	—	Received payout exemption

Note: Dashes mean not applicable.

Sources: Annual full cost rates are from U.S. Department of the Interior, Bureau of Reclamation, *Acreage Limitation: Draft Environmental Impact Statement, Westwide Report Appendix* (Denver, Colo., Water and Power Resources Service, 1981), pp. F-3–F-5. Annual "full cost" rates applicable under the Reclamation Reform Act of 1982 (RRA), the remaining repayment period, and the interest rate applicable for "full cost" are from records of Bureau of Reclamation records, U.S. Department of the Interior, Denver, Colo.

[a] Annual rate for full cost as of 1978 using a future interest rate of 8.49 percent and a forty-year amortization period. Does not include annual operation and maintenance costs. Historical interest rates used are the same as in table 2-3.

[b] Annual rate as of 1986 for qualified recipients (individuals) receiving water before October 12, 1982. Does not include annual operation and maintenance costs.

[c] The Reclamation Reform Act established a 7.5 percent minimum interest rate for calculating "full cost."

[d] Status as of June 1987, two months after the "hammer clause" took effect.

[e] Incorporates expenditures (less repayments) from 1979 to 1986. The net present worth of additional expenditures during this period is amortized over a forty-year period using an interest rate of 11.4 percent, which is the average of the interest rates applicable under the Reclamation Reform Act for the years from 1979 to 1986.

[f] Value as of 1978 was $42.40.

[g] For lands irrigated by a gravity irrigation system.

[h] For lands irrigated by pumped irrigation water.

[i] Values shown are average for district.

[j] Value as of 1978 was $142.70.

[k] Rate per acre-foot, instead of per acre. At a water application rate of 2.5 acre-feet per acre, actual full financial cost would be $134.12 per acre and RRA "full cost" would be $74.25 per acre. Excludes cost of distribution system ($10.11 per acre-foot for RRA "full cost").

[l] Value as of 1978 was $44.24 per acre-foot ($110.60 per acre).

[m] Full cost rate for the Westlands Water District. Full cost rates (excluding operation and maintenance costs) for other districts in the San Luis Unit are $47.01 per acre-foot for the San Luis Water District, $23.55 per acre-foot for the Panoche Water District, and $25.41 per acre-foot for the Pacheco Water District.

[n] Original contract.

[o] Supplemental contract.

of the act) "which enables the district to receive supplemental or additional benefit" cannot remain under prior law. Supplemental or additional benefits are defined in the RRA regulations as those contract actions that require expenditure of additional funds or commitment of additional water supplies to a district, or which substantially modify contract payments due the United States.

Exemptions from Acreage Limitation

To secure passage of the RRA, a number of legislative exemptions were fashioned. Even before passage, a small number of districts had been exempted from acreage limitation, including districts in the Colorado–Big Thompson Project, the Truckee Storage and Humboldt projects in Nevada, and the San Felipe Division of the Central Valley Project in California. There were statutory modifications of acreage limitation on at least two dozen other projects (see U.S. Department of the Interior, Bureau of Reclamation, 1981, pp. I-iii–I-iv). In 1980 the U.S. Supreme Court ruled that the Imperial Irrigation District in California was also exempt from acreage limitation based on specific legislative directives of the Boulder Canyon Project Act relating to the water rights held by Imperial before the construction of Hoover Dam (*Bryant v. Yellin et al.*). This decision removed about 465,000 acres from the application of acreage limitation. The Reclamation Reform Act of 1982 greatly expanded the number of exempt districts.

Exemption for Corps of Engineers projects. Acreage limitation on certain projects constructed by the Corps of Engineers in the Kings River, Kern River, and Tulare Lake areas in the southern Central Valley in California had been a source of controversy for years. These service areas contained a number of the largest farming operations in the reclamation program: J. G. Boswell, 109,793 acres; Tenneco West, 64,941 acres; Salyer Land, 29,060 acres; Southlake Farms, 26,816 acres; Westlake Farms, 19,817 acres; and George W. Nickel, Jr., 16,686 acres (U.S. Congress, House of Representatives, Committee on Interior and Insular Affairs, 1980, p. 65). The Isabella, Pine Flat, Success, and Terminus projects supplying these areas were authorized under the Flood Control Act of 1944. According to Section 8 of this act, Reclamation law was to apply to irrigation water that was a supplemental supply from these projects. However, the districts built their own distribution systems and believed that, consequently, they were exempt from the provisions of Reclamation law. After years of dispute with the Bureau of Reclamation over this issue, a test case was filed in 1963 and the parties agreed to abide by the outcome. In 1972 the District Court ruled in favor of the landowners, but this decision was overturned in 1976 by the Appeals Court, which found that

> There can be no doubt . . . that in proposing section 8, the Senate subcommittee intended to adopt the [Roosevelt] Administration's position that the Reclamation laws, and specifically the acreage limitation, should apply to irrigation uses of all projects authorized by the bill, including the Kings River project, even though the projects were built by the Corps of Engineers.

The Ninth Circuit refused to review the decision, as did the U.S Supreme Court in 1977.

The districts refused to comply with the outcome and within five years had succeeded in getting a legislative exemption written into the Reclamation Reform Act. Projects constructed by the Corps of Engineers are exempted by the RRA, unless they have been made part of a federal reclamation project explicitly by statute. In addition to exempting the Kings River Water District, the Tulare Lake Basin Water Storage District, and the Tulare Lake Canal Company (a total of about 1,085,000 acres), this provision exempted thirty-eight other irrigation districts.

Exemption for religious and charitable organizations. The Reclamation Reform Act clarifies that individual religious or charitable entities, such as a parish or ward, are subject to the same restrictions under the law as a private individual, regardless of whether they are affiliated with a larger religious organization. This provision of the RRA was added principally to protect the existing landholdings of individual wards of the Mormon Church. According to the RRA, the agricultural income from such lands must be used only for charitable purposes and not for the private benefit of any individual. As of 1985, the Mormon Church owned approximately 23,000 acres of irrigated land in reclamation projects, although some 14,000 of these acres were in districts exempt from acreage limitation.

Exemption for lands in the Central Arizona Project. A major exemption was granted to lands to be irrigated by the Central Arizona Project. Although under construction, this project was not ready to deliver water at the time the RRA was passed.[8] The drafters of the RRA judged that it was equitable to grant lands in the Central Arizona Project an exemption from the new provisions of the RRA until ten years after the date that such lands became eligible to receive irrigation water.

Exemption upon payout. The ownership and pricing limitations do

---

[8] Deliveries of water to the Phoenix area began in November 1985.

not apply after a district has completed its repayment obligation. Accelerated repayment to achieve payout is not allowed. As of 1986, fifty districts in the reclamation program had been granted a payout exemption, includng fifteen in the Mid-Pacific region, twelve in the Pacific Northwest region, and ten in the Upper Missouri region (refer also to the last column of table 4-6).

Exemption for trusts. The ownership and pricing limitations do not apply to the lands held by an individual or corporate trustee acting in a fiduciary capacity, as long as the holding of each beneficiary of the trust complies with such limitations.

Exemption for temporary supplies. The ownership limitations of Reclamation law are not to apply to lands that receive a temporary one-year supply of water that is not storable for project purposes.

In summary, under pressure from those who would suffer most from regulations implementing the acreage limitation provisions of the 1902 act, Congress dramatically liberalized the restrictions on entitlements to federally supplied water. The residency requirement was abolished, the acreage limitation was raised to 960 acres, leasing was explicitly allowed (although "full cost" had to be paid on lands in excess of 960 acres), and numerous categories of land were exempted from acreage limitation. However, both the Secretary of the Interior and congressional leaders had expressed the view that in liberalizing these provisions, it was meant that the new limitations would be administered more vigorously and would represent an upper limit on the benefits of receiving subsidized water. Senator James McClure of Idaho expressed these sentiments while endorsing the Senate bill:

> We must recognize that what we are trying to do in this legislation is get away from the building-block concept that allows an almost infinite multiplication of 160 acre units depending upon how many members of the family you can get involved, to put a real cap on the size. (*Congressional Record,* July 16, 1982, p. S 8469)

Again in addressing the Senate in support of the Conference Report, Senator McClure stated:

> The conference report establishes an absolute limit on the amount of subsidy that an individual or legal entity may receive from the reclamation program. (*Congressional Record,* September 24, 1982, p. S 12198)

Implementation of the act, however, would prove otherwise.

From Proposed to Final Regulations in 1983

For those affected by acreage limitation, the subsequent development and administration of regulations offered other opportunities for relief. Both before publication of the proposed rules to implement the

RRA and during the comment period on them, those water users most affected exerted considerable pressure to weaken the impact of the new law. Indeed, several accommodations were made regarding trusts, the ownership entitlement under prior law, water rates under extended recordable contracts, and provisions relating to the payment of operation and maintenance costs. These are discussed in turn.

Trusts

Although the RRA exempts fiduciary trusts from acreage limitation, it does not provide additional detail on which trusts may qualify. Before the passage of the Reclamation Reform Act of 1982, trusts involving land in reclamation projects had to meet seven criteria established in a 1962 opinion of the solicitor of the Department of the Interior. It was suggested before the RRA rules were published that they explicitly incorporate these criteria. The following brief account illustrates their importance.

In 1962 some of the ten-year recordable contracts executed in California were set to expire. These contracts, in accordance with Reclamation law, specified that the lands held in excess of the acreage limitation had to be sold at a price low enough that the value of the federally supplied water would not accrue to the original owner. Some of the contracts involved substantial excess acreage held by corporations. One corporation, instead of selling its excess land, proposed to place the land (about 1,900 acres of a vineyard) into a trust. Solicitor Frank J. Barry issued an opinion on this arrangement, and the opinion was approved by Secretary Stewart L. Udall (U.S. Department of the Interior, Opinion of Solicitor Frank J. Barry, March 19, 1962, approved by Commissioner Floyd E. Dominy and Secretary Stewart L. Udall, December 21, 1962). It held that, in reviewing trust agreements, the elements of the trust "must be carefully considered in order that the arrangement may not take on the character of 'business as usual' for the excess owners or may not present unacceptable burdens of supervision and policing by the Bureau." It went on to establish seven minimum requirements for trusts. Among these were (1) that the trust be irrevocable and convey all control over a specific parcel of land to the beneficiary of the trust; (2) that each undivided interest, when taken in proportion to the total acreage of the trust, not exceed 160 acres; (3) that the trustee not acquire any beneficiary interest in the trust (only compensation for management of the trust); and (4) that each beneficiary of the trust have the right, at his or her option, to partition his or her interest in the trust. These criteria were designed to ensure that trusts were not used merely as a means to escape acreage limitation, such as by being established on a temporary, revocable basis or by allowing the original landholders to maintain control over land placed into a trust.

It was finally decided, however, not to incorporate the seven criteria (applied to 960 acres, rather than 160 acres) in the proposed rules for the Reclamation Reform Act (U.S. Department of the Interior, Bureau of Reclamation, 1983a). Instead, in addition to limiting each undivided interest in a trust to the act's ownership entitlement (an explicit requirement of the law), the proposed rules imposed the same ownership entitlement on the entire trust. Banks objected strenuously on the grounds that through foreclosure or execution of a will, they might involuntarily become the trustees of excess lands on which lessees would have to pay "full cost," thereby lowering the rental value of the land. As a result, the final rules were changed to provide that neither a corporate nor an individual trustee would be subject to the ownership or pricing limitations of the RRA and that acreage limitation would apply only to the interests of each beneficiary of a trust. By this change, a provision originally intended to protect banking operations came to apply to all trusts. During the preparation of final rules, it was also argued that it was not necessary to include Solicitor Barry's criteria because the laws of the state of California regarding trusts were restrictive enough that the department had no reason to expect situations in which trustees were also the beneficiaries of the trust or any other situation that might be considered an abuse of the trust provisions. Notwithstanding this claim, shortly after the publication of the final rules, the Bureau of Reclamation offices in California were asked to approve the Richards family trust.

The Richards Family Trust. (The actual names are not used in this example.) At one time Richards Ranch, Inc., owned about 7,000 acres of irrigable land in excess of the 960-acre limitation. All of this land was eligible to receive project water because it had been placed under recordable contracts. As the ranch's recordable contracts began to mature, the ten-member Richards family formulated a plan by which ownership of all the land could remain in the family, while avoiding payment of "full cost" on any of it.

An outline of the Richards plan is shown in table 4-7. Under the plan, each family member would make an irrevocable election increasing his ownership entitlement to 960 acres. The great grandmother, the grandmother, and four adult grandchildren would collectively own 969 acres through Richards Ranch, Inc. In addition, a trust (designated as Trust 1 in table 4-7) consisting of 4,571 acres would be owned by the same six individuals, bringing their individual ownership entitlements close to 960 acres each. The beneficiaries

Table 4-7. Richards Family Trust

Family member	Relation	Richards Ranch, Inc. (acres)	Trust 1 (acres)	Trust 2 (acres)	Own name (acres)	Total (acres)
Elizabeth Richards	Great grandmother	483	478			961
Rebecca Fawcett	Grand-mother		960			960
Mr. and Mrs. Gerard	Adults	121	833			954
Harvey Richards	Adult	123	832			955
Michael Richards	Adult	121	832			953
John and Sue Crawford	Adults	121	636		221	978
Deborah Crawford	Child			663		663
John Gerard	Child			663		663
James Gerard	Child			663		663
Linda Gerard	Child			663		663
Total		969	4,571	2,652	221	8,413

Note: Once excess land sales are completed, ownerships may vary in acreage from the values shown here.

Source: Records as of 1986 of Bureau of Reclamation, U.S. Department of the Interior. The actual names have been changed.

would be the trustors. Trust 2, consisting of 2,600 acres, would be established for four great grandchildren, ranging in age from five to fourteen years, who would own approximately 663 acres each.[9] In accordance with the requirements of the Reclamation Reform Act of 1982, the Richards family indicated that these minor children were not dependents as defined by the Internal Revenue Service. Richards Ranch, Inc., would set up a farm management agreement to farm the land in Trust 1 and could legally do the same for the land in Trust 2.

The Richards family submitted this plan to the Bureau of Reclamation for approval in 1984. The family members have delayed making irrevocable elections until absolutely necessary (until all the recordable contracts expire). While final approval of the plan could not be given until all family members made irrevocable elections, the bureau approved the proposal in concept.

[9] The 1979 land tenure survey indicated that there were 238 minor beneficiaries of trusts in the Westlands Water District and fifty minors who were members of corporations owning land (U.S. Bureau of Reclamation, 1981, *Westside Appendix,* p. D-58).

Westwide Application of Ownership Entitlement Under Prior Law

The RRA specifies that for districts with new or amended contracts, a landowner's acreage in each of several districts must in total comply with acreage limitation. However, it does not explicitly state that a similar westwide ownership limitation is meant to apply to farmers residing in districts that choose to remain under prior law.

The proposed regulations specified that the 160-acre entitlement would be applied on a westwide basis for those under prior law, a point that led to a great deal of controversy (U.S. Department of the Interior, Bureau of Reclamation, 1983b, Response to Public Comments, p. 54,756). The final rules adopted a compromise position: for farmers remaining under prior law, westwide application is to be made only for those lands acquired after December 6, 1979. This is the date of the opinion of Interior Solicitor Leo Krulitz (M-36919), which states that the ownership limitation applied on a westwide basis (the opinion was intended to apply to all lands, regardless of when they were acquired). Therefore, through the rule-making process, a compromise was adopted that accommodated, in part, the past practice of multidistrict ownership.

Water Rates for Lands Under Extended Recordable Contracts

Since 1926, Reclamation law has required landowners with excess acreage to enter into recordable contracts to sell the acreage within ten years if they wish to remain eligible for federally supplied water. In the National Land for People lawsuit in 1976, the court enjoined the Bureau of Reclamation from further processing of sales of excess land in the Westlands Water District until a decision was reached on whether the bureau's procedures conformed with Reclamation law. This moratorium was in effect from August 13, 1976, to May 7, 1984.

The Reclamation Reform Act gave landowners affected by the moratorium more time to sell their land,[10] specifically, the length of time remaining on each recordable contract when the moratorium was first imposed. In effect, this granted many districts a period of eighteen years (the normal ten years plus eight years of the moratorium) to sell their excess land. However, the act provided that the extension was not meant to further postpone the imposition of "full cost" charges on excess lands. Rather, it allowed lands under recordable contract to receive water at less than "full cost" for a period of only ten years from the date that the recordable contract had been established,

---

[10] The Reclamation Reform Act granted an extension of time not only to excess land in Westlands affected by the court injunction, but also to excess land in all districts for which the processing of excess land sales was suspended for any reason.

without regard to any extensions (refer to Section 205(c) of the RRA). The House and Senate conferees further clarified this provision:

> Any extension of time for the disposal of lands under recordable contract is not to be considered as also extending the period of time in which subsidized water may be delivered to the lands under recordable contract (U.S. Congress, House of Representatives, 1982).

During the public comment period, six commentors claimed that only those landowners who became individual electors or those that resided in districts amending their contracts should be subject to this requirement. These concerns were accommodated in the final rules: landowners remaining under prior law were allowed to continue to pay the contract rate, rather than the "full cost" rate, on their excess landholdings during the entire period of the extended recordable contract.

Bureau of Reclamation estimates are that under existing patterns of landholdings, this modification in the rules cost the United States about $79 million in "full cost" revenues in the Westlands Water District and about $1 million in the Arvin-Edison Water Storage District.[11] Among some of the chief beneficiaries of this change in Westlands were Southern Pacific Land Co. (which has about 81,000 acres of land under recordable contract, accounting for about 45 percent of the total revenue loss estimate)[12] and Boston Ranch (which has around 24,000 acres under recordable contract, accounting for about 12 percent of the total revenue loss estimate).[13]

Interpretation of Operation and Maintenance Costs Provisions

Another change between draft and final rules also directly modified the revenues payable to the United States under the RRA, particularly within the Central Valley Project in California. Section 208 of the RRA relates to O&M charges for districts with new or amended contracts:

> Section 208(a). The price of irrigation water . . . shall be at least sufficient to recover all operation and maintenance charges which the district is obligated to pay to the United States.

[11] If landholders rearranged their landholdings to avoid the "full cost" charges, the estimated loss in revenues would be less.

[12] Southern Pacific Land Co. has about 220 recordable contracts ranging in size from 160 acres to 747 acres.

[13] Boston Ranch is owned by James G. Boswell, Roseland Boswell, the J. G. Boswell Co., the James Boswell Foundation, and Nay & Co. Most of its land is held under one recordable contract.

Section 208(b). Whenever a district enters into a contract or requests that its contract be amended . . . and each year thereafter, the Secretary shall calculate such operation and maintenance charges and *shall modify the price of irrigation water delivered under the contract as necessary to reflect any changes in such costs* by amending the district's contract accordingly. [emphasis added]

Section 208(a) requires that water rates on new or amended contracts at least cover O&M costs. Section 208(b) can be interpreted to require more than that. As an illustration, suppose that the water service contract of a district in the Central Valley Project obligated the district to pay a fixed rate of $3.50 per acre-foot for water and that its forty-year contract expired in 1992. Suppose that at the time the contract was written, O&M costs were $0.50 per acre-foot, with the remainder credited toward capital repayment. Over time, however, O&M costs increased because of inflation. Also suppose that at the time the district amended its contract to take advantage of the expanded ownership limitation, O&M costs had risen to $3.00 per acre-foot, with only $0.50 per acre-foot left for capital repayment. Finally, suppose that the O&M costs increased by $0.25 per acre-foot per year following amendment. This example is illustrated in table 4-8.

The year after the district amended its contract, Section 208(b) would allow the Bureau of Reclamation to charge $3.75 per acre-foot; that is, the rate would be modified to reflect the changes in O&M costs. Under this interpretation, the bureau could maintain receipt of that small portion of the contract rate that goes to repay capital on those water service contracts not yet failing to cover O&M ($0.50 per acre-foot in the example). This, in fact, was the interpretation under

Table 4-8. Example of Capital Repaid for Operation and Maintenance Charges Under Proposed Rules and Final Rules, 1983
(dollars per acre-foot)

| | | | Proposed rules | | Final rules | |
Year	Existing contract rate	Actual O&M costs	Amended contract rate	Capital repaid	Amended contract rate	Capital repaid
1987[a]	3.50	3.00	3.50	0.50	3.50	0.50
1988	3.50	3.25	3.75	0.50	3.50	0.25
1989	3.50	3.50	4.00	0.50	3.50	0.00
1990	3.50	3.75	4.25	0.50	3.75	0.00
1991	3.50	4.00	4.50	0.50	4.00	0.00
1992	3.50	4.25	4.75	0.50	4.25	0.00

[a]Or first year of contract amendment or individual election.

the proposed rules. However, there were fourteen comments in opposition, and the 1983 final rules adopted the alternate interpretation—that the rates would be modified only enough to recover O&M. In the example, the rate would stay at $3.50 per acre-foot until such time as the O&M costs exceeded $3.50. Clearly, this second interpretation is disadvantageous to the United States, since it further erodes financial recovery in the Central Valley Project. The staff of the solicitor's office in the Department of the Interior held that either interpretation could be defended. The one chosen favored the water users. In this case, it is estimated that the loss in revenues is not large. If all districts amended their contracts in 1987, the difference in revenues between the two interpretations would be around $133,000 (about $100,000 in present worth). Since some farming operations are small enough that they may decide not to become individual electors, the expected difference in revenues would be less than $100,000 in present worth.[14]

Hammer Clause

One other change between draft and final regulations offered a major advantage to water users: namely, the final regulations issued in December 1983 contained nothing that would implement the hammer clause. The rationale was that this provision did not take effect under law until April 12, 1987, so it was not necessary to provide regulations until that time. Of course, it could also be argued that it was essential for water users to understand far in advance exactly what terms and conditions would apply if they did not amend their contracts before April 12, 1987. Indeed, without Section 203(b), there is little incentive for water districts to amend their contracts at all, since they can enjoy the benefits of unlimited leasing without paying "full cost" under the prior law provisions of the RRA. Omitting the sections implementing 203(b) was in part symbolic, because it was this section that most angered water users. Beyond this, however, the four-and-one-half-year grace period not only gave water users the opportunity to arrange their landholdings for the transition, it also provided an extended period for Congress to amend the RRA in their favor or for the courts to decide that, as the water users contended, the

---

[14] Of course, a larger number of farmers might have become individual electors before 1987 if there had been greater legal certainty as to (1) the nature of the final regulations (especially those regarding Section 203(b)), (2) the administration's intent to limit subsidies on larger farming operations, or (3) the outcome of lawsuits regarding the constitutionality of the act. If more farmers had become individual electors at an earlier date, the financial importance of this provision of the regulations would have been considerably greater because a greater portion of the current contract rates would have been creditable to capital charges.

hammer clause was unconstitutional. For example, Secretary of the Interior William Clark openly supported repeal of Section 203(b). Congress, however, did not amend the law.

Two principal lawsuits on the 203(b) issues were filed in 1986. In *Peter D. Peterson et al. v. United States Department of the Interior,* the parties (several California districts, including the Glenn-Colusa Irrigation District, the Westside Water District, the Arvin-Edison Water Storage District, and the Dunnigan Water District) claimed that Section 203(b) was unconstitutional because it unilaterally raised the water rates that must be paid by some members of the district in violation of existing long-term contracts with the Bureau of Reclamation. However, on April 13, 1987, Federal District Court Judge Raul Ramirez advised the parties that he would issue a written decision in favor of the United States.

> There has been no taking. . . . The Court cannot find and does not find the implementation of 203(b) in any way, shape, or form will cause an effect on reasonable investment-backed expectations.
>
> It has now come full bore some 85 years later, where these individuals are being required to pay the cost—the reasonable cost of the water that is being distributed—no more, no less. And although it comes at a time when contracts are in existence, when persons, and entities and corporations have gotten long use to—if you'll excuse the phrase—a free ride on the issue of water.
>
> I find nothing of an unconstitutional nature, or nothing of such an abhorrent nature that would allow this Court to bring into play . . . theories which somehow point the finger of guilt at the Federal Government for now legislating, 85 years later, which in hindsight probably should have been legislated some 50 years earlier than that.

His decision was rendered on July 15, 1987, but the parties have filed notices of appeal.

In a separate legal action in the Columbia Basin Project in Washington (*Balcom & Moe, Inc., et al. v. United States Department of the Interior*), the parties contended that Section 203(b) violates the terms of some existing long-term leases between landowners and farm operators because of the "full cost" water rates it would impose. On May 28, 1987, after issuance of the new rules, the parties dropped their case.

Finally, deferment of regulations to implement Section 203(b) until 1987 provided the opportunity to reopen the entire set of regulations to revision, not just the sections referring to 203(b). This provided those water users most affected by the act yet another chance to influence its implementation through modifications in the rules.

Revised Final Regulations in 1987

In 1986 the decision was made to address not only regulations needed to implement Section 203(b), but to look at potential revisions in all sections of the regulations in order to take advantage of what had been learned from administering the law for nearly four years. For example, it was found that because the Reclamation Reform Act explicitly restricts leasing by its "full cost" provisions, greater use was being made of farm management agreements and trusts.

Farm Management Agreements

The Reclamation Reform Act of 1982 makes no explicit reference to farm management agreements, that is, agreements under which a landowner or lessee pays a company to manage his farm. This type of arrangement was not uncommon before passage of the RRA, but it clearly raises a question about acreage limitation, since a single farm management company could be managing the landholdings of several individuals, each holding land within the acreage limitation. In fact, individuals whose holdings currently exceed the acreage limitation could establish a new farm management agreement in order to maintain their large landholding and to avoid paying "full cost." For example, ownerships have been established in the names of Mr. and Mrs. R. J. Smith, Sr. (919 acres), Mr. and Mrs. R. J. Smith, Jr. (906 acres), Mr. Edward Smith (626 acres), Ms. Alice Smith (874 acres), and Mr. Tom Jones (143 acres). (The actual names are not used.) The acreage owned by each is in accordance with the RRA. The total landholdings are maintained in a single farming operation of 3,468 acres using the "custom farming" services of the R. J. Smith Company, which owns an additional 40 acres. The individuals maintain that each farms his or her acreage individually and assumes the associated financial risks, rather than the R. J. Smith Company.

Another example, Vaquero Farms, was highlighted in an article in the Oakland Tribune (reproduced in *Congressional Record,* Extension of Remarks, February 3, 1987, p. E335):[15]

> Without tight regulations, lawyers will subvert the act by establishing phony management companies and trusts that divide large farm operations into sham parcels under the 960-acre limit.
>
> Don Villarejo, executive director of the California Institute for Rural Studies in Davis, has turned up several possible examples of this subterfuge.

[15] For an expanded account of practices during the period after the 1983 rules were published, see Villarejo (1986).

In western Fresno County, for example, seven business entities farm adjacent lands near to or only slightly above the 960-acre limit. They thus stand to benefit from continued subsidies. Yet according to Villarejo, "all seven report the same address, telephone number and name of contact person. A telephone call to that number produced the response from the person answering, 'Hello, Vaquero Farms.' " Vaquero Farms was the operator of record before the 1982 act.

Other farm management arrangements consolidate holdings of up to 20,000 acres.[16]

Proposed Changes

The proposed regulations issued in November 1986 would have strengthened the department's enforcement capability in a number of areas. Farm management agreements would be presumed to be leases unless the rates paid for management were comparable to rates paid for custom services in the same geographic area. To qualify for exemption, trusts would have to be irrevocable and would have to submit a copy of the trust for review, along with copies of the tax returns of the grantor and the beneficiaries. Owners falling under prior law would be charged at least the full O&M cost for water delivered to land under extended recordable contract. The O&M cost provisions would be interpreted to perpetuate the contribution to capital that remained at the time of contract amendment.

In addition, farm operators would be required to disclose the landholdings and leases that they managed. Each landowner and lessee within a Bureau of Reclamation project must submit a certificate setting forth the number of acres owned and leased and indicating his compliance with the provisions of the RRA. The form developed by the bureau (and approved by the Office of Management and Budget) for this purpose is actually a booklet requiring name, social security number, and a detailed description of owned and leased land. The 1986 proposed rules required that these forms be completed by farm operators as well as by owners and lessees as a means of checking the farming operation records against the records of the owners and lessees. This reporting requirement was considered important because it required farm operators that were neither owners nor lessees to register. It was feared that without such a requirement, some operators would disappear from regulatory purview by being converted to farm mangement agreements or trusts.

The affected water users, in commenting on the proposed regulations, objected to these various changes on the grounds that they went

[16] The potential use of farm management agreements to avoid acreage limitation had been a concern even before publication of the 1983 rules. See, for example, Martin (1978).

beyond the explicit authority of the law and the intention of Congress. The water users believed that the provisions they had come to expect since 1983 should be retained. With two exceptions, the final set of rules, issued April 13, 1987 (when the hammer clause was to take effect), restored provisions identical to those in the 1983 rules.[17] The two exceptions were (1) the retention of the O&M cost recovery provision that was more favorable to financial recovery by the United States and (2) a somewhat different set of qualifications for farm management agreements. Under the final rules, farm management agreements are not presumed to be leases, the landowner must be entitled to retain the profits of the farming enterprise, and the details of the agreement must be provided to the Secretary of the Interior if requested. In addition, the reporting requirement for farm operators was dropped, increasing the regulatory burden on Bureau of Reclamation personnel responsible for policing acreage limitation.

Recent Developments

Congress intervened in the bureau's interpretation of the pricing provisions for extended recordable contracts. As previously discussed, the language of both the law and the conference report could be construed to mean that "full cost" should apply to extended recordable contracts. However, in both the 1983 and 1987 rules, the bureau decided not to apply "full cost" to such contracts. The bureau's rationale was that Congress meant such provisions to apply only to amending districts and individual electors. Congress evidently disagreed. In the Budget Reconciliation Act of 1988, passed in December 1987, Congress expressly required the application of "full cost" to all extended recordable contracts. In 1988 several of the affected parties in the Westlands Water District filed suit, alleging that the provisions constituted a taking.

In addition to returning to most of the provisions of the 1983 rules, Bureau of Reclamation leadership apparently decided to take action against the staff that had proposed the 1986 provisions strengthening

---

[17] One California newspaper account dubbed the final regulations, "Reclamation's rubber hammer" (*Fresno Bee,* April 14, 1987). Upper-level departmental officials apparently wanted to distance themselves from the approval of the rules amid the controversy the rule-making created. A special amendment to the departmental manual was executed a few days before the final rules were to be published, delegating the responsibility for issuing the rules from the Secretary of the Interior, to the Assistant Secretary for Water and Science, down to the Commissioner of Reclamation, C. Dale DuVall. The 1983 proposed and final rules and the 1986 proposed rules had been signed by Secretaries of the Interior James Watt, William Clark, and Donald Hodel, respectively.

the original rules. The bureau announced that its Acreage Limitation Branch, which was located in Denver, would be moved to Washington, D.C.[18] In addition, on July 31, 1987, the Department of the Interior announced that many of the day-to-day decisions for administering acreage limitation would be removed from this branch and placed under the control of a special policy committee composed of the bureau's regional directors and headed by the bureau's assistant commissioner for planning and operations. Although the department portrayed these steps as being designed to strengthen the bureau's enforcement of acreage limitation, they were perceived by the acreage limitation staff and by outside interests as just the opposite. For example, Representative George Miller of California, who had been one of the key architects of the Reclamation Reform Act, opposed the move, along with representatives Sam Gejdenson and Patricia Schroeder in a June 16, 1988, letter to Secretary of the Interior Donald Hodel. The House also included a prohibition against the move in the Budget Reconciliation Act of 1988. Although this provision was removed in the House-Senate conference, the Washington move was never actually implemented. As part of the Bureau of Reclamation's overall reorganization effort in 1988, however, the Acreage Limitation Branch was abolished, branch chief Phillip Doe was reassigned to another division with responsibilities unrelated to acreage limitation, and two of the seven members of his staff were assigned to yet another branch with unrelated responsibilities. The remaining staff, while retaining their prior duties, were folded into part of a larger division, the Lands Branch.

Conclusions

Once Congress had established an interest subsidy for irrigation water supplies, not only was it difficult to limit the percentage of the subsidy through a short repayment period, it was also difficult to limit the amount of the subsidy accruing to any one farming operation. Originally, Congress sought to widely distribute the benefits of the irrigation subsidy by limiting ownership of land receiving federally supplied irrigation water to 160 acres and by requiring residency. However, these provisions were not strictly enforced, particularly where the reclamation program brought water into an area where larger landholdings had previously existed.

Today, more than eighty years after the reclamation program was first established, it is still an open question as to how acreage limita-

---

[18] This was ironic, since the bureau had already announced that it was planning to move most of its Washington staff to Denver.

tion will ultimately be enforced on Bureau of Reclamation projects. During these eight decades, the affected water users have been successful in securing administrative, legislative, and judicial actions that in one way or another either exempt some categories of project lands from the application of acreage limitation or expand the acreage entitlement, thereby protecting the property and financial interests of larger farming operations. (For a further illustration of administrative accommodation, see the appendix to this chapter, which describes the department's negotiated settlement of a water rate and contract dispute with the Westlands Water District.)

The success of these actions shows the degree to which federal water supplies become regarded as de facto property rights, defended with much the same conviction as the protection of private property interests. As covered in chapter 5, any reforms proposed to encourage more efficient use of federally supplied water need to take this history into account and acknowledge these property interests.

References

Frampton, Mary L. 1979. "The Enforcement of Federal Reclamation Law in the Westlands Water District: A Broken Promise," *University of California, Davis, Law Review* vol. 13, no. 1, pp. 89–122.

Hall, Bruce F., and E. Phillip LeVeen. 1978. "Farm Size and Economic Efficiency: The Case of California," *American Journal of Agricultural Economics* vol. 60, no. 4, pp. 589–600 (November).

LeVeen, E. Phillip, and George E. Goldman. 1978. "Reclamation Policy and the Water Subsidy: An Analysis of the Distributional Consequences of Emerging Policy Choices," *American Journal of Agricultural Economics* vol. 60, no. 5, pp. 929–934 (December).

Martin, William E. 1978. "Economics of Size and the 160-Acre Limitation: Fact and Fancy," *American Journal of Agricultural Economics* vol. 60, no. 5, pp. 923–928 (December).

Sax, Joseph L. 1965. "Selling Reclamation Water Rights: A Case Study in Federal Subsidy Policy," *Michigan Law Review* vol. 64, no. 13, pp. 13–46 (November).

Seckler, David, and Robert A. Young. 1978. "Economic and Policy Implications of the 160-Acre Limitation in Federal Reclamation Law," *American Journal of Agricultural Economics* vol. 60, no. 4, pp. 575–588 (November).

U.S. Congress, House of Representatives. 1982. *Conference Report to Accompany S. 1409* Report No. 97-855 (September 22).

U.S. Congress, House of Representatives, Committee on Interior and Insular Affairs. 1980. *Report Together with Additional and Dissenting Views to Accompany H.R. 6520* Report No. 96-1158 (July 15).

————. 1982. *Report Together with Additional and Dissenting Views to Accompany H.R. 5539* Report No. 97-458 (March 15).

U.S. Congress, Senate, Committee on Energy and Natural Resources. 1982. *Report to Accompany S. 1867* Report No. 97-373 (April 29).

U.S. Department of the Interior, Bureau of Reclamation. 1981. *Acreage Limitation: Draft Environmental Impact Statement, Westwide Report Appendix* (Denver, Colo., Water and Power Resources Service).

————. 1983a. "Acreage Limitation; Proposed Rules," 48 *Federal Register* 19900–17 (May 3).

————. 1983b. "Acreage Limitation: Rules and Regulations; Final Rule," 48 *Federal Register* 54748–86 (December 6).

Villarejo, Don. 1986. *How Much Is Enough? Federal Water Subsidies and Agriculture in California's Central Valley* (Davis, California Institute for Rural Studies, Inc.).

Appendix

Contract Dispute
with Westlands Water District

The pressures to avoid the acreage limitation provisions of Reclamation law and to reduce or avoid the impacts of the operation and maintenance and the "full cost" pricing provisions of the Reclamation Reform Act (RRA) did not end with passage of the act or with the promulgation of regulations under it. Rather they continued during implementation of the regulations and administration of Bureau of Reclamation contracts. The outcome of a contract dispute between the United States and the Westlands Water District exemplifies the situation.

Westlands is a large water district in the San Joaquin Valley of California. It encompasses some 600,000 acres (550,000 of which receive water service) and is the largest single contractor within the Central Valley Project (refer to table 3-1). Actual water deliveries vary by year, but recently contractual entitlements have been about 1,150,000 acre-feet of water annually, approximately one-fourth of the total irrigation deliveries in the project. Because the district contains a high proportion of large farming operations, it was a major presence during the passage of the RRA. Since then, it has sought to relax those provisions of the act that most affect its farming operations. This appendix discusses the actions taken by Westlands regarding its 1963 water supply contract in its attempt to maintain the original water rates charged to it.[1]

History of the Contract Dispute

The Westlands Water District has been involved in a long-standing dispute with the Department of the Interior over its 1963 water supply contract. Since 1964 it has sought to obtain a firm contract for additional delivery of

The author wishes to thank Richard C. Ready of the Office of Policy Analysis for his assistance in preparing the tables in this appendix and for reviewing the text.

[1] For another account of the settlement of this contract dispute, see Mosher (1986).

107

water. After 1982 it sought to do this without signing a new or amended contract, since that would bring all of its acreage under the provisions of the Reclamation Reform Act, which requires districts to pay water rates that at least cover operation and maintenance costs. A brief review of this dispute is necessary to appreciate the controversy surrounding the final 1986 settlement.

In 1963 the Westlands Water District, which consisted of about 400,000 acres at that time (table 4-A-1), signed a long-term contract with the Department of the Interior for delivery of an amount of water that was subject to adjustment based on certain groundwater studies. This amount was subsequently determined to be 900,000 acre-feet per year after 1980. The contract extended to 2007 and established a water rate of $7.50 per acre-foot plus a drainage charge of $0.50 per acre-foot beginning at such time as drainage facilities (the San Luis Drain) were placed in service. It also provided that Westlands could request surplus quantities of water at the same price when such water was available in the Central Valley Project.

Westlands was considering a merger with the adjacent Westplains Water District, which had 160,000 acres within the original San Luis service area. In a 1964 memorandum to the Secretary of the Interior, Assistant Secretary for Water and Power Development Kenneth Holum recommended that the merger be allowed and that the same water rates be extended to the new area, provided Westlands would assume the operating cost (but not the capital cost) of the Pleasant Valley Canal and Pumping Plant, a facility necessary to raise water to some parts of the new service area. Holum also recommended several other amendments to the 1963 contract. For example, he suggested that only 35–45 percent of the additional water provided be committed on a long-term basis, with the remainder subject to withdrawal to meet prior commitments to other Central Valley Project contractors. In addition, he suggested setting per-acre-foot limits on the amount of water supplied, based on the cropping pattern. Secretary of the Interior Stewart L. Udall approved the proposal to

Table 4-A-1. Number of Acres in Various Portions of the Westlands Water District

	(A) Inside original San Luis service area	(B) Outside original San Luis service area	Total
(I) Original Westlands Water District	284,000	116,000	400,000
(II) Former Westplains Water District	160,000	40,000	200,000
Total (current Westlands Water District)	444,000	156,000	600,000

Source: Records of Bureau of Reclamation, U.S. Department of the Interior, Sacramento, Calif.

reopen contract negotiations and to amend the contract "with the understanding that execution of the contract will be withheld until negotiations have been successfully completed and until we have reviewed the outcome of these negotiations and have approved the contract."

In 1965, state legislation merging the two water districts was signed by the governor of California. The merger required expansion of the federally financed water distribution system, as well as increased water deliveries. Drafts of water service contracts amending the 1963 contract for the purpose of accommodating the expanded service area were exchanged with Westlands in 1967, 1968, and 1969 (U.S. Department of the Interior, Bureau of Reclamation, 1978, p. 61), but no final agreement was reached. To move negotiations forward, the district proposed in 1969 to advance funds for completion of the distribution system and to be repaid through a reduction in the future water charges payable to the federal government. There was controversy within the administration, however, over whether to allow a subsidy in any form to an entity that could borrow its own funds for such a purpose. After five years of internal discussion, the Office of Management and Budget rejected the proposal because of objection by the Department of the Treasury. After removal of the advance funding provision, the water service contract was approved by the Secretary of the Interior in 1975, eight years after the original amendatory contract was proposed.

Secretarial approval was apparently granted despite recognition at the time that the $0.50-per-acre-foot charge for repaying the cost of the San Luis Drain would be inadequate to cover the cost of drainage facilities. An April 13, 1970, memorandum from regional director Robert J. Pafford to the commissioner of reclamation stated that the bureau had informed representatives of Westlands and other districts in the San Luis Unit "that we are reviewing the drainage service charge and we may wish to increase the charge." Later that same year the acting regional director notified the commissioner that the drainage rate was "grossly inadequate and may need to be adjusted." The approved contract also failed to contain any rate adjustment provisions for water deliveries, even though such provisions were adopted by the bureau's Mid-Pacific Region the same year. The newly adopted provisions required adjustment every five years to account for changes in O&M costs and in the twentieth and thirtieth years to account for changes in capital costs.

After secretarial approval, the 1975 amendatory contract was submitted to Congress for the ninety-day review period required by the San Luis Act of 1960. Joint committee hearings of the Senate Select Committee on Small Business and the Senate Committee on Interior and Insular Affairs revealed public criticism centering on the large number of excess landholdings in Westlands and on the effects on water quality in the Sacramento–San Joaquin Delta. Consequently, during 1975 and 1976 the department and the district proposed various changes in the amendatory contract. On January 19, 1977, Assistant Secretary Jack O. Horton approved the contract on the condition that the water rate be adjusted every five years to cover all O&M as well as capital costs. (Despite all of these proposed adjustments to the original

contract from 1964 through 1977, Westlands argued in 1986 that it should
have the right to water for its expanded service area at the rate specified in
the 1963 contract.)

Congress intervened in the rate question in 1977. In June, P.L. 95-46 (46
Stat. 225) authorized an additional $31 million to expand distribution and
drainage systems within the Westlands Water District. (These drainage
systems are distinct from the San Luis Drain flowing from the district's
drainage system to Kesterson Reservoir.) The Bureau of Reclamation proceeded with expansion of the district's distribution and drainage facilities
even though no contract with Westlands was signed to cover repayment. P.L.
95-46 also established the San Luis Task Force to examine a number of
repayment, excess lands, and authorization issues and to submit a report to
Congress by January 1978. Among the issues to be examined was "the
desirability of maintaining present repayment timetables or of modifying
them in order to ensure that an equitable burden of repayment falls on all
project beneficiaries." The final task force report reiterated the recommendation of Assistant Secretary Horton that contract rates be adjusted every five
years to cover O&M and capital costs. However, the Westlands Water District
never agreed to such a provision. Water deliveries to Westlands continued at
the $8.00-per-acre-foot rate under a series of temporary one-year contracts,
rather than under the 1963 contract.

Even though no water had been delivered under the 1963 water service
contract, on June 1, 1978, Interior Solicitor Leo Krulitz ruled that the 1963
contract was valid, but only for delivery of water within the original service
area of the San Luis Unit (areas IA and IIA in table 4-A-1) and only if the
$0.50-per-acre-foot drainage charge was replaced by a new repayment con-
tract for drainage facilities. Krulitz's ruling on the service area excluded
about 116,000 acres of the original Westlands Water District and about
40,000 acres of the former Westplains Water District (areas IB and IIB in
table 4-A-1). Krulitz held that the 1964 Holum memorandum did not obligate
the department to deliver water to areas IB and IIB at the same $8.00-per-
acre-foot rate. His rationale was that the Holum memorandum did not constitute a contract, but was merely a recommendation to the secretary. In turn,
the secretary indicated that contract negotiations were to be reopened and
final approval was to have secretarial review. Secretarial approval was
granted in 1975, but enough criticism had surfaced during congressional
review that the department put forth a revised set of contract provisions,
including five-year rate adjustments. Solicitor Krulitz also held that the
$0.50-per-acre-foot drainage service charge was an inappropriate way to
repay for drainage under Reclamation law and that a new repayment contract, establishing fixed annual payments instead of per-acre-foot charges
(and presumably ensuring more timely revenue recovery) was necessary.
Krulitz's opinion, in effect, recognized the district's entitlement to receive
water outside of the original Westlands Water District under the 1963 contract, but only for that area of the former Westplains Water District that lay
within the original San Luis Unit. As a result, Westlands still lacked clear
contractual rights to serve all of its service area thirteen years after the
contractual dispute began.

Two other reports during this period focused attention on the fact that water rates being charged to CVP contractors were too low to ensure adequate repayment. In 1978 and 1979 the Inspector General's Office of the Department of the Interior (formerly the Office of Audit and Investigation) issued reports criticizing the financial and rate-setting practices in the Central Valley Project. These reports heightened the realization that the fixed-rate contracts in the project were leading to a situation where many contract rates would fail to cover even operation and maintenance costs (for a more detailed discussion, refer to chapter 3).

The Threatened Shutoff of Water and the Ensuing Lawsuit

In 1981 the Assistant Secretary of the Interior for Land and Water Resources Garrey Carruthers established several points to serve as the basis for ongoing negotiations with Westlands: (1) 1.15 million acre-feet of Central Valley Project (CVP) water would be provided, (2) rates should be adjusted every five years consistent with the CVP rate-setting policy in effect at the time of adjustment, and (3) the total cost of the distribution system should be repaid over a period of less than forty years consistent with Westlands's ability to pay.

Westlands did not agree to these terms, and Carruthers threatened not to renew its temporary one-year contracts, thereby shutting off its water deliveries. The district went to court to ensure that it continued to receive water. Under a 1981 court-stipulated agreement between the Department of the Interior and the district, Westlands received 1.15 million acre-feet of water annually and paid the bureau's "cost-of-service" rate—a rate sufficient to cover both the operation and maintenance cost and the capital cost for all the water it received, including that water delivered to the original Westlands Water District. But Westlands contended that, consistent with its interpretation of the Holum memorandum, it was obligated to pay only the original $8.00-per-acre-foot rate on all of its water. Under the agreement, Westlands paid the $8.00-per-acre-foot rate directly to the bureau and paid the disputed portion into an escrow fund. Specifically, in 1982 Westlands paid $8.00 per acre-foot directly to the Bureau of Reclamation for about 1.1 million acre-feet of water annually from the San Luis Unit and put an additional $5.30 per acre-foot into escrow. The moneys in the fund were to be invested by the district. Similarly, for about 50,000 acre-feet of water delivered from the Mendota Pool, Westlands paid $4.00 per acre-foot directly to the United States and an additional $5.30 to the escrow fund. The total rates ($13.30 and $9.30) were adjustable by the department in subsequent years to reflect changes in the "cost of service." The stipulated agreement also provided that, after a final judgment or settlement, the escrow fund would be used to pay the United States any additional amount due for water already delivered, plus interest. By mid-1985, $29 million had accrued in the escrow account.

The Reclamation Reform Act of 1982 also affected final settlement of the Westlands dispute. The RRA requires that districts with new or amended contracts pay a rate at least sufficient to cover O&M costs and that this rate be adjusted annually to cover any changes in O&M costs. Even where entire districts do not amend, farmers desiring the benefits of the expanded ownership limitation (960 acres instead of 160 acres) can become individual electors. Individual electors are required to pay water rates that at least cover O&M costs. The 1983 regulations written pursuant to the act provide that when districts seek amended contracts to receive supplemental or additional benefits, their new contract rates should be consistent with the then-current rate-setting policies (that is, "cost-of-service" rates, covering both O&M and capital).

In November 1985 the Mid-Pacific regional director of the Bureau of Reclamation, David G. Houston, reached a proposed settlement with the district and forwarded it to the secretary for approval. The principal provisions of the proposed settlement covered the quantities of water the United States would be obligated to deliver, the rates Westlands would be obligated to pay for water, and cost-sharing for future drainage facilities.

Adoption of the settlement necessitated the reversal of the Krulitz opinion, which was accomplished through a new opinion issued by Solicitor Ralph Tarr. In particular, the proposed settlement recognized the entire Westlands service area as included within the original San Luis Unit authorization and accepted the $0.50-per-acre-foot service charge as a valid means of repaying the cost of existing drainage facilities. Perhaps the most important and revealing provision of the proposed settlement was one that allowed Westlands to avoid the minimum water rates imposed by the Reclamation Reform Act. Specifically, the proposed settlement allowed Westlands to establish one or more improvement districts within its boundaries. That way, the district could avoid executing a new or amended contract and thereby avoid the provisions of the Reclamation Reform Act requiring repayment of full annual operation and maintenance costs. In the absence of this device, the district might also have been obligated to pay "cost-of-service" rates for its water, since the additional water deliveries to the expanded service area could be regarded as supplemental or additional benefits under the Reclamation Reform Act.

The use of an improvement district was designed to allow irrigators in the original Westlands Water District (areas IA and IB in table 4-A-1) to preserve their $8.00-per-acre-foot rate for water for up to 900,000 acre-feet of water (actual deliveries to the original Westlands area are expected to range from 775,000 acre-feet in 1986 to 815,000 acre-feet by 2007; see tables 4-A-2a and 4-A-2b). Additional improvement districts might also be established to contract for expanded drainage service. Irrigators in the original district who became individual electors would pay rates that covered O&M costs. The proposed settlement envisioned a separate long-term contract for water to be supplied to the former Westplains area. This additional water would be charged at the "cost-of-service" rate, the bureau's term for a rate applicable to a new contract and subject to annual adjustments. That portion of the 900,000 acre-feet of water under the 1963 contract that is delivered within the former Westplains area (areas IIA and IIB in table 4-A-1) would also be charged at the same "cost-of-service" rates as under a new contract. Westlands would give up its rights under the 1963 contract to receive surplus water from the Central Valley Project at the original $8.00-per-acre-foot rate.

Table 4-A-2a. "Cost of Service" and Settlement Rates, Westlands Water District, 1986

Source	Destination	Projected use (acre-feet)	New contract rate[a] (dollars)			Settlement rate (dollars)
			Capital rate	Operation and maintenance	Total	
San Luis Canal	Original Westlands (I)	775,000	6.88	9.19	16.07	8.00
San Luis Canal	Westplains (II)	400,000	6.88	9.19	16.07	16.07
Mendota Pool	Westplains (II)	32,000	4.61	6.85	11.46	11.46

Source: Projected use and contract rates are from records for Central Valley Project water rates, Bureau of Reclamation, U.S. Department of the Interior, Sacramento, Calif.

[a]"Cost-of-service" rates. In accordance with Reclamation law, repayment of construction costs is on an interest-free basis.

Table 4-A-2b. "Cost of Service" and Settlement Rates, Westlands Water District, 2007

Source	Destination	Projected use (acre-feet)	New contract rate[a] (dollars)			Settlement rate (dollars)
			Capital rate	Operation and maintenance[b]	Total	
San Luis Canal	Original Westlands (I)	815,000	6.88	20.94	27.82	8.00–20.94[c]
San Luis Canal	Westplains (II)	400,000	6.88	20.94	27.82	27.82
Mendota Pool	Westplains (II)	50,000	4.61	15.61	20.22	20.22

Source: Projected use and contract rates for capital repayment are from records for Central Valley Project water rates, Bureau of Reclamation, U.S. Department of the Interior, Sacramento, Calif.

[a]"Cost-of-service" rates. In accordance with Reclamation law, repayment of construction costs is on an interest-free basis. After 2007 the current contract expires and all rates will be "cost-of-service" rates.

[b]Projected for 2007 using 1986 costs and a 4 percent rate of inflation.

[c]Range reflects the fact that some irrigators will pay $8.00 per acre-foot, while individual electors under the Reclamation Reform Act of 1982 must pay operation and maintenance costs.

Table 4-A-2a shows the bureau's calculated "cost-of-service" rates as of 1986 and the rates that would prevail under the proposed settlement. "Cost of service" from the San Luis Canal is estimated at $16.07 per acre-foot ($9.19 per acre-foot for operation and maintenance costs plus $6.88 per acre-foot to recover capital). Following the pattern of the original 1963 contract, the proposed settlement would provide up to 900,000 acre-feet of this water at a rate of $8.00 per acre-foot. However, projected use for 1986 is only 775,000 acre-feet. Additional water from the San Luis Canal delivered to the former Westplains area (areas IIA and IIB in table 4-A-1), projected at 400,000 acre-feet per year, would carry the full "cost-of-service" rate (estimated at $16.07 per acre-foot for 1986). Water delivered from the Mendota Pool requires less conveyance pumping and carries lower capital and operation and maintenance charges: the estimated cost of service is $11.46 per acre-foot for up to 50,000 acre-feet per year, although projected use for 1986 is only 32,000 acre-feet.

Over time, operation and maintenance costs can be expected to escalate. Table 4-A-2b shows the rates estimated to prevail in 2007 (the year in which the 1963 Westlands contract expires), assuming a rate of inflation of 4 percent per year. The range of water rates shown for 2007 reflects the fact that under the proposed settlement, farmers in the original Westlands Water District would fall into one of two classes. Those who became individual electors would pay full O&M costs, estimated at $20.94 per acre-foot in 2007. Those who did not (for example, those with operations less than 320 acres owned by husband and wife) could maintain the original $8.00-per-acre-foot rate.

Since the establishment of the San Luis Unit, the member water districts have wanted the United States to complete the San Luis Drain. With the closing of Kesterson Reservoir, Westlands is very concerned about how future drainage will be handled (see chapter 7). However, it was unable to get the United States to commit to the construction of drainage facilities as part of the proposed settlement. But it did offer, through contributions to a new trust fund to be established under the proposed settlement, to provide 35 percent up-front cost-sharing for future drainage facilities, up to $15 million per year and a total of $100 million, provided that the United States maintain a certain schedule in planning for and constructing such facilities. It also assumed the obligation to pay the operation and maintenance costs of such facilities; however, when it does so, the United States forgoes the $0.50-per-acre-foot drainage charge it now collects. Westlands also sought a long-term contract for an additional 100,000 acre-feet of water to the former Westplains area. The proposed settlement did not guarantee Westlands this water, although it did acknowledge the district's request for additional water.

Analysis of Settlement and Litigation Outcomes

Once these settlement terms were proposed, the Secretary of the Interior had the option to accept them; to press for terms more favorable to the United States; or, if Westlands was unwilling to agree to a change in terms, to proceed with litigation. Table 4-A-3 summarizes various possible outcomes of the contract dispute: adoption of the November 1985 settlement proposal, the November settlement proposal modified by the requirement that Westlands pay O&M costs for all of its water, several litigation scenarios, and the final settlement approved by the secretary in June 1986.[2] The table shows the basic components of each scenario, the estimated financial value to the United States in present worth terms, and a comparison with the November settlement proposal, which is used as a baseline.

November 1985 Settlement Proposal and the Final Settlement

The November 1985 settlement proposal would have provided revenues with an estimated present worth of $368 million from water sales and such other sources as repayment for distribution systems and for the cost of the San Luis

---

[2] This settlement was adopted by all of the parties involved and became final by court action on December 30, 1986.

Drain facilities. This estimate assumes that 70 percent of the acreage in the district would fall under individual elections by 1987; that the remainder of the former Westplains portion of the district would fall under an amended contract in 1990 (the assumed date for executing a new contract for additional water); and that the remainder of the original Westlands portion of the district would become subject to amended contracts for improvement districts in three equal stages in 1995, 1997, and 1999 as new drainage facilities are placed in service.[3]

To get some idea of the importance of paying operation and maintenance costs, another settlement scenario is presented—one that requires all water users in the original Westlands Water District to pay O&M charges beginning immediately (the second column of numbers in table 4-A-3). This scenario yields additional revenues of $5 million. Because such a settlement permits no improvement districts, it would have satisfied those who criticized the use of improvement districts as a means of avoiding the O&M cost provisions of the Reclamation Reform Act. The importance of a provision that requires payment of O&M costs is also indicated by the last row of table 4-A-3. If the hammer clause of the Reclamation Reform Act were repealed or successfully challenged in court, or if revised RRA regulations reduced the percentage of individual electors, then the costs recovered under the November 1985 settlement proposal would be reduced by about $11 million in present worth. Under these conditions, a settlement that required payment of operation and maintenance costs could be worth about $16 million more to the United States compared to the original November 1985 settlement proposal.

The bureau's negotiators believed that farmers in the original Westlands Water District felt so strongly about their rights under the original 1963 contract that they would not voluntarily agree to pay operation and maintenance costs. At $9.19 per acre-foot, O&M costs already exceeded the $8.00-per-acre-foot rate stipulated in the 1963 contract, and they would continue to escalate. As a compromise, the department negotiated a substitute revenue increase of $11 million through requiring accelerated repayment for some of the district's distribution and drainage facilities provided for by P.L. 95-46 (see the third column of numbers in table 4-A-3). Even if the hammer clause were nullified after the final settlement, revenue recovery would be only $5 million short of recovering all O&M costs (equivalent to the November 1985 settlement with the hammer clause intact).

---

[3] These three assumptions were suggested by Westlands in the district's presentation to the department concerning the proposed settlement. The current pattern of farming operations might indicate that an even higher percentage would become individual electors in 1987, at least under a tightly constructed set of regulations implementing the Reclamation Reform Act. Currently, 98 percent of farming operations exceed the 320 acres allowable under the hammer provision without paying "full cost." If all of these operations executed individual elections in 1987, then revenues would be nearly equal to those shown in table 4-A-3 for the November 1985 settlement proposal with payments for operation and maintenance costs required.

Table 4-A-3. Westlands Water District Contract Dispute—Possible Outcomes as of Early 1986

		Settlement proposal Nov. 1985	Settlement proposal With O&M required	Final settlement June 1986	Litigation scenario[a] (I) L-Holum, service area	(II) W-Holum, L-service area	(III) W-Holum, service area	(IV) W-Holum, service area, past and future rates
Water rates[b]								
1986								
775,000 AF (SLC to Westlands)	($/AF)	8.00	9.19	8.00	8.00	8.00	9.19	16.07
400,000 AF (SLC to Westplains)	($/AF)	16.07	16.07	16.07	8.00	16.07	16.07	16.07
32,000 AF (DMP to Westplains)	($/AF)	11.46	11.46	11.46	4.00	11.46	11.46	11.46
2007								
815,000 AF (SLC to Westlands)	($/AF)	8.00–20.94	20.94	8.00–20.94	8.00–20.94	8.00–20.94	20.94	27.82
400,000 AF (SLC to Westplains)	($/AF)	27.82	27.82	27.82	8.00–20.94	27.82	27.82	27.82
32,000 AF (DMP to Westplains)	($/AF)	20.22	20.22	20.22	4.00–15.61	20.22	20.22	20.22

Improvement districts allowed		yes	no	yes	yes	yes	no	no
New contract for San Luis Drain		no[c]	yes[c]	no	no[c]	no[c]	yes	yes
Present worth of future revenues[d] (less court costs)	($ millions)	368[e]	373	379	333	367	385	456[f]
Gain or loss from November settlement baseline	($ millions)	0	5	11	-35	-1	17	88
Effect of repeal of "hammer clause"								
Present worth of future water revenues	($ millions)	357	373[g]	368	322	356	385[g]	456[g]
Gain or loss from November settlement baseline without repeal	($ millions)	-11	5[g]	0	-46	-12	17[g]	88[g]

Note: Abbreviations: AF, acre-foot; L, U.S. losses; W, U.S. wins; SLC, San Luis Canal; DMP, Delta-Mendota Pool.

Source: Tables 4-A-2a and 4-A-2b, November 1985 settlement proposal, final June 1986 settlement.

[a]Litigation costs are assumed to be $1 million.

[b]Contract rates and cost-of-service estimates are from tables 4-A-2a and 4-A-2b.

[c]Drainage charge of $0.50 per acre-foot is included in existing water rate.

[d]Excludes "full cost" revenues, which should be approximately the same under all outcomes listed. Discounted at 8 percent.

[e]Baseline value.

[f]Includes increased revenue recovery of $30 million to United States from escrow fund.

[g]Repeal of Section 203(b), the "hammer clause," would have no effect on settlement and litigation outcomes in which the district is required to pay operation and maintenance costs.

Possible Litigation Outcomes

If the settlement had been rejected and the department had gone back to court, the outcome would, of course, have been uncertain. However, one can get some idea of the range of possible litigation outcomes and can, with some certainty, estimate the revenue implications of each.

Litigation Scenario I. Before the settlement, Westlands claimed that all of the lands in the district (including the former Westplains area and the area outside the original San Luis service area) were authorized for water service from the federal project. It further claimed that the Holum memorandum extended its $8.00 rate to water used to irrigate all of these additional lands. If the district had prevailed in these claims in litigation, then the revenues would have been considerably lower than under the final settlement, some $35 million lower in present worth (see litigation scenario I in table 4-A-3). However, this scenario was regarded as unlikely because the claims to rights under the Holum memorandum appeared weak. As previously discussed, in contract negotiations subsequent to the memorandum, Westlands sought to confirm some aspects of the memorandum (such as the pricing recommendations), but not others (such as establishment of a duty of water for the water delivered to each crop or the long-term commitment of only 35–45 percent of the water). Therefore, by implication, the terms of the memorandum had not been taken as a binding contract. More important, the memorandum was couched only in terms of several *recommended* changes to a proposed contract as the basis for further negotiations. It clearly indicated that the final contract would have to be submitted for secretarial approval. An amended contract was approved by the secretary in 1975, but it did not meet with approval during the required congressional review period. A revised 1977 contract rejected the Holum memorandum rates by requiring rate adjustments every five years consistent with the "cost of service."

Litigation Scenario II. The second possible litigation scenario shown in table 4-A-3 is that the United States wins on the Holum memorandum issue but that the court recognizes the improvement district concept as a valid means of complying with the Reclamation Reform Act and finds the current service area to be authorized. This outcome would have been similar to the November 1985 settlement proposal, except that the United States would have incurred litigation expenses (valued at $1 million in the table). Compared with the final settlement, the United States would also have lost the accelerated repayment of the additional distribution and drainage funds.

Litigation Scenario III. A third possible outcome is that the United States wins on the Holum memorandum issue and on the service area question. Then, as a quid pro quo for supporting authorization of an expanded service area in Congress and for delivering water to that service area, either the Department of the Interior or Congress could demand that a new contract for the entire district be written, requiring rates that would at least cover O&M costs on the water delivered within the original Westlands Water District, and that a new repayment contract be written to recover the costs of the San Luis Drain (the $0.50-per-acre-foot charge embodied in current contracts is far short of providing adequate revenue recovery for the facilities). Under this scenario, the United States would have recovered revenues with a present worth of $385 million, some $17 million more than under the original November 1985 settlement proposal and $6 million more than under the final settlement.[4]

Litigation Scenario IV. The third litigation scenario is closely related to a fourth possible outcome: the United States wins on both the Holum memorandum and service area issues. As a result, either the Department of the Interior or Congress requires that a new contract be written with Westlands requiring payment of capital, as well as O&M charges, on all water deliveries to Westlands, including whatever portion of the original 900,000 acre-feet is delivered within the original Westlands Water District. Under this outcome, it would have been likely for the court to find such rates applicable retroactively to the date the escrow fund was established (1981). If so, the escrow fund payments would have reverted to the United States.[5] Overall, the fourth litigation scenario would have yielded an increase of $88 million to the United States over the November 1985 settlement proposal and $77 million over the final June 1986 settlement. If the department or Congress had required that "cost-of-service" rates be applied only to *future* water deliveries, then the escrow fund payments would have reverted to Westlands and the present worth of revenues under this scenario would have dropped $37 million.

The principal values for all the litigation scenarios are based on the assumption that the hammer clause would remain in effect. However, under the settlement, Westlands preserves its right to contest the hammer clause. If Westlands were successful, those water users who became individual electors because of the hammer clause would undoubtedly seek to reverse their individual elections. This could lead to a situation in which water users subject to the $8.00-per-acre-foot rate were paying rates insufficient to cover O&M costs, at least until such time as new facilities were constructed. This would lead to a loss by the United States of about another $11 million in present worth under litigation scenarios I and II. In contrast, under those settlement or litigation outcomes that require the district to pay full O&M costs or O&M plus capital, no similar erosion of revenues would occur. From this analysis, it appears that the Department of the Interior, through litigation, may have had a fair chance of securing an additional $5 million (present worth) in O&M costs and possibly $77 million of O&M plus capital costs.

[4] Another way of arriving at nearly this same outcome would be for the United States to win on the Holum memorandum issue and to lose on the service area question, but for the court to hold that the additional water delivered under the settlement constitutes a supplemental or additional benefit under the Reclamation Reform Act. Such benefits require amended contracts that recover at least operation and maintenance costs.

[5] Under other litigation and settlement scenarios, the escrow fund of $30 million reverts to Westlands and, in addition, the United States is obligated to refund an additional $6.8 million to Westlands because of overcharges relative to the historical rates applicable under the settlement.

Bureau Support for the Settlement

The Bureau of Reclamation defended its proposed and final settlements on the following grounds.

1. The 1963 contract had always been regarded as valid and should be honored. The settlement honors the water rates in this contract up to the first 900,000 acre-feet but charges "cost of service" for the remaining water.

The opposite side of this argument is that the 1963 contract was regarded as insufficient almost as soon as it was written because it did not provide for water to be delivered to an expanded service area. For example, the Holum memorandum dates from 1964, and the expansion of Westlands that required additional water deliveries was approved by the state in 1965. Solicitor Krulitz held the 1963 contract to be valid, but only for delivery of water to the original service area. In his view, a new or amended contract was required for the delivery of water to an expanded service area.

If the department had required Westlands to sign a new or amended contract, the Reclamation Reform Act would require revised repayment provisions. The bureau contended that the settlement accommodates these provisions by establishing improvement districts for any additional water services to be provided. It also maintained that the use of improvement districts is common under western water law and that such districts were contemplated by Congress in drafting the Reclamation Reform Act. However, prior to the settlement, the RRA regulations had been applied differentially to an improvement district only once, and the district had existed before the regulations were issued. The improvement districts in Westlands were to be formed after the settlement was finalized and more than four years after the issuance of RRA regulations. Allowing improvement districts in Westlands also posed another risk to the United States: a potential precedent for other districts to avoid districtwide application of the pricing provisions of the RRA.

2. The bureau argued that the offer by Westlands to share costs on future drainage service is of immense value to the United States. It is true that if the department had returned to litigation, this commitment would almost certainly have been withdrawn. However, the bureau's argument ignores that cost-sharing for drainage facilities could be negotiated at some future date and that the same levels could be demanded. The type of drainage facilities, their ultimate cost, and whether they will ever be built have yet to be determined. Therefore, unless one believes that Congress or the courts would make future drainage for Westlands a nonreimbursable financial obligation of the United States, it is questionable whether this cost-sharing aspect of the settlement added appreciably to its value to the United States.

3. Regional director David Houston contended that if the United States won litigation on the service area issue, it would have great difficulty in Congress in securing authorization of the full service area currently receiving water. He envisioned opposition from environmental interests because of the problems at Kesterson Reservoir (refer to chapter 7) and because of a desire to keep additional water flowing to the Sacramento–San Joaquin Delta rather than diverting it for irrigation. He also envisioned opposition to an expanded service area by Congressman George Miller, a long-time critic of

the department's dealings with Westlands.[6] Given the large amount of federal and private investment in the San Luis Unit outside of the original service area and the historical delivery of water to these areas, it seems unlikely that Congress would refuse to authorize continued irrigation deliveries. Federal investment in distribution and drainage systems in these areas totals $59 million, and the scheduled future repayment has a present worth of about $18 million.

4. Houston maintained that there was no viable litigation scenario that led to more revenue than the settlement and contended that litigation scenarios III and IV had little likelihood of success. He further maintained that the rate for water delivered to the original Westlands Water District ($8.00 per acre-foot) was not at issue. However, an examination of the history of this controversy indicates that recovery of capital costs for this water had in fact been at issue since at least 1977, when Assistant Secretary Horton made approval of the amendatory contract conditional on the inclusion of appropriate capital rates. Capital-recovery rates were also one of Assistant Secretary Carruthers's bases for negotiation in 1981, which eventually lead to litigation with Westlands. The court stipulation itself required Westlands to pay rates sufficient to cover the current "cost of service," including capital, on the full amount of water delivered (including the water delivered to the original Westlands area) and to hold the share under contention in escrow. The court would not have required escrow of these funds for the original service area if the rates for water delivered there were not at issue.

If the department had proceeded with litigation and the court had decided the case in favor of the department, the United States would have received the approximately $30 million currently in the escrow account and avoided a refund of past overcharges relative to the rates under the settlement (see table 4-A-3). The United States would also have begun receiving immediately the capital repayment deferred by the settlement on future water delivered within the original Westlands Water District. At $6.88 per acre-foot, these capital charges would have amounted to $5.3 million in 1986 and about $5.6 million annually by 2007.

5. The bureau maintained that if the United States prevailed in litigation and required the district to pay either higher O&M or capital rates on a new contract, then the original Westlands area could successfully preserve its rights under the 1963 contract by voting to be separated from the overall Westlands district or by voting to reject a new contract. It is not known what difficulty Westlands might have faced in attempting to obtain state legislation to separate into two districts—the original Westlands and Westplains areas. Certainly it would have incurred financial costs and some losses of efficiency in its current management of integrated distribution and drainage systems. Also significant is that under article 21 of the 1963 contract, the district would have had to secure the bureau's permission to change its acreage by more than 12,500 acres. As indicated in table 4-A-1, dropping the Westplains area would have removed about 200,000 acres from the district.

---

[6] Miller subsequently introduced legislation providing for authorization of an expanded service area.

Therefore, it seems that this provision would have given the department the discretion to declare the 1963 contract invalid if the district separated into two districts.

The Bureau of Reclamation determined that the settlement, including the use of improvement districts, was in compliance with the Reclamation Reform Act, although the use of improvement districts is likely to be regarded by some interests as creating a loophole by departmental action.[7] Provided the hammer clause of the Reclamation Reform Act is not repealed, the final settlement will return revenues worth at least as much in present worth as several of the other possible outcomes, except litigation scenarios III and IV. Under these scenarios, the United States would have recovered $5 million–$77 million in additional revenue (on a present worth basis). Of course, the settlement also avoided possible litigation outcomes under which the department could have lost $12 million to $46 million in revenues. However, the loss of $46 million appears unlikely because Westlands's chances of winning on the Holum memorandum issue appear weak. Therefore, by adopting a negotiated settlement rather than pursuing litigation, the department accommodated in large part the concerns of water users in the Westlands district but lost a good chance of obtaining much higher revenue recovery through litigation.

If the secretary had decided to pursue the litigation alternative, the department would have had to make vigorous use of its various legal tools: the Reclamation Project Act of 1939, which requires that water service revenues recover O&M costs; the Reclamation Reform Act of 1982, which imposes the same requirement on new or amended contracts; the rejection of the use of improvement districts to comply with the Reclamation Reform Act; Westlands's need for a new water service contract, as well as other supplemental and additional benefits (such as drainage and an expanded distribution system); and the 1963 contract, which prohibits changes of more than 12,500 acres in the contracting organization without the bureau's consent.

CONCLUSIONS

This case study of the contract dispute with the Westlands Water District indicates the considerable amount of administrative discretion afforded to the Secretary of the Interior and his designated representatives in the Bureau of Reclamation in matters of repayment. It also illustrates that the terms of repayment for public sector projects are subject to continuing renegotiation and adjustment. The dispute with Westlands began soon after the 1963 contract was signed. The district annexed additional acreage in 1965 and sought irrigation water for this acreage at the district's original $8.00-per-acre-foot water rate. It became clear to various federal officials and

---

[7] The secretary had sufficient legal authority to disallow the use of improvement districts for purposes of compliance with the Reclamation Reform Act.

agencies (including the Senate Select Committee on Small Business and the Senate Committee on Interior and Insular Affairs in 1975, Secretary of the Interior Horton in 1977, the federal San Luis Task Force in 1978, Interior Solicitor Krulitz in 1978, the department's Office of Inspector General in 1978 and 1979, Assistant Secretary of the Interior Carruthers in 1981, and the authors of the Reclamation Reform Act in 1982) that the $8.00-per-acre-foot rate would fail to cover operation and maintenance costs and capital costs for the water, as well as repayment for the San Luis Drain. Each of these parties made some attempt to modify the repayment terms to require Westlands to pay at least the operation and maintenance costs of its federally supplied water and to bring repayment more into line with sound business practices. Despite these measures, over the twenty-one-year period extending from 1965 to 1986, the water users in the original Westlands Water District were successful in maintaining their original repayment terms for up to 900,000 acre-feet of water. The result is that some farmers in Westlands will continue to pay the United States $8.00 per acre-foot for water even though the operation and maintenance costs alone are $9.19 for 1986 and may increase to $20.94 per acre-foot by 2007.

The Westlands contract dispute shows how tenaciously water districts defend what they believe to be their property rights in federally supplied water and how successful they can be in dealing with the public sector. Westlands made itself felt at all levels—with the bureau's regional directors in Sacramento; with representatives in Congress; and directly with departmental officials at the level of the assistant secretary, the solicitor, and the secretary. These officials often feel that they must defend their constituents' interests to the Office of Management and Budget when it performs its final review of proposed departmental actions. Westlands pleaded its case to departmental officials not only through its legal representatives, but also through Kenneth Khachagian, who at the time was a speechwriter for President Reagan (see *National Journal,* 1985; Mosher, 1986; and Kirschten, 1986). Clearly, when the financial assets at stake are considerable, a wide range of resources will be brought to bear to protect them.

This twenty-one-year history of administrative accommodation may well extend at least that far into the future. Further renegotiations and accommodations are likely to be made in determining the financial responsibility for repaying the costs of containing the selenium contamination in Kesterson Reservoir (see chapter 7), in providing additional drainage service to Westlands, and in developing a new contract for Westlands when the original one expires in 2007.

References

Kirschten, Dick. 1986. "White House Kibitzers," *National Journal* vol. 18, no. 24, pp. 1496–1497 (June 14).

Mosher, Lawrence. 1986. "Paying for Water," *National Journal* vol. 18, no. 22, pp. 1313–1315 (May 31).

National Journal. 1985. "Inside Washington," vol. 17, no. 49, p. 2749 (December 7).

U.S. Department of the Interior, Bureau of Reclamation. 1978. *Special Task Force Report on San Luis Unit, Central Valley Project, California* (Washington, D.C., Government Printing Office).

Part II

Policy Recommendations to Facilitate Water Marketing

5

Promoting More Efficient Use of Federally Supplied Water

The main reason why federally supplied water in the arid West is not always managed efficiently is that it is sold far below the cost of providing it, a characteristic that does not engender wise husbandry. For example, several long-term contracts in the Central Valley Project provide water for only $3.50 per acre-foot (refer to table 3-1), whereas new sources of supply such as the Auburn Dam would cost the federal government or the state $200–$300 per acre-foot per year for construction costs alone (see chapters 2 and 3 for estimates of the construction cost subsidy for irrigation). Clearly, it makes little sense to construct expensive new facilities if contractors are not using efficiently the water they have.

The Reclamation Act of 1902 was originally intended to facilitate settlement of the arid West with small family farms. But today it is largely outdated, and the trend has been toward administrative and legislative relaxation or removal of acreage limitations and residency requirements. Alongside this has been a shift away from the original social goals of the reclamation program. The West is settled, and concerns today focus on meeting new demands for water by a growing population for urban and industrial uses, as well as for recreational and other instream uses such as maintenance of fish and aquatic wildlife habitat. Increasing competition for limited water supplies and the rising cost of new supplies have heightened awareness that water must be used more efficiently. In this chapter various proposals for promoting more efficient use of federally supplied water are examined and evaluated.

Alternative Means for Promoting More Efficient Use of Low-Cost, Federally Supplied Water

Raising Prices

Some of the traditional means for promoting water conservation have met with only limited success on Bureau of Reclamation projects. Pricing a commodity to reflect its marginal cost of production or its market value engenders conservation. However, for several reasons, the chances are slim that federal water prices could be raised. As covered in part I of this book, the entitlements to inexpensive water are vigorously defended, and any attempt to raise prices would undoubtedly anger the Bureau of Reclamation's constituents and prompt direct forestalling actions from their representatives in Congress. For example, when the White House formed a task force in 1982 to study raising the rates of federally generated hydropower, including options to raise rates to market value, Congress passed a funding resolution that prohibited any federal funds from being spent even to study the proposition. The task force meetings stopped.

An example related more directly to water pricing is the "full cost" pricing requirement of the Reclamation Reform Act of 1982. This was touted as promoting water conservation on land in excess of 960 acres on large farming operations. However, most landowners are likely to avoid "full cost" charges by reorganizing their holdings into operations of 960 acres or less.

More fundamentally, long-term contracts for federally supplied water prevent prices from being raised on the basic 960-acre entitlements because they customarily fix the repayment terms over a forty- or fifty-year period. Furthermore, since this contracting takes place under legislation that provides substantial subsidies, there is likely to be little change in future contracting policies unless there is a change in the terms of the underlying legislation.

Conservation Requirements

A second way to promote more efficient water use is to require that water users implement certain conservation measures. Some Bureau of Reclamation contracts were originally written to require the contractor to develop a water conservation program acceptable to the bureau's contracting officer. According to bureau directives established in 1979, all new contracts are to require conservation programs that contain "definite goals, appropriate water conservation measures, and time schedules for meeting the water conservation objectives." The Reclamation Reform Act of 1982 further extended and codified these requirements by making them mandatory on existing and future contracts. The act states that conservation measures should be encouraged "where such measures are shown to be economically feasible for . . . non-Federal recipients [of water]." Therefore, the specific measures can vary from one location to another, as appropriate.

Standardization of such requirements would be inappropriate because the value of water, as well as the financial resources available to farming operations, varies from one location to another. Conservation measures in irrigation could easily range in cost from $5 per acre-foot of water saved to $100 per acre-foot or more (for example, see Wahl and Davis [1986] for the range of costs for conservation measures that could be undertaken in the Imperial Irrigation District in California). It would make little sense to require a district to undertake conservation measures that cost $80 per acre-foot to install and maintain if the water conserved were only worth $40 per acre-foot. Conservation plans probably will be useful in making water districts aware of the measures that similarly situated districts are undertaking. However, the current conservation plan requirement is deficient because it gives little basis (other than "economic feasibility") for deciding which measures a district should be required to adopt, it provides no real incentive for the conservation measures to be adopted, and it provides no financial resources for the measures to be implemented.

Voluntary Water Transfers

Raising prices of federally supplied water and implementing conservation measures can be contrasted with what, by this analysis, promises to be a more effective approach, namely, facilitating voluntary market transfers of federally supplied water. The idea is to allow contractual deliveries in federally supplied water to be traded among water users at whatever prices they may establish. Such changes in location or end use of Bureau of Reclamation water that is already under contract are undertaken voluntarily by the parties involved for their mutual benefit. A potential buyer would only enter into such a transaction if the purchase provided a less expensive water supply than other sources. Likewise, the seller would enter the transaction only if the sale provided more income than the current water use. The price paid by the purchaser could be used to finance conservation measures, such as canal lining. For example, in 1985 the Metropolitan Water District of Southern California (MWD) offered the Imperial Irrigation District $10 million per year to fund water conservation measures that would salvage 100,000 acre-feet of water annually for use by MWD. The price offered, $100 per acre-foot in this case, is a measure of the scarcity of water and indicates which conservation measures are economical to undertake.

Voluntary market transfers differ from water pricing and conservation requirements in several respects. The latter two are likely to be resisted by water users because they impose a financial burden. They also imply extensive governmental regulation and intervention. In fact, raising water prices could necessitate breaking long-term federal water contracts, a step that would be politically difficult if not legally problematic (for example, refer to the discussion of the contract dispute with the Westlands Water District in the appendix to chapter 4). Certain provisions of Reclamation law virtually guarantee the renewal of these contracts once they expire. The act of July 2, 1956 (70 Stat. 483), provides federal irrigation contractors with the right to renew water service contracts that were executed under the Reclamation Project Act of 1939 (53 Stat. 1187)—the bureau's principal contracting authority—provided the contractor renegotiates to pay current water charges.[1] Once project costs have been repaid, water delivery rights become permanent. These provisions of Reclamation law reinforce the notion that long-term property rights are conferred to federal water contractors. The use of voluntary water transfers recognizes such contractual rights and seeks to facilitate efficient water use by further clarifying these rights and by relying on the economic incentives for trading between water users (for additional discussion of the rationale for market transfers of water, see Hartman and Seastone, 1970; Meyers and Posner, 1971; U.S. National Water Commission, 1973, pp. 260–270; Phelps, Moore, and Graubard, 1978; California Assembly Office of Research, 1982; Frederick, 1982; Environmental Defense Fund, 1983; Stavins and Willey, 1983; Anderson, 1983a, b; and Saliba and Bush, 1987).

Voluntary exchanges can be as effective as appropriate pricing in leading to efficient water use. If a farmer pays only $10 per acre-foot for water but can sell water for $60 per acre-foot, he is likely to value the water at $60 per acre-foot. Furthermore, the $60-per-acre-foot effective value of the water is realized without the political difficulty of imposing a price increase on the current water user.

The flexibility to transfer water is also important because the life of water projects is often 50–100 years or more. No matter how well a project is planned, it would be impossible to forecast the pattern of water demands accurately over such a long period of time. Therefore, water transfers provide one means to accommodate new patterns of

[1] The act of June 21, 1963 (77 Stat. 68), provides similar rights to contractors for municipal and industrial water supply.

agricultural production, population settlement, and industrial growth and to allow water to be used where it is most needed.

It should be emphasized that voluntary transfers of water are not necessarily sales of water rights. They would most often be leases or sales of contractual deliveries, without the actual water rights changing hands. In our federal system of government, states were granted responsibility over the allocation of water within their borders, with some exceptions—for instance, the federal government holds reserved water rights for certain "reserved" federal lands like Indian reservations and national forests.[2] With the "appropriative" system of water rights, which in the West is the most common, states grant use of water to citizens and associations that appropriate water and place it to beneficial use in conformance with rules and procedures established by the state. Today, these requirements often include filing a permit to use water and subsequently establishing that the water is put to beneficial use. Technically, actual water users do not own the water outright, but possess a usufructuary right to it. In some ways, water rights holders can treat their water rights as real property that can be sold to other water users, but states retain the authority to determine the nature of beneficial use and to regulate the assignment or transfer of water rights to other locations.

On some Bureau of Reclamation projects, irrigation water rights are held by the water districts served.[3] More commonly, the water rights are held by the bureau, which filed for the rights under state law. The bureau, in turn, contracts with water districts for water delivery from its storage and conveyance facilities. In voluntary market transactions, a water contractor reassigns a portion of the contractual deliveries to another water user in exchange for monetary or other compensation. These reassignments can be short-term leases, annual rentals, long-term leases, or permanent sales. The actual water rights can be retained by the Bureau of Reclamation or the district selling the water. However, in those cases where a district holds water rights, there can be permanent and more secure transfers in which some or all of the actual water rights are sold. In either case, the bureau is involved in the transfer process, since bureau facilities

---

[2] In addition to retaining jurisdiction over interstate questions such as navigation and interstate allocation of surface water, the federal government regulates water quality. For an accessible treatment of western water law, see Getches (1984). For a briefer account of the principal tenets of the appropriation doctrine, as well as its establishment in the early West, see Webb (1931, pp. 431–452).

[3] For additional detail on project water rights held by the water districts and by the Bureau of Reclamation, see table 6-2 and the surrounding text.

are usually necessary for water storage and, in many cases, water delivery. Also, Bureau of Reclamation approval of the transfer is required by bureau contracts, and, in some cases, contract amendments are necessary (more detail is provided on the bureau's role in transfers in chapter 6).

The Government Role in Regulating Market Transactions

Voluntary transfers of water supplied by Bureau of Reclamation facilities do not imply a "free market" in water. Administration of water transfers and water rights requires considerable regulation because of the return-flow aspects of the water resource. When a gallon of gasoline is sold and consumed, its utility is gone, but water is used over and over again. Before it reaches the ocean, water melting from high mountain snow may be used by a fisherman, turn the turbines of a power plant, be diverted to a meadow for irrigating pasture, be used by a city's households, pass through a sewage treatment plant, be diverted once again for irrigating field crops, and so on. A consequence of this is that one person's pattern of use and return flow affects another's. For example, when a farmer diverts 5 acre-feet of water from a stream to an acre of his field, 20 percent of the water might be consumed by evapotranspiration of plants, 40 percent might be runoff that returns almost directly to the streamcourse, and 40 percent might percolate into the soil to become groundwater that is either pumped by another water user or that eventually returns to the stream channel. Such return flows become the basis of the water rights of downstream users or of neighboring farms that depend on groundwater pumping. Therefore, under most state laws, a farmer would not be allowed to lease or sell 100 percent of his diversions, but only the amount of his consumptive use and, then, only in a way that did not harm other water users. For example, if a farmer proposed to sell 400 acre-feet of his consumptive use to another farmer (or to a city) with a diversion point upstream of his own, this would deprive the stream of that quantity of water between the original and final diversion points. Such a reduction in stream flow could affect the water rights of other water rights holders in that reach of the stream, as well as reduce the water available for instream recreational uses and for fish and wildlife habitat. Therefore, state government routinely plays a necessary role in measuring consumptive use and return flows and in settling disputes over effects on third-party water users (water users who are not the trading parties directly involved in the exchange).

Government has one other role. There are recreational, aesthetic, and public benefits associated with instream use of water, uses that are not protected by the current pattern of privately held water rights.[4] States serve a function in protecting these public benefits, and most western states have explicit authority to protect the public interest in approving water transfers.

Examples of Transfers Involving Federally Supplied Water

The voluntary transfer of federally supplied water is not new, and the rest of this chapter covers a variety of past transfers (adapted in part from Wahl and Osterhoudt, 1986). As will be revealed, the bureau's policy has not been uniform from one transfer to another or from region to region or project to project. In chapter 6, various changes to Bureau of Reclamation policy and Reclamation law are recommended that would facilitate the transfer of bureau water and standardize the bureau's approach to processing transfer requests.

The Idaho Water Supply Bank

Water rentals utilizing the system of Bureau of Reclamation reservoirs on the Upper Snake River in Idaho reach back to the 1930s. The arrangements were recognized in Bureau of Reclamation contracts with water users. However, some concern developed among water rights holders that renting their water might jeopardize their water rights under state law (that is, renting water might be considered evidence that the owner was not putting the water to beneficial use). Motivated in part by this concern, the state legislature formally authorized rental agreements by establishing state water banking legislation in 1980. This legislation provided for statewide banking operations through either short-term or long-term leases. Initially, however, the only active banking operation was the one established prior to the act on the Upper Snake River above Milner Dam, utilizing the American Falls, Jackson Lake, and Palisades Reservoirs within Water District No. 1.

Leasing arrangements arose in part because of the supplemental nature of the federal water supplies. Because rates for federally supplied water are very low, about $0.19 per acre-foot, some space holders maintain large water holdings as insurance against water-short years and defray their costs by placing unneeded supplies in the bank. Water transfers are also facilitated by the fact that one water

---

[4] This is not to say, however, that greater use could not be made of private rights to instream flows as a means to supplement the role of the state. Methods to increase the role of private water rights in protecting instream water uses are discussed in Anderson (1983a) and in Western Governors' Association (1987).

user cannot gain rights to the return flows from stored water used by another.

The bank, managed by a local "Committee of Nine," leases storage space in Bureau of Reclamation facilities. The bureau currently requires the price set by the Committee of Nine to be based on space-owner costs and requires leases to be restricted to one year. The following priorities for leasing water have been established by the Committee of Nine: (1) existing canal companies that own storage space, (2) agricultural users who have traditionally used rental pool water, (3) new agricultural users, and (4) any other user (such as a power company).

To encourage early commitments of water to the bank, water made available before July 1 is sold first, and revenues from sales are divided proportionally. Water made available after July 1 is sold on a first come, first served basis, and the water owners are reimbursed in a like manner. The sale price set by the committee is the sum of annual capital and operating costs. The established price rose from $0.30 per acre-foot in the 1950s to $0.50 per acre-foot up until 1977. Since then it has increased to $2.50 per acre-foot (see table 5-1), which includes a $0.50 per-acre-foot charge accruing to the bank for updating its equipment for measuring water. Therefore, water users placing water in the bank are able to more than offset their annual capital obligations to the Bureau of Reclamation for the year, which average about $0.19 per acre-foot. Water supplied to the bank has exceeded 800,000 acre-feet in some years, although the amount actually sold by the bank is usually considerably less (see table 5-1). The

Table 5-1. Water Transfers on the Upper Snake River, Idaho, 1979–1986

Year	Water supplied (acre-feet)	Total water pur-chased (acre-feet)	Irriga-tion pur-chases (acre-feet)	Power purchases (acre-feet)	Percent power	Price (dollars/acre-foot)
1979	88,870	73,960	23,960	50,000	67.6	1.19
1980	72,190	14,575	14,575	0	0.0	1.19
1981	170,107	149,039	24,039	125,000	83.9	1.60
1982	290,426	203,515	3,515	200,000	98.3	2.30
1983	540,606	353,084	3,084	350,000	99.1	2.40
1984	806,400	277,433	2,433	275,000	99.1	2.50
1985	497,302	362,169	12,169	350,000	96.6	2.50
1986	895,642	159,735	9,735	150,000	93.9	2.50

Source: Records of Idaho Water District No. 1 (Idaho Falls) and the Bureau of Reclamation, U.S. Department of the Interior, Boise, Idaho.

principal purchases from the bank have been made by the Idaho Power Company, to control the timing of water releases for generation of hydroelectric power at its facilities. For example, from 1982 through 1985, the bank leased more than 96 percent of the water sold (in quantities exceeding 200,000 acre-feet per year) to the Idaho Power Company at prices ranging from $2.30 to $2.50 per acre-foot. Irrigation constituted the remainder of the purchases during these and other years.

To increase the flexibility of the bank's operation and to provide a basis for long-term investments related to water use, the Bureau of Reclamation has been requested to allow lease terms longer than one year and to permit the price for water to be established on a basis other than cost. In November 1985, the bureau granted permission for longer leases, but no contract amendments were executed during 1986 to take advantage of the change. The Bureau of Reclamation is also considering giving the bank more flexibility in establishing the rental price of water.

The Northern Colorado Water Conservancy District

Perhaps the most widely known, best-established market for water operates in the Northern Colorado Water Conservancy District (NCWCD) in the Fort Collins area. The district was founded in the 1930s to contract with the Bureau of Reclamation to serve the water demands on the east slope of the Continental Divide by using the more abundant water supplies from Colorado's west slope. The bureau's Colorado–Big Thompson Project (C-BT) diverts water at the headwaters of the Colorado River and transports it through the Continental Divide to supplement the water supplies of about 720,000 acres of irrigated land as well as the supplies of several east-slope cities. From 1957 to 1982, the C-BT provided an annual average of 220,000 acre-feet of water, or about 25 percent of the total 865,000 acre-feet of water used by the district (Northern Colorado Water Conservancy District, 1982).

There are three principal types of water rights in the NCWCD area: rights to C-BT water imported from the west slope, rights to water stored in irrigation company reservoirs, and direct flow rights from east-slope streams. Water companies within the NCWCD typically hold one or more of these three. Although water rights from each category have been transferred, C-BT water is the most easily marketed. It is diverted under water rights filed for and owned by the Bureau of Reclamation and sold under contract to the district. Each year the NCWCD divides the amount of available C-BT water proportionally among the owners of its 310,000 shares or units. Shares can be bought, sold, and leased within the district. For example, about

65,000 acre-feet—some 30 percent of the water delivered to the district by the C-BT—moves through the rental market every year (Howe, Schurmeir, and Shaw, 1986). Annual rentals require no more than a postcard to the NCWCD to shift the water to a different use or location. Sales of water on a permanent basis are also relatively frequent and straightforward, and a number of realtors specialize in brokering such transactions.

The price of shares of C-BT water has varied widely. The average price for permanent rights to C-BT water (all expressed in 1980 dollars) was $99 per acre-foot equivalent in 1961; $504 in 1970; $2,895 in 1980; $2,445 in 1981; and about $900 in 1985 (Wahl and Osterhoudt, 1986). In the rental market, prices have risen slightly from 1961 to 1983, but less than the rate of inflation. The predominant annual rental price is $5–$7 per acre-foot. Prices are slightly lower in the early part of the irrigation season than later on (Howe, Schurmeir, and Shaw, 1986). The rental market has been stimulated by cities within the district that regularly acquire water in excess of present demands so as to ensure sufficient supplies for the future. For instance, the current development of the Windy Gap Project in the C-BT—funded by municipal and industrial interests—will add about 48,000 acre-feet of water annually to the district's supplies, but municipalities are expected to lease the water to irrigators until needed.

The fact that C-BT water is a supplemental supply appears to have played an important part in its marketability. Different areas in the NCWCD have different demands for the additional water, and a mandatory, uniform assignment of water to land was not deemed appropriate when the district was established. Freely transferable allotments allow farmers to recover water costs whenever they have no need for their supplemental supply. Transfers are further facilitated by the fact that return flows of C-BT water are retained by the United States for use by the district (a provision of the NCWCD contract with the bureau). This arrangement was possible because C-BT water was diverted from the west slope, and since it was new to the region, no rights to return flows had developed (Howe, Schurmeir, and Shaw, 1986).

Federal Water Banking Operations in California During the 1976–1977 Drought

Drought conditions can intensify interest in water exchange possibilities. Water users who would suffer the greatest damage from a water shortage may be able to purchase water from those willing to reduce water use temporarily, provided sufficient compensation can be paid. The year 1976 was the fourth driest in more than a century in California, and 1977 was the driest year ever recorded. Statewide precipitation was 65 percent of normal in 1976 and 45 percent of normal in 1977, with the most severe water shortages experienced by the northern two-thirds of the state (see California Department of Water Resources, 1978, and U.S. Department of the Interior, Bureau of Reclamation, 1978). After the 1976 drought and in view of the worsening situation developing for 1977, Congress enacted Public Law 96-18 on April 7, 1977, which authorized the operation of federal water banks during the drought. Rules and regulations were published in the *Federal Register* on April 16, 1977, to implement the law. The Secretary of the Interior was to assist willing sellers in transferring water to irrigation water buyers. The program was to be carried out so that no "undue benefit or profit" would accrue to sellers. Toward that end, the secretary was directed to establish a transfer price that would recover all costs of acquiring the water and that would also cover the estimated net income usually derived from the water. The rules also established allocation priorities among purchasers: (1) preservation of orchards and perennial crops; (2) irrigation of support crops for dairy and beef cattle herds and other breeding stock; and (3) irrigation of all other crops. The rules also allowed interest-free loans to be used by irrigation purchasers for repayment over a period not to exceed five years.

With these rules, the Bureau of Reclamation established water banking operations in the Central Valley Project during the 1976–1977 drought. The prices paid by the bank to purchase water ranged from $15 per acre-foot to about $84.50 per acre-foot (see table 5-2). Various methods were used to establish the prices paid. For example, the $25-per-acre-foot price paid to Reclamation District No.

Table 5-2. Sellers of Water to the Federal Water Bank in California During the 1976–1977 Drought

Seller	Water sold to bank (acre-feet)	Total cost (dollars)	Price per acre-foot (dollars)
Department of Water Resources	8,185	691,729	84.51
Pleasant Grove–Verona Mutual Water Company	15,752	1,102,640	70.00
Chaplin-Lewis-Lewis	1,279	44,765	35.00
Reclamation District No. 108	5,000	125,000	25.00
Pelger Mutual Water Company	4,425	110,625	25.00
Natomas Central Mutual Water Company	6,000	90,000	15.00
Sacramento River Water Contractors' Association	5,797	86,955	15.00
Total	46,438	2,251,714	

Source: Records of Contracts and Repayments Branch, Bureau of Reclamation, U.S. Department of the Interior, Washington, D.C.

108 represented the estimated cost to the district of pumping ground-water in lieu of its usual diversions from the Sacramento River. The $70-per-acre-foot price for Pleasant Grove–Verona Mutual Water Company's supply was intended to compensate farmers for forgoing rice production ($60 per acre-foot) and to compensate those land-owners who would normally have sold the associated tailwater (water coming off the end of irrigation rows, which was valued at $10 per acre-foot). The $85-per-acre-foot price paid to the state of California was based on State Water Project rates for operation, maintenance, and capital repayment, plus the power costs associated with compensatory water diversions from the Colorado River to southern California.

In total, the Federal Water Bank spent about $2.3 million to purchase 46,438 acre-feet of water both from the State Water Project and from the bureau's Central Valley Project water contractors. The water rights associated with these supplies were quite broad in their geographic extension and allowed exchanges to be readily accomplished in accordance with state water law. Of the 46,438 acre-feet purchased by the bureau's Water Bank, 42,544 acre-feet were sold (see table 5-3). The balance of 3,894 acre-feet represents deductions for return flow losses and conveyance losses. The average price paid by purchasers for water was about $61 per acre-foot, with prices ranging from about $55 to around $142 per acre-foot. The high end of the price range reflects the significant conveyance and pumping costs necessary to transport the water to the purchaser.

The Arvin-Edison Water Storage District Exchange Pool

The Arvin-Edison Water Storage District, located on the east side of the San Joaquin Valley in California, operates an ongoing "water exchange pool" among its contractors (Davis, 1985). The pool is activated each year with offers and requests for water received by December 15. If there is a surplus of offers to sell water, then the pool is open to additional requests for water until February 1, after which time any surplus is made available on a first come, first served basis. Conversely, if requests to purchase water exceed offers, then the exchange pool remains open until February 1 for additional water to be offered for sale. If requests still exceed offers by that date, then the available water is prorated among the requesters. As shown in table 5-4, the water-short years of 1974 and 1977 showed the largest excess of demands over offers. Exchanges in the pool have run as high as 7.6 percent of the district's firm water supply of 128,300 acre-feet. Water purchasers pay for their allocation from the exchange pool at the district's normal water rate. Those offering water for sale receive

Table 5-3.   Purchasers of Water from the Federal Water Bank in California During the 1976–1977 Drought

Purchaser	Water purchased (acre-feet)	Total revenue (dollars)	Price per acre-foot (dollars)
Hills Valley ID	76	10,825.63	142.44
Stone Corral ID	124	17,232.37	138.97
Tri-Valley WD	135	18,688.19	138.43
Delano-Earlimart ID	200	27,294.09	136.47
Lindsay-Strathmore ID	300	40,545.50	135.15
Terra Bella ID	503	67,452.91	134.10
Mustang WD	112	7,168.29	64.00
San Luis WD (San Luis Canal)	1,144	72,746.07	63.59
Romero WD	120	7,482.57	62.35
Broadview WD	120	7,387.98	61.57
Hospital ID	1,389	85,269.35	61.39
Kern Canyon WD	605	36,894.35	60.98
Arvin-Edison WSD	500	30,356.38	60.71
Davis WD	304	18,208.69	59.90
Salado WD	500	29,538.97	59.08
Centinella WD	329	19,404.67	58.98
Orestimba WD	843	49,503.97	58.72
Quinto WD	435	25,310.10	58.18
Del Puerto WD	1,326	76,986.73	58.06
Westlands WD	22,362	1,295,098.78	57.92
Foothill WD	1,100	63,539.13	57.76
San Luis WD (Delta-Mendota Canal)	5,469	314,926.32	57.58
Plain View WD	1,180	67,870.11	57.52
Sunflower WD	1,205	68,718.19	57.03
Contra Costa WD	1,250	70,252.02	56.20
Panoche WD	891	49,859.16	55.96
Glenn-Colusa ID	22	1,208.46	54.93
Total	42,544	2,579,769.98	

Note: Abbreviations: ID, irrigation district; WD, water district; WSD, water storage district.

Source: Records of Contracts and Repayments Branch, Bureau of Reclamation, U.S. Department of the Interior, Washington, D.C.

refunds at the end of the year for water distributed by the pool. Water exchanges are limited to the boundaries of the district.

Water deliveries can also be exchanged after the district's water year begins on March 1 (refer to the last column of table 5-4). This is done by submitting written notice to the district requesting or offering water. The dispatcher's office serves as the clearinghouse for such

Table 5-4. Preseason Water Exchange Pool and In-Season Transfers, Arvin-Edison Water Storage District, 1970–1987

Year	Offers (acre-feet)	Requests (acre-feet)	Pro rata share[a] (percent)	In season transfers[b] (acre-feet)
1970	9,725	9,720	100	n.a.
1971	3,223	3,623	89	n.a.
1972	2,212	3,147	70	n.a.
1973	3,531	5,202	68	n.a.
1974	1,071	7,631	14	n.a.
1975	1,124	1,124	100	n.a.
1976	2,953	2,953	100	n.a.
1977	1,509	7,868	19	1,743
1978	3,788	3,788	100	2,644
1979	3,937	3,937	100	11,759
1980	4,604	7,872	58	7,940
1981	5,862	5,862	100	13,695
1982	3,165	5,591	57	5,730
1983	6,225	6,225	100	3,812
1984	7,814	3,192	100	n.a.
1985	4,175	4,175	100	12,424
1986	12,306	1,942	100	11,246
1987	19,249	812	100	12,000

Note: n.a. means not available.

Source: Data from 1970 to 1984 are from U.S. Geological Survey, *National Water Summary 1985,* Water Supply Paper 2300, p. 120. Data for subsequent years are from the Arvin-Edison Water Storage District.

[a]Percent of acre-foot request received by each purchaser.

[b]The district's water year begins on March 1.

"posted" transfers. In addition, water exchanges are worked out between individuals without the aid of the posting process, and the district is subsequently notified in writing. In-season transfers have run as high as 11 percent of the district's firm water supply. It is not surprising that in-season exchanges are sometimes more heavily used than preseason exchanges because of the risk involved in forecasting water needs several months in advance of the growing season.

Water Transaction Between the Emery Water Conservancy District and the Utah Power and Light Company

In 1972 the Utah Power and Light Company obtained the equivalent of a forty-year lease on 6,000 acre-feet of water from the Bureau of Reclamation's Emery County Project. This water, formerly used for irrigation, is now used in a coal-fired steam electric plant, principally for cooling purposes. The plant lies in Huntington Canyon, about 150 miles southeast of Salt Lake City, Utah. Two irrigation companies in the Emery Water Conservancy District agreed to reduce their allotments of project water in order to enable the district to allot project water to the power company. The original 1962 contract between the United States and the district was for irrigation water use only. However, the Emery County Project of the Bureau of Reclamation is a unit of the Colorado River Storage Project, which had been established by Congress for irrigation and broader purposes. The bureau used this legislation as authority for executing an amendatory contract with the conservancy district to allow it to contract for water for municipal and industrial purposes.

The 1972 amendatory contract reduced the irrigation repayment obligation of the Emery Water Conservancy District from $2,935,000 to $2,433,600 and added $4,440,000 for industrial water, a net increase in the total repayment obligation of $3,938,600 deriving from the interest charges associated with municipal and industrial use. In turn, the power company assumed repayment of its corresponding share of project costs. The United States receives $120,000 a year from the power company for the 6,000 acre-feet of water transferred ($20 per acre-foot per year), plus a proportionate share of the annual operation and maintenance costs. As a result of the transaction, the irrigable acreage in the district was reduced by 4,604 acres (of a total of 18,755 acres). There was little local objection to this reduction in agricultural use, partly because the local economy depends heavily on coal production.

Transaction Between the Casper-Alcova Irrigation District and the City of Casper

Increasing urban demands for water in the city of Casper, Wyoming, led to a mutually beneficial transaction with the Casper-Alcova Irrigation District (Wahl and Osterhoudt, 1986; Engels, 1986). From the inception of the Kendrick Project, the district had difficulty meeting its repayment obligation. Although the original project was intended to irrigate 66,000 acres, today only about 24,000 acres are being irrigated. Under a 1982 water exchange agreement, the municipality paid off the district's outstanding repayment obligation of $750,000 to the United States in three years. In addition, the city is paying $150,000 annually to the district for rehabilitation and canal lining on portions of the district's 59-mile canal and its 190-mile lateral system in order to reduce seepage. Reducing seepage allows for a lesser quantity of water to be diverted for agricultural use while maintaining the same quantity of water delivered to crops. This arrangement is designed to eventually provide Casper with an additional water supply of 7,000 acre-feet per year from the North Platte River. In addition to the payments already described, the city will pay the Bureau of Reclamation $24 per acre-foot for the water. Casper estimates that the total annual cost of the water will be about $105 per acre-foot.

Since only the amount of conserved water is transferred, the reassignment was not considered a change of use under Wyoming law. Rather, a "secondary supply permit" was used to reassign storage rights from the Bureau of Reclamation's Seminoe and Alcova reservoirs, which are the sources of supply for the irrigation district. During the environmental impact review process, there was some concern that the proposed rehabilitation and improvement project would eliminate the wetlands that currently exist because of canal seepage. As a result of public concern, 4 of the larger seepage areas (out of 100) were maintained.

Negotiations Between the Imperial Irrigation District and Metropolitan Water Users in Southern California

An agreement similar in effect to the Casper-Alcova arrangement has been reached in southern California. Since March 1984 the Metropolitan Water District of Southern California, which supplies water to twenty-seven member agencies on the Pacific coastal plain, has been holding discussions with the Imperial Irrigation District (IID) about providing financial assistance for conservation improvements in exchange for receiving the conserved water.

The Imperial Irrigation District diverts 2.9 million acre-feet annually from the Colorado River (nearly one-fifth of the average flow) through the All-American Canal (a Bureau of Reclamation project) and through 1,627 miles of main canals and laterals to irrigate 450,000 acres of farmland. In 1980 one of the district's farmers, whose lands were being threatened by the rising levels of the Salton Sea (which receives the return flows from the district), filed a complaint with the state alleging that wasteful use of water by the district was a contributing factor. In accord with state law, the California Department of Water Resources investigated and prepared a 1981 report estimating that up to 437,000 acre-feet of water could be conserved in IID by various means, including canal lining, spill interceptor canals, tailwater recovery systems, system automation, an increased number of regulatory reservoirs, and a more flexible system of deliveries. The annual costs of these measures were estimated to range from $8 to $115 per acre-foot conserved in 1981 dollars (California Department of Water Resources, 1981; also see U.S. Department of the Interior, Bureau of Reclamation, 1983). In June 1984 the State Water Resources Control Board used the Department of Water Resources report in deciding that IID's use of water was "unreasonable" and that conservation measures should be implemented.

The Metropolitan Water District of Southern California (MWD) is interested in the water conserved by IID because MWD has been taking Colorado River water allocated to, but unused by, Arizona. In November 1985 the Central Arizona Project was completed to the extent that deliveries to the Phoenix area could commence. Under the set of priorities governing the usage of the Colorado River, as the Central Arizona Project increases its diversions, MWD will suffer a corresponding decrease in the availability of surplus flows from the Colorado River. Under the recent MWD/IID proposal, IID would reduce its diversions from the Colorado River via the All-American Canal in order to allow a corresponding increase in MWD diversions upstream at the Colorado River Aqueduct.

Financing of the conservation measures in IID appears to provide water to MWD at less cost than would several of MWD's other alternatives (see Stavins and Willey, 1983; Wahl and Davis, 1986). During fall 1988, the two districts reached an agreement intended to provide the first 100,000 acre-feet of potential conservation. In exchange for the salvaged water, MWD will pay IID $92 million for the construction of conservation facilities, $3.1 million annually for operation and maintenance, and $23 million in five annual installments for indirect costs. In this case, the possibilities of a successful transaction were enhanced by (1) the fact that irrigation return flows are causing increased costs to some farmers, (2) the State Water Resources Control Board order to IID that necessitated financing certain improvements in order to increase the efficiency of water use, (3) the high value that is placed on the water by potential urban wholesalers, (4) the fact that the Imperial Irrigation District holds rights to Colorado River deliveries, and (5) state legislation encouraging water transfers.

Conclusions

Voluntary water transfers of federally supplied water appear to offer significant potential for increasing the efficiency of use of federally supplied water in the western states, especially when compared with mandatory conservation plans or attempts by the federal government to raise water prices. As discussed in this chapter, several such voluntary transactions have already taken place. But there is reason to believe that the number of transactions has been unnecessarily con-

strained by several factors. The procedures that would govern transfers of federally supplied water were not well understood by most
water users on federal projects. This is not surprising given the lack of
any clear policy prior to December 1988 on the part of the Bureau of
Reclamation concerning transfers or of any written procedures for
processing transfer requests.[5] The result is that Bureau of Reclamation policy has varied widely from one situation to another and from
one regional office to another. This is particularly true in the case of
bureau policy regarding increased income from transfers. For example, water from the Colorado–Big Thompson Project is routinely sold
at market rates in the Northern Colorado Water Conservancy District. In the bureau's banking operation during the 1976–1977
drought in California, the bureau placed a limit on the selling price of
water, which was intended to reflect the value forgone in its original
use. However, except for those two years, the bureau has only allowed
water in the Central Valley Project to be transferred among districts
at the federal contract rates. In the ongoing banking operations on
the Upper Snake River in Idaho, the bureau imposes a ceiling on the
price of water transferred, which is set somewhat higher than contractor costs. Chapter 6 will address in more detail steps that the
Bureau of Reclamation can take to facilitate transfers of federally
supplied water.

References

Anderson, Terry L. 1983a. *Water Crisis: Ending the Policy Drought* (Wash-
    ington, D.C., Cato Institute).
_____, ed. 1983b. *Water Rights: Scarce Resource Allocation, Bureaucracy,
    and the Environment* (Cambridge, Mass., Ballinger).
California Assembly Office of Research. 1982. *A Marketing Approach to
    Water Allocation* (Sacramento, Calif.).
California Department of Water Resources. 1978. *The 1976 California
    Drought—A Review* (Sacramento, Calif.).
_____. 1981. *Investigation Under California Water Code Section 275 of Use of
    Water by Imperial Irrigation District,* Southern District Report (Los An-
    geles, Calif.).
Davis, Robert K. 1985. "The Arvin-Edison Water Storage District: The Ori-
    gins, Development and Operation of a California Irrigation District."
    U.S. Department of the Interior, Office of Policy Analysis (Washington,
    D.C.).

[5] On December 16, 1988, the Department of the Interior issued a set of principles
designed to guide Bureau of Reclamation review and approval of water transfer requests. These principles are reproduced as an appendix at the end of this book.

Engels, David. 1986. "Augmenting Municipal Water Supplies Through Agricultural Water Conservation," in Natural Resources Law Center, *Western Water: Expanding Uses/Finite Supplies* (Boulder, University of Colorado School of Law).

Environmental Defense Fund. 1983. *Trading Conservation Investments for Water* (Berkeley, Calif.).

Frederick, Kenneth D., with James C. Hanson. 1982. *Water for Western Agriculture* (Washington, D.C., Resources for the Future).

Getches, David. 1984. *Water Law in a Nutshell* (St. Paul, Minn., West Publishing).

Hartman, L. M., and Don Seastone. 1970. *Water Transfers: Economic Efficiency and Alternative Institutions* (Baltimore, Md., The Johns Hopkins University Press).

Howe, Charles W., Dennis R. Schurmeir, and William D. Shaw, Jr. 1986. "Innovations in Water Management: Lessons from the Colorado–Big Thompson Project and Northern Colorado Water Conservancy District." *Water Resources Research* vol. 22, pp. 439–445 (April).

Meyers, Charles J., and Richard A. Posner. 1971. "Market Transfers of Water Rights: Toward an Improved Market in Water Resources." Legal Study No. 4 prepared for the U.S. National Water Commission, Washington, D.C. (Available from National Technical Information Service, Springfield, Va. NWC-L-71-009).

Northern Colorado Water Conservancy District. 1982. Annual Report. (Loveland, Northern Colorado Water Conservancy District).

Phelps, Charles E., Nancy Y. Moore, and Morlie H. Graubard. 1978. *Efficient Water Use in California: Water Rights, Water Districts, and Water Transfers* (Santa Monica, Calif., Rand Corporation).

Saliba, Bonnie C., and David B. Bush. 1987. *Water Markets in Theory and Practice: Market Transfers, Water Values, and Public Policy* (Boulder, Colo., Westview Press).

Stavins, Robert, and Zach Willey. 1983. "Trading Conservation Investments for Water," in *Regional and State Water Resources Planning and Management* (Bethesda, Md., American Water Resources Association), pp. 223–230.

U.S. Department of the Interior, Bureau of Reclamation. 1978. *Report on the Emergency Drought Act of 1977* (Washington, D.C.).

_____. 1983. "Water Conservation Opportunities: Imperial Irrigation District, California." Draft Special Report (Washington, D.C.).

U.S. National Water Commission. 1973. *Water Policies for the Future* (Washington, D.C., Government Printing Office).

Wahl, Richard W., and Robert K. Davis. 1986. "Satisfying Southern California's Thirst for Water: Efficient Alternatives," in Kenneth D. Frederick, ed., *Scarce Water and Institutional Change* (Washington, D.C., Resources for the Future).

Wahl, Richard W., and Frank H. Osterhoudt. 1986. "Voluntary Transfers of Water in the West," in U.S. Geological Survey, *National Water Summary 1985,* Water Supply Paper 2300 (Washington, D.C., Government Printing Office).

Webb, Walter Prescott. 1931. *The Great Plains.* Reprint. (Lincoln, University of Nebraska Press, 1981).

Western Governors' Association. 1987. *Water Efficiency: Opportunities for Action* (Denver, Colo.).

6

Federal Policy Changes to Facilitate Voluntary Water Transfers

A good deal has been written about the steps states could take to facilitate voluntary water transfers. For example, they could reduce the high transactions costs of state approval processes, clarify in state law that the transfer of water does not constitute evidence of failure to put water to beneficial use, define water rights in terms of consumptive use rather than only in terms of withdrawals, and quantify the consumptive uses associated with existing rights.[1] This chapter takes state water law and institutions as given and examines what changes in federal law and policy would facilitate voluntary water transfers within the context of existing state law. The matter is important given the large quantities of water that are supplied by the Bureau of Reclamation in many western states and the interest by some states in facilitating transfers. The bureau supplies about 27 million acre-feet of water for irrigation use annually in the seventeen western states, about 3 million acre-feet for municipal and industrial uses, and about 1 million acre-feet for other nonagricultural uses (U.S. Department of the Interior, Bureau of Reclamation, 1986, p. 2). About 22 percent of the irrigated acreage in these states receives at least supplemental supplies of federally supplied irrigation water, and this percentage exceeds 40 percent in Idaho and Washington (refer to tables 1-2 and 1-3).

---

[1] For additional discussion of these points, see Hartman and Seastone, 1970; Meyers and Posner, 1971; U.S. National Water Commission, 1973, pp. 260–270; Phelps, Moore, and Graubard, 1978; California Assembly Office of Research, 1982; Frederick, 1982; Environmental Defense Fund, 1983; Stavins and Willey, 1983; Anderson, 1983a,b; Saliba and Bush, 1987).

Chapter 5 reviewed a number of past transfers of Bureau of Reclamation water. However, the bureau's policies regarding transfers have not been consistent from transfer to transfer or from region to region. This chapter examines in detail the present legal, contractual, and administrative provisions with which a voluntary water transfer must comply. These categories are important because they represent different levels of discretion for the bureau. The bureau can modify its administrative policies and amend its existing contracts to facilitate voluntary water transfers, provided such changes are allowable within the provisions of Reclamation law. Changes in Reclamation law itself would require a wider consensus.

This discussion reveals that the Bureau of Reclamation has considerable discretion within existing law to adopt administrative policies that would facilitate voluntary water transfers and, where necessary, to amend contracts for the same purpose. The bureau's administrative policies are pivotal because Bureau of Reclamation contracts require the approval of the federal contracting officer for any assignment of rights under the contract. In the course of this chapter, specific administrative steps are proposed that the federal government could take to facilitate voluntary transfers of federally supplied water. Certain changes in federal law that could ease transfers are also suggested. Finally, the consequences of adopting such measures are considered.

Provisions Related to Voluntary Water Transfers and Recommended Changes

Legal Provisions

It is sometimes presumed that there are general legal prohibitions against the resale of water by federal contractors. However, this presumption appears to derive from administrative practice rather than specific legal mandates. This section reviews federal legislative provisions that may have some potential bearing on market transfers of federal water with the goal of clarifying what type of transfers can take place within the existing framework of Reclamation law.

Water Appurtenant to Land. Section 8 of the Reclamation Act of 1902 (32 Stat 388; 43 U.S.C. 391) requires that federally supplied water be "appurtenant to the lands irrigated." This provision, if applicable, could severely impede water transfers because it could restrict water to the lands currently receiving project deliveries for irrigation use. However, it is generally held that numerous subsequent acts providing for reclamation water for nonirrigation purposes, such as the Reclamation Project Act of 1939 and the Water Supply Act of 1958, have repealed by implication the appurtenancy requirement. The bureau has acknowledged this position at least as far back as 1971 (see Meyers and Posner, 1971, pp. A3–A4).

Residency.   Section 5 of the Reclamation Act of 1902 required that a recipient of irrigation water be "an actual bona fide resident on such lands, or occupant thereof residing in the neighborhood of such land." The residency requirement was repealed by the Reclamation Reform Act of 1982.

Beneficial Use.   Section 8 of the 1902 act provides that "beneficial use shall be the basis, the measure, and the limit of the right." There is no definition of "beneficial use" in federal Reclamation law. It is unclear whether a federal or a state definition of beneficial use is intended by the statute, but the Department of the Interior has generally held that state definitions of beneficial use are controlling: Section 8 of the 1902 act provides that "nothing in this act shall be construed as affecting . . . or to in any way interfere with the laws of any State or Territory relating to the control, appropriation, use, or distribution of water." State laws differ in the procedures for establishing beneficial use and for processing prospective transfers of water to new beneficial users. If state jurisdiction over beneficial use is controlling, then it does not appear that making changes in the treatment of beneficial use in federal law would further facilitate water transfers.

Irrigation Efficiency of Projects.   The most comprehensive contracting authority for the Bureau of Reclamation is the Reclamation Project Act of 1939 (53 Stat. 1187; 43 U.S.C. 485). Section 9(c) of this act authorizes the Secretary of the Interior to contract for municipal and industrial water supply, for the sale of electric power, and for the lease of power privileges from reclamation projects, provided that such contracts "will not impair the efficiency of the project for irrigation purposes." This provision echoes similar restrictions embodied in earlier legislation. Section 4 of the Town Sites Act of 1906 (34 Stat. 116; 43 U.S.C. 567) authorized the development and lease of surplus power from irrigation projects, provided that the lease did not "impair the efficiency of the irrigation project." The Miscellaneous Purposes Act of 1920 (41 Stat. 451; 43 U.S.C. 521) authorized the Secretary of the Interior to contract for water from irrigation projects for purposes other than irrigation, provided that he first obtain the permission of the existing water user associations in the project and that the delivery of water for these other purposes is not "detrimental to the water service for such irrigation project or to the rights of any prior appropriator."

At first glance it may appear that provisions concerning the priority of the irrigation function of projects would significantly limit water transfers. However, in actual practice, the bureau has encountered little difficulty in entering into contracts to supply municipal and industrial water or to sell hydropower under the authority of the Reclamation Project Act. Furthermore, the provisions of the 1939 act have been utilized to facilitate transfers—for example, the transfer of water between the city of Casper, Wyoming, and the Casper-Alcova Irrigation District discussed in chapter 5. The original project had been established for irrigation by secretarial order under the authority of the Reclamation Act of 1902. When a portion of the water was shifted to municipal and industrial use, the bureau conditioned the agreement on delivering the same amount of water to crops—a strict interpretation of the provision of the 1939 act that the contract not "impair the efficiency of the project for irrigation purposes." Various interpretations of this provision are possible, particularly where an irrigation district is willing to forgo use of some of its water. In the Casper-Alcova case, however, the bureau interpreted the measure in such a way that other alternatives, such as retiring marginal lands from production, were not permitted. It would be desirable for the bureau to have clear legislative authority to permit transfers of irrigation water to any other uses even where it decreased the project acreage devoted to irrigation, provided that the various parties agreed to such a transfer and that the transfer complied with other provisions of federal and state law.

Profitability of Resale. Essential to a viable market transfer policy for water is the profitability of lease or resale. With the exception of Warren Act contracts, there appear to be no explicit legislative provisions that would prohibit reclamation water users from participating in the income gains from resale. Indeed, such practice is common in some districts, such as the Northern Colorado Water Conservancy District.

The Warren Act contracts deserve additional discussion. When "storage or carrying capacity has been or may be provided in excess of the requirements of the lands to be irrigated under any project," the Warren Act of 1911 (36 Stat. 925; 43 U.S.C. 523) allows the Secretary of the Interior to contract out the excess storage and carrying capacity to nonproject individuals, districts, or associations. One of the conditions of the act is that the contracting party shall not levy a charge for storage or delivery in excess of actual cost, except to the extent that an additional charge may be necessary to cover the contractor's own cost of carriage and delivery of water. This would appear to prohibit the resale of water at a profit by Warren Act contractors. However, this may not be as significant a barrier to most water transfers as it first appears. For one thing, only about 400 out of some 4,000 reclamation contracts have been executed under the authority of the Warren Act, and these are mostly concentrated in a few projects and regions, namely, the Klamath Project in the Mid-Pacific region and the Boise, Minidoka, and Yakima projects in the Pacific Northwest region. Therefore, water transfers in more arid parts of the country are not affected.[2] Furthermore, a 1985 ruling by the Department of the Interior (August 23 opinion of Associate Solicitor Keith E. Eastin, U.S. Department of the Interior, Bureau of Reclamation, 1985, LBR ER 0259) indicates that many of the 400 presumed Warren Act contracts may not have properly utilized the authority of the act. Consequently, the number of Warren Act contracts may be considerably less than 400 after the bureau completes its review of these agreements.

Even for the relatively small number of contracts to which it does apply, the Warren Act may not limit the income gains from transfers. One of the principal purposes of the act was to allow delivery of water to irrigation districts outside of a government project, provided excess storage and carrying capacity were available. The solicitor's opinion referenced above held that the act does not apply to delivery of project water but only to delivery of water to which a contractor holds his own "permitted or adjudicated right under State water law." Seen in this light, the act's prohibition against making excessive charges for delivery of water was an attempt to prevent irrigation districts and water companies from charging their own customers an undue fee merely for the carriage of water through federally constructed facilities. However, the act does not appear to prevent the nonfederal owners of the water rights from charging whatever price they desire for the privilege of utilizing the nonfederal water rights, whether by sale or lease.

Project Service Area and End Use of Water.   Legislative restrictions relating to the geographic areas where project water may be used and the end uses of water (irrigation, municipal and industrial, hydropower, and so on) need to be examined on a project-by-project basis in response to any particular transfer proposal. Many project authorizations specify the end uses of project water but are quite general in defining the service area of the project. For example, the

---

[2] There are only thirty-five Warren Act contracts in the Upper Colorado region, nine in the Lower Missouri region, four in the Lower Colorado region, and one each in the Upper Missouri region and the Southwest region.

Colorado River Basin Project Act of 1968 authorizes the Central
Arizona Project for furnishing irrigation water and municipal water
supplies to "the water-deficient areas of Arizona and western New
Mexico." Even where specific details regarding service area are included in authorizing legislation, a 1986 opinion of the interior solicitor (opinion no. M-36901, Supp. I, by Solicitor Ralph Tarr, June 17,
1986) indicates that the secretary may have considerable discretion.
An act passed in 1960 authorized the San Luis Unit of the Central
Valley Project in California "for the principal purpose of furnishing
water for the irrigation of approximately five hundred thousand acres
of land in Merced, Fresno, and Kings Counties." Currently, about
650,000 acres are irrigated in the San Luis Unit, of which 560,000
acres lie within the Westlands Water District alone (U.S. Department
of the Interior, Bureau of Reclamation, 1986, table 3). However, Solicitor Tarr held that the authorizing language did not limit the acreage
to 500,000 acres since it did not use such restrictive terms as "no more
than," "not to exceed," or "only."[3]

Even in light of this opinion, however, the authorizing language for
a project can limit transfers. For example, water from the Central
Valley Project is not authorized for delivery to southern California
outside of Central Valley. Where project authorizations are tied to
specific feasibility or planning reports, service areas are more restricted. Prior to the 1940s, most reclamation projects were authorized by the Secretary of the Interior under the general authority of
the Reclamation Act of 1902 and subsequent legislation. Even where
secretarial authorizations were based on planning reports, the fact
that the projects were authorized by administrative action rather
than directly by Congress would probably provide some flexibility in
adjusting the service area.

Reclamation law itself gives flexibility to the bureau in complying
with service area and end-use restrictions. The Warren Act of 1911
allows the bureau to deliver water outside of project service areas,
provided the water rights are not held by the Bureau of Reclamation
(and provided there is surplus storage and conveyance capacity available). This is a geographic extension, of sorts, of the services that can

---

[3] The increase from 500,000 acres in the authorizing act to 650,000 acres had been a
source of controversy surrounding the Bureau of Reclamation contracts with Westlands (refer to the appendix to chapter 4). Solicitor Tarr's opinion overturned the June
1, 1978, opinion of former Interior Solicitor Leo Krulitz (U.S. Department of the
Interior, 1979, pp. 254–275, opinion M-36901), who had held that contracts with
Westlands were limited to the delivery of water to 500,000 acres because of the
authorizing legislation (see also U.S. Department of the Interior, Bureau of Reclamation, 1978).

be provided by a Bureau of Reclamation project.[4] The Reclamation Project Act of 1939 allows the bureau to contract out water for municipal and industrial purposes or for hydropower, provided the irrigation uses are protected. This provision was used to facilitate the transfer of water between the city of Casper, Wyoming, and the Casper-Alcova Irrigation District. The original project was established for irrigation by secretarial order under the authority of the Reclamation Act. Because the city of Casper lies outside the boundaries of the district, as part of the agreement, the bureau executed a contract with the city under the authority of the 1939 act, as well as an amendatory contract with the irrigation district.

There is no clear authority under existing legislation for allowing project water users to sell or lease water for uses and locations not envisioned in project authorizations. Therefore, either the bureau has to be involved in such transactions by contracting for water delivery for the new use or location (such as in the Casper-Alcova example), or legislative action must be solicited to facilitate such transfers.

Transfer of Title to Project Works. The Bureau of Reclamation has authority to transfer the responsibility for operation and management of project facilities to water districts, but, even in such cases, it retains title to project works. Section 6 of the Reclamation Act of 1902 provides for district management and operation of "irrigation works" but reserves title to and management and operation of "reservoirs and the works necessary for their protection and operation" to the government "until otherwise provided by Congress." Section 5 of the Reclamation Extension Act of 1914 (38 Stat. 687; 43 U.S.C. 492, 499) makes clear that the transfer of management and operation extends to all project works, such as canals and distribution systems, but makes no reference to transfer of title of such works ("the Secretary is hereby authorized . . . to transfer . . . the care, operation, and maintenance of all or any part of the project works").

While title to project works does not relate to water transfers as directly as some of the other provisions examined, it is probably safe to say that water transfers would be easier for districts if the districts had clear title to their facilities at project payout. Districts would then

---

[4] Delivery of project water to lands outside project boundaries is another matter. Although many contracts have been written by the bureau to deliver project water outside of the project service area, purportedly under the authority of the Warren Act, the 1985 solicitor's opinion discussed in the previous section indicates that this is not a valid use of the act. Even if such contracts were improperly executed and are not Warren Act contracts, they are valid for the delivery of water because of Section 225 of the Reclamation Reform Act of 1982, which validates all existing agreements for the delivery of project water through nonproject facilities.

be free to modify their facilities or to retire them at will in response to transfer requests, without having to secure further bureau or congressional approval. Before payout is complete, however, it probably makes sense for the bureau to retain title to ensure payout of project costs (for additional discussion on transfer of title to project works, see Wahl and Simon, 1988).

Acreage Limitation. The Reclamation Reform Act of 1982 (96 Stat. 1263; 43 U.S.C. 390) abolished the residency requirement of the Reclamation Act of 1902 and offers farmers a choice. Either they can stay with the 160-acre limitation of the 1902 act or they can elect an expanded ownership limitation of 960 acres, provided that they pay "full cost" for any water delivered to leased lands in a farming operation larger than 960 acres. Farmers staying with the ownership limitation of the 1902 act have had to pay "full cost" since April 12, 1987, for any water deliveries to leased land in a farming operation over the 160-acre limit. Following is a summary of the provisions that the Reclamation Reform Act imposes on agricultural purchasers of water (it imposes no additional restrictions on municipal and industrial purchasers):[5]

1. The recipients of water have to submit certification forms setting forth the size and location of land ownerships and leases for their farming operations.

2. Individuals (and corporations benefiting twenty-five or fewer individuals) are required to pay "full cost" (a rate that incorporates interest charges on the unpaid irrigation allocation) for project water delivered to farming operations in excess of 960 acres of class I lands, or the equivalent acreage of land in other (less productive) land classes.

3. Agricultural corporations benefiting more than twenty-five individuals are required to pay "full cost" for all project water unless the limited recipient was receiving water on or before October 1, 1981, in which case water deliveries to lands in excess of 320 acres, or their equivalent, are assessed "full cost."

4. Individuals who own more than 960 acres of land and who wish to receive federal water on this "excess land" are required to sign recordable contracts agreeing to dispose of their ownerships in excess of 960 acres within five years at a price set by the secretary. This price excludes the value of the federal water supply. Corporations owning more than 640 acres are subject to a similar requirement.

---

[5] For additional detail on provisions of the Reclamation Reform Act of 1982, see chapter 4.

5. Lands receiving transferred water on any sustained basis require land classification to ensure repayment potential and to ensure that the land has long-term productivity under an irrigation regimen.

6. Water districts are required to develop and implement conservation plans that meet with the bureau's approval.

Agricultural purchasers not previously subject to Reclamation law, such as those outside a bureau project, are subject to these provisions. The stipulations have no impact on water sales to current federal water contractors holding contracts established or amended after 1982, because the purchasers are already subject to them. Likewise, the act imposes no additional restrictions on agricultural sellers of federally supplied water with new or amended contracts. However, it can impose further restrictions on agricultural buyers and sellers of water who are federal water contractors but who do not have contracts amended or established after the date of the act—those choosing to remain under prior law. Most such purchasers can be categorized as receiving supplemental or additional benefits as the result of a water transfer, thereby requiring an amended contract to which the provisions apply. For example, federal contractors receiving increased income from a water transfer fall into this category because of the additional benefit accrued. In addition, contractors not already paying water rates sufficient to cover the bureau's annual operation and maintenance charges are required to do so upon amending their contracts.[6]

One implication of the RRA restrictions is that the market value of water for agricultural use is generally less for federally supplied water than for nonfederally supplied water with the same cost to the seller. This is especially true for water transferred to farms larger than 960 acres because of the "full cost" requirement, but there is some burden on smaller operations as well because of the reporting and land classification requirements and because of the limitations on resale to large farming operations.

Summary and Recommended Changes in Law.   It appears that there is considerable latitude for voluntary water transfers under existing Reclamation law. Apparently, there are no general legislative prohibitions against such transfers or against the potential income gains from them. However, federal legislation must be reviewed in response to any specific transfer proposal because project authori-

---

[6] This provision has its principal impact in the Central Valley Project in California (see chapters 3 and 4 and the appendix to chapter 4).

zations often limit project service areas and end uses of water. Where necessary, legislation could be developed on a case-by-case basis to accommodate a transfer that was agreed to by the parties but that required modification of authorized service areas or end uses of water. Even with regard to these two legislative restrictions, however, general Reclamation law appears to provide some contracting authority for new uses of water that do not "impair the efficiency of the project for irrigation purposes." It is not clear, however, that this provision will be interpreted to allow marginal lands to be retired from production in order to facilitate an exchange. For example, in the transfer of water between the Casper-Alcova Irrigation District and the city of Casper, Wyoming, the Bureau of Reclamation interpreted this provision to mean that the same amount of water had to be delivered to crops. Therefore, it would be useful to have some general legislative authority for water contractors to voluntarily transfer water to other end uses, whatever they might be, if the district voted to do so and if the federal costs were paid for the new end use of the water. Such an amendment to general Reclamation law might also clarify that federally supplied water need not be appurtenant to the lands irrigated. The amendment could go one step further by indicating that transfers to other beneficial uses recognized by state and federal law would not lead to forfeiture of a right for failing to use the water for its original purpose. It would also be useful for general legislation to indicate that the title to project facilities would transfer to the water users once a district's contractual obligation was repaid. At present, congressional transfer of title is required in most cases.

Contractual Provisions

The Bureau of Reclamation delivers water under more than 4,000 water contracts.[7] Over the years, certain sections of the contracts have become relatively standardized, while others vary considerably from one contract to another. To gain some idea of the provisions that might impinge on water transfers, a sample of bureau contracts was reviewed. Of particular interest were provisions in the contracts that placed restrictions on water transfers over and above those imposed by Reclamation law, for it is these provisions that the Bureau of Reclamation could change through contract amendment. Several contracts were included from projects in which there had been past water transfer activity, such as the Central Valley Project, the Minidoka-Palisades Project (which participates in the Idaho Water Supply

---

[7] For a discussion of the two basic types of contracts provided for by the Reclamation Act of 1939, see chapter 3.

Bank), and the Colorado–Big Thompson Project, to show how contractual provisions affected water transfers in those projects and how such provisions were accommodated. The sample is not a random one, but rather was chosen with the assistance of the bureau's contracting officials to represent a wide variety of geographic areas and contracting circumstances. Those contracting provisions judged relevant to voluntary water transfers were categorized under the headings shown in table 6-1. The contracts are referenced in the table both by Bureau of Reclamation project and by contractor. For convenience, they are usually referred to in the text by their project designation only. However, contract provisions can differ among districts in the same project (for example, among the five contracts listed in the Central Valley Project), so the provisions discussed below may not apply to all contracts in a project. The table indicates relatively standardized provisions with an "X." Less standardized provisions are summarized.

Assignment Limited. Of the thirty-four contracts reviewed, all contain a standardized provision limiting the assignment of rights under the contract. The usual language of this provision is as follows:

> The provisions of this contract shall apply to and bind the successors and assigns of the parties hereto, but no assignment or transfer of this contract or any part thereof or interest therein shall be valid until approved by the Secretary.

This provision indicates that the administrative policy of the bureau with regard to water transfers (discussed later in this chapter) is pivotal: contracts give the bureau the right to refuse district requests for reassignment of water deliveries. On the other hand, the assignment-limited provision does not present anything more than an approval requirement and therefore does not necessarily impede water transfers. Of course, elimination of the requirement from bureau contracts would further facilitate trading, but such a step does not seem appropriate. The bureau has a legitimate role in ensuring that repayment for assigned water is forthcoming. Furthermore, it has legislative mandates, such as enforcement of the acreage limitation provisions of Reclamation law, that cannot be adequately executed without knowing to whom water deliveries are assigned.

Beneficial Use. Beneficial use of water is explicitly mentioned in only eleven of the thirty-four contracts cited. However, it applies as a requirement in all contracts since it is a condition imposed by Reclamation law (refer to the discussion in the section on legal provisions, above). Therefore, its presence or absence in contracts does not affect the transferability of water.

Table 6-1. Provisions Relevant to Voluntary Water Transfers, Taken from a Sample of Bureau of Reclamation Contracts

Project–Contractor	Assignment limited	Beneficial use	U.S. retains title to facilities	Service restrictions		Limitations on increased income	Ownership of return flows	Subcontracting/transfer provisions
				Lands	Type of use			
Boise–Pioneer Ditch Co.	X	X	X	X	Ag.		U.S. for project use	None
Boulder Canyon–Imperial Irrigation District	X		X	X				None
Central Arizona–Central Arizona Water Conservancy District (master contract)	X		X			Excess revenues of subcontractors go to U.S. for district's repayment obligation	Subcontractors may sell those captured	Allows three-party water service contracts with entities within boundaries of district
Central Arizona–Central Arizona Water Conservancy District (master subcontract)	X			X	Ag.; restrictions on use for M&I	Excess revenues from water transfers go to U.S. for district's repayment obligation	(See master contract)	This is a master subcontract

					Allows sale of water outside district (with approval of C.O.) and contracts with other parties for water supplies
Central Valley– El Dorado Irrigation District	X			X	
Central Valley– G. H. Russell	X	Ag.	X		None; only with land transfer can water be transferred
Central Valley– Glenn-Colusa Irrigation District	X	Ag;; other with U.S. consent	X		Contracts between district and others for water service if U.S. agrees
Central Valley– Kanawha Water District	X	Ag, M&I	X		Water exchanges allowed with secretarial approval, if provide additional water to district or if with other project contractors

(continued)

Note: Abbreviations: Ag., agriculture; dom., domestic; ind., industrial; mun., municipal; M&I, municipal and industrial; F&W, fish and wildlife; O&M, operation and maintenance; rec., recreational; misc., miscellaneous; C.O., federal contracting officer.
Source: Contracts with Bureau of Reclamation, U.S. Department of the Interior, on file in Washington, D.C.

Table 6-1 (*continued*)

Project–Contractor	Assignment limited	Beneficial use	U.S. retains title to facilities	Service restrictions — Lands	Service restrictions — Type of use	Limitations on increased income	Ownership of return flows	Subcontracting/transfer provisions
Central Valley–Tehama Water District	X	X			Ag.; M&I		U.S. beyond district	Subcontracts/exchanges/transfers allowed with other parties having U.S. contracts for project water (with approval of C.O.)
Colorado–Big Thompson–Northern Colorado Water Conservancy District	X (no mention of approval)		X		"Primarily" Ag. and Dom.; also M&I	Excess revenues to fund and to U.S. for district's repayment obligation	U.S. for district use	Water not needed for use in district may be provided for ag. and dom. uses outside district with secretarial approval
Colorado River Storage–Utah International, Inc.	X	X			Ind. (coal)	"No brokerage" provision implies no profit to contractor		U.S. reserves right to market water reserved and on standby for contractor to third parties making bona fide offers

					Use		
Colorado River Storage–Public Service Company of New Mexico	X	X	X		Ind. (coal, thermal electric energy)	"No brokerage" provision implies no profit to contractor	None
Columbia Basin–East Columbia Basin Irrigation District	X		X	X	Ag., incidental dom., M&I, misc.	U.S. for project use, if needed, otherwise for district use on district lands	District may enter into additional or new water service contracts (subcontracts) upon forms approved by the secretary
Emery–Emery County Water Conservancy District	X	X	X	X	Ag., ind.		None
Fort Peck–Montana Department of Natural Resources and Conservation	X	X	X		Ind., but others can be allowed		Subcontracts with industrial water users allowed with C.O. approval
Fryingpan–Arkansas–Southeast Colorado Water Conservancy District	X	X	X	X	Mun., ag.	District for use and benefit of district	Water cannot be resold by district users (unless user is a municipality, but municipalities cannot resell return flows)

Table 6-1 (*continued*)

Project–Contractor	Assignment limited	Beneficial use	U.S. retains title to facilities	Service restrictions		Limitations on increased income	Ownership of return flows	Subcontracting/transfer provisions
				Lands	Type of use			
Grand Valley–Grand Valley Water Users' Association	X		X	X	Ag.	Excess revenues from temporary deliveries to unproductive lands disposed "as required by law"	U.S. for project use	None
Kendrick–Casper-Alcova Irrigation District	X	X	X	X	Ag.	Revenues to U.S. until capital costs have been repaid	U.S. for project use	None
Kern River–North Kern, Buena Vista, and Tulare water storage districts, and Hacienda Water District	X		X		Ag.	Subcontracting charges are limited to no more than district's obligation to U.S.		Allows subcontracting without consent of other districts or U.S.
Kings River–Alta Irrigation District	X		X		Ag.			None

District		District title at pay-out	Authorized purposes			
Lower Rio Grande–Hidalgo and Cameron counties Water Control & Improvement District No. 9	X					None
Lower Yellowstone–Lower Yellowstone Irrigation District No. 1	X			Profits from sale or lease of surplus water under Warren Act contracts may not be distributed until repayment and secretary decides "equitable proportion"		None
Milk River–Malta Irrigation District	X	X			U.S.	None
Minidoka–Palisades–Island Irrigation Company	X	X	X	Water rental rates may not exceed annual costs under obligation to U.S.		Allows rental of water to others at rates and terms approved by secretary

(continued)

Table 6-1 (*continued*)

Project-Contractor	Assignment limited	Beneficial use	U.S. retains title to facilities	Service restrictions		Limitations on increased income	Ownership of return flows	Subcontracting/ transfer provisions
				Lands	Type of use			
Mountain Park Reclamation– Mountain Park Master Conservancy District	X				M&I, F&W, rec.	Revenues to U.S. until repayment complete; revenues from nonintegrated district-financed activities to district	U.S. and district	Contracts by district (subcontracts) for sale or use of project water are subject to approval of C.O.
Newlands– Truckee-Carson Irrigation District	X		X	X	Ag. for nondistrict lands; not explicit			Contracts by district (subcontracts) for O&M and water delivery are subject to secretarial approval
Pick-Sloan Missouri Basin–Belle Fourche Irrigation District	X	X	X	X	Ag.; others with approval	Revenues to U.S. with exception of district's O&M expenses	U.S. for project use	None

165

Project					
Pick-Sloan Missouri Basin–Farwell Irrigation District	X	X			None
Rio Grande–El Paso County Water Improvement District No. 1	X		Ag.		None
Rio Grande and San Juan–Chama–City of Albuquerque	X			Revenues of city may not exceed storage charge going to U.S.	None
Seedskadee–State of Wyoming	X		M&I	50% of excess revenues over subcontractor costs go to U.S. for repayment obligation	State allowed to contract with others (subcontract) to provide M&I water, use of storage capacity
Truckee Storage–Washoe County Water Conservation District	X	X			None

(continued)

Table 6-1 (*continued*)

| Project–Contractor | Assignment limited | Beneficial use | U.S. retains title to facilities | Service restrictions | | Limitations on increased income | Ownership of return flows | Subcontracting/transfer provisions |
				Lands	Type of use			
Weber Basin–Weber Basin Water Conservancy District	X	X	X		Ag., mun., misc.	Excess revenues may be used by district without U.S. claim	U.S. for project use	Contracts by district (sub-contracts) for water delivery/distribution are subject to secretarial approval
Yakima–Kennewick Irrigation District	X	X	X	X	Ag.		U.S. for project use	Contracts by district (sub-contracts) for water delivery to new lands are subject to secretarial approval
Yuma–Yuma County Water Users' Association	X	X	X	X	Ag., park watering	Project profits to project costs, association fund	U.S. and association	Contracts for water must be validated by secretarial approval

Restrictions on Lands Served. Sixteen of the thirty-four contracts examined restrict water use to particular lands, usually those of the district. This will clearly limit the potential transferability of water until such time as the bureau indicates its willingness to amend these provisions to make them consistent with those of Reclamation law (see section on legal provisions relating to project service area and end use of water, above). Such amendment is possible, as illustrated by a sequence of contracts with the Emery County Water Conservancy District on the Emery Project. Article 30 of the original 1962 contract specified that the district "shall not use any of the Project water . . . on any lands other than those irrigable lands which are situated within the project." However, as discussed in chapter 5, a 1972 amendatory contract with the district affirms the district's agreement to sell 6,000 acre-feet of water to the Utah Power and Light Company.

The following provisions vary considerably from one contract to another.

Restrictions on End Use of Water. Twenty-six of the thirty-four contracts contain some limitation on the end use of water (whether agricultural, domestic, industrial, or the like). Eleven of the contracts specify a single use of water; the remaining fifteen provide for more than one use (see table 6-1). Clearly, contracts specifying multiple uses of water can provide more flexibility for water transfers without the need for amending the contract. Flexibility of use is explicitly indicated in some contracts. For example, the Central Valley Project contract with the Glenn-Colusa Irrigation District, the Fort Peck contract with the Montana Department of Natural Resources and Conservation, and the Pick-Sloan Missouri River Basin contract with the Belle Fourche Irrigation District all indicate that additional uses of the water may be permitted with approval. Even in cases where the current contract does not specify flexibility of end use, approval could be granted by the bureau through contract amendment (such as in the Emery County Water Conservancy District example), provided the new use is consistent with other provisions of Reclamation law.

Limitations on Increased Income from Water Transfers. Fifteen of the thirty-four contracts place explicit conditions on the increased income from water resales by a contractor. These provisions are far from standardized, but in six cases they specify that any additional revenues secured by the contractor must be paid to the United States to further reduce the district's repayment obligation (refer to table 6-1). After the repayment obligation is satisfied, additional revenues presumably could go to the district to cover expenses or to reduce charges to customers. The Lower Yellowstone contract (not in this group of six) indicates that the district can share in profits from sale or lease of surplus water once repayment is complete.

Between-district water transfers would be natural in those projects that serve a number of water districts from a common water supply or through interconnected facilities, such as the Central Valley Project in California or the Central Arizona Project. However, contractual provisions in the Central Arizona Project rule out increased income for the subcontractor from such transactions, and, as discussed below, administrative policy has played a similar role in the Central Valley Project. Provisions requiring that extra revenues be paid to the United States reflect the bureau's desire to secure prompt repayment for a project, but the provisions are probably self-defeating since they almost completely remove the incentive for transfers to take place. Transfer of water to a new user with greater economic demand for water could, in fact, provide a more sound basis for repayment.

Some contracts restrict transfers by prohibiting resale at a price higher than the contract rate, regardless of whether the surplus revenues are turned over to the United States. The two contracts from the Colorado River Storage Project contain a "no brokerage" provision preventing profit to a contractor. The Kern River contract limits subcontracting charges to the amount the district must pay the United States. A similar provision is contained in the contract with the city of Albuquerque (Rio Grande and San Juan–Chama projects). The Minidoka-Palisades contracts (with districts that participate in the Idaho Water Supply Bank) provide for annual rentals of water, but the rates charged may not exceed annual costs under contract obligations to the United States. As noted in chapter 5, these provisions have been interpreted to allow a modest markup in price. More specifically, the "annual costs" provision is interpreted to include not only the annual capital costs that the contractor must pay to the Bureau of Reclamation, but also the operation and maintenance costs charged by individual districts for water deliveries.

To facilitate water transfers, the bureau could adopt a policy that would allow the increased income from transfers to be used by water districts, so long as the currently established financial obligations of Reclamation law are met. Furthermore, the bureau could indicate its willingness to amend its contracts to allow such use of the revenues from transfers. It is interesting in this regard that three of the contracts surveyed recognize some sharing of revenues between the United States and the district. Under the Seedskadee project contract with the state of Wyoming, the state shares excess revenues with the United States on a 50-50 basis. The Lower Yellowstone contract specifies that once the district repayment is complete, the profits from sale or lease of surplus water under the Warren Act may be distributed according to an "equitable proportion" decided on by the secretary. (This provision is, of course, a weaker and more uncertain procedure for sharing income from resales than that in the Seedskadee project.) Also notable is the Weber Basin contract, which allows excess revenues to be used by the district without claim by the United States.

Those contracts that prohibit extra income to the district for selling water do not prohibit profitable resales within the district. For example, as discussed in chapter 5, there is a thriving market for water within the Northern Colorado Water Conservancy District in the Colorado–Big Thompson Project, where the resource is sold at market values far above the cost paid to the Bureau of Reclamation.

To facilitate transfers between water users, the Bureau of Reclamation could develop standardized contract language that would permit a water district to receive any additional income from the resale or lease of the water it currently has under contract, provided that the United States recovers its project costs. This would also mean a revenue increase to the United States for water shifting to municipal and industrial use (see the section "Increased Revenues to the Federal Government," below). State legislation authorizing the establishment of water districts customarily prohibits districts from making profits. However, the proceeds from a water sale or lease could be used to fund conservation measures and to pay other district expenses, or could be passed on to district members through a reduction in their water rates.

Subcontracting and Transfer Provisions.   Nineteen of the bureau contracts reviewed contain provisions relating specifically to subcontracting or to water transfers. They vary as to the types of subcontracting allowed, the approval required for a transfer, and the location where subcontracted water may be used.

Two of the contracts reviewed explicitly prohibit resales: in the Fryingpan-Arkansas Project and in the Central Valley Project contract with G. H. Russell. The latter indicates that water can be transferred only with a transfer of title to the land, a provision that probably prohibits a purchaser of the land from transporting the associated water elsewhere. The Utah International contract in the Colorado River Storage Project comes under a different category: it allows the water held on standby for the contractor to be resold by the United States.

Subcontracts require bureau or departmental permission in thirteen of the nineteen cases with subcontracting or transfer provisions. In the Columbia Basin Project, the Secretary of the Interior merely provides the forms for the subcontract. In the Central Arizona Project, the United States is a party to a three-way contract involving the contractor and subcontractor. The Kern River Project contract specifies that subcontracting may take place without the consent of the United States. Certainly, the fewer the restrictions on subcontracting, the easier it is for districts to lease or resell water.

As to the locations to which subcontracted water can be transferred, six of the contracts specifically mention the right of the district to subcontract for water outside the district. Three other contracts were established under conditions allowing transfer of water to a wide geographic area: water rental in the Minidoka-Palisades Project and subcontracting from the Fort Peck and Seedskadee projects by the states of Montana and Wyoming, respectively. The master contract in the Central Arizona Project limits subcontracting to the district boundaries, whereas seven other contracts provide no guidance as to where subcontracting or water transfers will be allowed. Even where transfers are limited by contract to the district service area, these areas are in some cases quite extensive. The Northern Colorado Water Conservancy District encompasses several irrigation companies and municipalities on Colorado's east slope. The Central Arizona Water Conservancy District subcontracts with more than seventy municipal and industrial contractors, twenty irrigation districts, and twelve Indian tribes in central Arizona. In this case, there appears to be more flexibility in Reclamation law than in the contracts. Although the Central Arizona Project contract limits subcontracting to the district boundaries, the Colorado River Basin Project Act of 1968, authorizing the project, only restricts water use to "the water deficit areas of Arizona and western New Mexico through direct diversion or exchange of water" (for further discussion of water transfer possibilities involving the Central Arizona Project, see chapter 8).

Even within the same project, subcontracting and transfer provisions vary widely. Three of the five contracts examined in the Central Valley Project specifically allow transfers to other districts in the same project but prohibit out-of-project exchanges. The fourth appears to allow sale outside the district, and the fifth—the G. H. Russell contract—restricts water transfers to transfers of title of the associated lands.

There are two additional contractual provisions that are, in some ways, less directly related to water transfers: those referring to transfer of title of facilities and those covering district control over return flows. These provisions may not be applicable to the existing situation in all projects, but, where they are, the recommendations discussed below would further facilitate water transfers.

Title to Project Works to Remain with the United States. It is the stated policy of the Bureau of Reclamation that water districts should assume responsibility for maintaining project works when they are able to do so. This is often accomplished through "transfer-ring" to the district maintenance responsibility for such project facilities as conveyance canals, diversion works, and storage facilities. However, the transfer is not a transfer of title, as indicated by the presence of the following provision in twenty-two of the thirty-four contracts reviewed (refer to table 6-1):

> Title to the transferred works shall remain in the United States until otherwise provided by Congress, notwithstanding transfer of the care, operation and maintenance of said works to the District.

This provision requiring congressional approval stems from general Reclamation law, and therefore its presence or absence in contracts does not limit the transferability of water. Interestingly, one of the contracts reviewed, on the Lower Rio Grande Project, indicates that the title to project works transfers to the district upon completion of payout.

An indication by the bureau that it is willing to seek congressional approval for transfer of title of facilities to water districts upon completion of repayment requirements could enhance the district's ability to arrange for water transfers (Wahl and Simon, 1988). For example, districts with title to their facilities would find it less cumbersome to seek outside financial support for maintaining or upgrading those facilities and would be free to abandon portions of facilities that would no longer be needed after a water transfer took place.

Return Flows. Most water uses result in less than total consumption of the water diverted. The fact that return flows form the basis for subsequent reuse is a complication of water rights that derives from the nature of the resource. Because rights to return flows would in most cases have been established by other water users, the seller would not be allowed to implement a proposed water exchange if it injured those rights. This leaves open the possibility that the seller could modify the proposed exchange or could compensate the potentially affected water users such that they would voluntarily agree not to object to the transfer. One rule of thumb that provides some protection of other established water rights is to permit the seller to transfer only the amount of his consumptive use, while maintaining the same return flows. For example, a user diverting 4 acre-feet per acre and returning 1 acre-foot to the stream and 1 acre-foot to groundwater sources might be allowed to sell 2 acre-feet per acre. This protects water users downstream from the diversion point but, in those cases where the diversion point is transferred upstream, may not protect water users between the initial and final points of diversion. These complications are avoided when the seller owns the rights to the return flows. For example, the fact that return flows in the Colorado–Big Thompson Project are retained by the United States for use by the Northern Colorado Water Conservancy District has facilitated the development of an in-project market there.

Fourteen of the thirty-four contracts examined contain provisions designating the ownership of return flows. In the Central Arizona Project, subcontractors are allowed to resell return flows (provided any excess revenues are returned to the United States). In the Fryingpan-Arkansas Project, the district is given the rights to return flows. However, the most common contract language (six cases in table 6-1) reserves the right to return flows to the United States for project use, and the district does not have specific control over their disposition.

In other contracts, the status of return flows is not so clearly delineated. For example, in the contracts on the Yuma Project and the Mountain Park Reclamation Project, the return flows are retained by the United States and by the district. In the contract on the Columbia Basin Project, the return flows are retained by the United States for project use if needed; otherwise they are for district use within the district.

Established uses of return flows naturally vary from one location to another. Therefore, it would not be possible for the bureau to adopt any standard contract provision related to return flows. However, in order to facilitate water transfers, the bureau could adopt a policy of giving the district the rights to return flows owned by the bureau where such flows have not already been dedicated to other water uses. Such situations are likely to be infrequent on established bureau projects. In summary, district control over return flows is not essential to market transfer of water, but, in those cases where return flows are retained by the United States and are not dedicated to use elsewhere, district control would facilitate water transfers.

Summary of Recommended Changes Regarding Contracts. To facilitate water transactions, the Bureau of Reclamation could develop standardized subcontracting provisions to be inserted into contracts upon a district's request. To facilitate transfers, these provisions should place the fewest geographic and administrative restrictions on the transfer process, consistent with existing legislation. For example, a minimum set of restrictions might be the following: transfers or subcontracting outside district boundaries would be specifically allowed if consistent with Reclamation law and state law, but (1) bureau approval would be required in those cases where water changed type of use (for example, irrigation to municipal use), since this would likely require a change in the amount of repayment, and (2) irrigation subcontractors would be required to file certification forms to ensure compliance with the Reclamation Reform Act. After both the district selling the water and the district purchasing the water had complied with Reclamation law, the bureau might remove itself from further involvement in the transfer process.

Water Rights

Ownership of the rights to water that a district receives from the bureau would enhance the district's ability to transfer water. Indeed, before initiating a water storage project, the Bureau of Reclamation had to ensure that the associated water rights were secure. In some instances it encouraged irrigation districts to file for the flow rights and the storage rights necessary for a project. In many cases, however, it filed for and obtained the rights itself. Discussions with bureau personnel indicate that there was no particular rationale or pattern to the decisions as to which party was to file, except in those cases like the Central Valley Project in California, where water from several sources was combined and subsequently distributed to several contractors. Then, the bureau appeared to be the logical locus of the water rights.

Table 6-2 presents a summary of the water storage rights on federal projects, aggregated by state.[8] This table was prepared from bureau records of the water rights of each project in the seventeen western states where the bureau operates. The rights tabulated are for all uses of bureau water, including irrigation, municipal and industrial, fish and wildlife, and recreation. The table reveals that, westwide, the bureau holds about 84 percent of the storage rights on its projects. In twelve states, it has title to more than 50 percent, and in eight states it has title to over 90 percent. It holds less than 50 percent of the storage rights on its projects in Oregon, Oklahoma, Colorado, Texas, and Kansas.

Unlike title to project works, which, as noted above, does not transfer to districts upon completion of their repayment obligation until such time as Congress so provides, it appears that title to project

---

[8] There are often flow rights associated with the water rights on Bureau of Reclamation facilities. These are not reflected in table 6-2.

Table 6-2. Water Storage Rights Held by the United States and by Nonfederal Interests on Bureau of Reclamation Projects

(thousands of acre-feet)

State	U.S.	Non-U.S.	Total	Percent U.S.
Montana	33,385	0	33,385	100.0
North Dakota	683	0	683	100.0
South Dakota	1,087	0	1,087	100.0
Washington	16,569	24	16,593	99.9
Idaho	8,975	16	8,990	99.8
Utah	6,551	215	6,765	96.8
California	47,313	2,944	50,257	94.1
Wyoming	7,256	691	7,947	91.3
Nevada	836	300	1,136	73.6
New Mexico	3,508	1,910	5,419	64.7
Arizona	6,456	3,531	9,987	64.6
Nebraska	2,041	1,480	3,521	58.0
Oregon	4,337	4,811	9,147	47.4
Oklahoma	91	272	362	25.0
Colorado	2,209	6,663	8,872	24.9
Texas	1,018	3,627	4,645	21.9
Kansas	11	795	806	1.4
Total	142,326	27,279	169,602	83.9

Note: There are also flow rights associated with some of the water rights on Bureau of Reclamation facilities. These are not reflected in the table.

Source: Compiled from records of Contracts and Repayments Branch, Bureau of Reclamation, U.S. Department of the Interior, Washington, D.C.

water does transfer to water users when they fulfill their repayment obligation. However, the exact status of water rights after repayment is somewhat unclear. The Reclamation Act of 1902 originally intended that the secretary would establish water rights charges for entry upon land supplied with water by a reclamation project. Section 5 of the act provides that "no right to the use of water for land in private ownership . . . shall permanently attach until all payments therefor are made." Water rights certificates or other contractual forms were established between the Bureau of Reclamation and individual settlers. When a settler had established residency and proof of cultivation of his land and when he had completed repayment of the water rights charges, he was entitled to a "final water rights certificate" or "patent" (Act of August 9, 1912; 37 Stat. 265; 43 U.S.C. 541).

Over time, as problems with repayment arose, the Bureau of Reclamation found that it had little recourse in trying to obtain repayment from individuals that defaulted. Thus, the reclamation program shifted to contracting with irrigation districts instead of individuals. These districts, as entities of the state, had the power to tax and assess liens against their members for recovery of water charges. This trend is first noted in the Reclamation Extension Act of 1914 (38 Stat. 686; 43 U.S.C. 471) and the act of May 15, 1922 (42 Stat. 541; 43 U.S.C. 511), both of which allowed, but did not require, the bureau to contract with irrigation districts rather than individual settlers. The Omnibus Adjustment Act of 1926 (which established a number of measures to remedy repayment problems on reclamation projects) carried the trend one step further by mandating that contracts be made only with water user organizations, both for new contracts and for amendments of existing contracts (44 Stat. 648; 43 U.S.C. 423d).

With the bureau's transition from relationships with individual settlers to relationships with irrigation organizations, it is not entirely clear whether the individual or the district receives title to the associated water rights when project repayment is complete. For example, the 1922 act indicates that when contracts with irrigation districts are used, the water rights applications of individuals may be dispensed with, although it is made clear that the water rights certificates themselves are not dispensed with. The act of July 2, 1956 (70 Stat. 483; 43 U.S.C. 485 h-1) provides that once construction charges have been repaid, an irrigation contractor has a permanent right to his share or quantity of the federal project's water for beneficial use on the irrigable lands within the boundaries of the contractor's district. Therefore, upon completion of project repayment, it appears that water rights held by the Bureau of Reclamation for irrigation use would still transfer either to individual settlers or to their district as trustee for its members.

As noted in chapter 5, in order for voluntary market transactions of federal water to take place, it is not essential that the actual water rights be held by the district because a market can develop in contracted deliveries. In fact, some bureau officials believe that it is immaterial who owns the rights "because the Bureau puts the water at the disposal of water users." However, one expects that water transfers would be facilitated if the rights of water users were more secure. In effect, where water rights are held by the bureau, contractors are currently in the position of "leasing" the water and are consequently restricted to "subleasing in order to implement a transfer." Leasing tenure of any property, such as housing or an automobile, restricts the lessee's freedom to reassign use of the property. Clearly, the bureau is in a stronger position to impose restrictions on the water for which it holds the rights than on that water for which the rights are held by water users. Therefore, water users would benefit from clarification of the bureau's policy regarding the transfer of water rights to a district, especially the policy that is to apply after a district completes repayment of its contractual obligation.

Current Administrative Policies and Recommended Changes

It is probably safe to say that much of the confusion over what type of water transfers are allowed by the Bureau of Reclamation (if any), or over which transfers can be implemented within existing Reclamation law, stems from past bureau administrative pronouncements and practices, which varied considerably from region to region and project to project.[9] Of particular interest to water users is not only whether the bureau will approve a transfer of water, but whether users will be allowed to receive increased income from the lease or sale of federally supplied water. Without this financial incentive, the number of transfers is likely to be relatively low. But, as discussed in chapter 5, there has been considerable variation in the allowable financial incentive. As a matter of administrative policy, rather than contract or law, water in the federal Central Valley Project in California can normally be transferred from one district to another only at the project's established contract rates; no profit is allowed. In the Idaho Water Supply Bank operations on the Upper Snake River, the bureau's policy permits some markup, although there is a bank-administered ceiling on the selling price of the water. At the other extreme, in the Colorado–Big Thompson Project, federally supplied water is routinely sold at market rates among agricultural water users at a profit or loss, depending on prevailing market prices.

It is important that the Bureau of Reclamation standardize its transfer policies. This is particularly important in order to lower the transactions cost of potential transfers. Although a number of transfers have already occurred, some—such as those involving the Utah Power and Light Company; the city of Casper, Wyoming; and the Metropolitan Water District of California discussed in chapter 5—have had to overcome high start-up or transactions costs. In each case, the substantial value of water to the purchaser made it worth the time and effort to investigate the procedural requirements for a transfer (requirements that are far from standardized) and to undertake what were often protracted negotiations. Also, because of the costliness of the negotiation process, such individually negotiated transactions usually involved fairly large blocks of water.

[9] On December 16, 1988, the Department of the Interior issued a set of principles designed to guide Bureau of Reclamation review and approval of water transfers proposed by water users. It is reproduced as an appendix at the end of this book.

While transfers that involve a rather substantial increase in the value of water can absorb high start-up costs, smaller transfers often cannot. For example, many transfers within the agricultural sector would involve increases in income of only $5–$10 per acre-foot, with relatively small quantities of water involved. Consequently, many potential transfers that would lead to increased productivity are probably thwarted simply because the procedures for making the transfers and the bureau's willingness to approve them are not clear. For this reason, and also because increasing competition for water is likely to lead to an increasing number of transfer requests, the Bureau of Reclamation needs to establish uniform and clearly defined administrative policies with regard to water transfers.

Administrative Clarification of Policy. The bureau needs to state to the public and to its personnel that it will facilitate voluntary water exchanges in those states where law and administrative practice support such exchanges, provided that the transfer complies with both state and federal law, including laws that protect third-party water interests (those that are not direct parties to the transfer). In most cases, state law would be the vehicle for ensuring that third-party water interests are protected, including the protection of instream flows.[10] In addition, water laws in several western states allow fairly broad judgment on the part of state authorities in disapproving water appropriations and transfers that are not "in the public interest." At the federal level, transfers would have to comply with the National Environmental Policy Act (NEPA). Minor transfers might receive a "categorical exclusion" or a "finding of no significant impact," whereas those with greater environmental effects would require environmental assessments or full-blown environmental impact statements. The NEPA process would provide such federal agencies as the Fish and Wildlife Service an opportunity to comment on and influence the decision regarding approval of the transfer. This would provide additional protection of recreational and wildlife values associated with instream flows. In approving the water transfer, the bureau would want to ensure that the transfer did not increase the operational expenses of other water users or harm their water rights, especially in those cases where the transfer did not require state approval (for example, a transfer that did not require state permission for a change in the place or time of use).

Transfers would also have to comply with federal legislation regarding repayment. The principal relevant provision is that water

[10] For a summary of different state approaches to the protection of instream flows, see Lamb (1986) and Lamb and Meshorer (1983).

shifting from irrigation to municipal and industrial or hydropower use would require increased payment to the United States, since neither the interest-free provision nor the "ability-to-pay" provision attached to irrigation would continue to apply. Additional revenues could be deposited in the Reclamation Fund. The effect would be to reallocate the cost of the project on a "use-of-facilities" basis. If 1,000 acre-feet of water were transferred from agricultural use to municipal and industrial use, then the corresponding percentage of repayment would shift from agricultural to municipal and industrial use for the duration of the transfer. This method would avoid the process of redoing the project cost allocations on the basis of separable costs and remaining benefits—the process now used by the bureau when planning new projects. The cost allocations and repayment obligations on most projects were established long ago and redoing them would be administratively cumbersome, especially given that many transfers might be temporary in nature. It would probably also be a reasonable policy that a transfer not decrease federal revenues—in other words, that any transfers of water to fish and wildlife uses (which are traditionally nonreimbursable) not decrease repayment. Reducing repayment would mean that the amount of repayment originally scheduled would no longer be met, and this might require congressional reauthorization of the project.

There should probably be one additional precondition for allowing water districts to resell federally contracted water: assumption by the district of complete financial responsibility for future operation and maintenance on the project, including rehabilitation and replacement work. It is the bureau's policy that project operation and maintenance become district responsibilities, but actual practice has fallen short of this, and, even after responsibility has been transferred, districts have successfully appealed to the Bureau of Reclamation for financial assistance for major rehabilitation work. Such practice leaves the federal government at some risk because federal financing of rehabilitation measures is normally accomplished through interest-free loans. It might prove politically unacceptable to allow a district that has made a substantial income gain on a water transfer to receive subsequent federal subsidies for rehabilitation work.

The Bureau of Reclamation should make any surplus capacity in its conveyance facilities available to facilitate possible water transfers, whether or not the transfer itself involves federal water. This is important simply because the extensive "plumbing" managed by the bureau in many western states could greatly increase the number of locations water could be transferred to—for example, the Central Valley and Central Arizona projects (for further discussion of the potential for water transfers that would utilize the conveyance facilities of the Central Valley and Central Arizona projects, see chapters 5 and 8, respectively). Of course, determination of "surplus" capacity would have to recognize prior commitments to the bureau's existing contractors. In allowing surplus capacity to be used, the bureau would need to determine appropriate "use" charges to recover additional operation and maintenance costs and administrative costs, and might also assess an allocable share of the capital cost of the conveyance facilities, especially on long-term transfers.

Willingness to Modify Contracts.   The bureau should also indicate its willingness to modify certain types of contractual provisions that inhibit the transferability of water. Provisions that prohibit the resale of water, impose service area restrictions or restrictions on the end use of water that are not embodied in legislation, or prohibit income gains on water transfers are examples (all discussed in more detail earlier in this chapter). In a limited number of cases, the bureau may also be able to amend contracts to give a district the use of its return flows.

Transfer of Water Rights.   The bureau holds a substantial portion of the water rights on its projects. Market transfers of contracted deliveries can take place regardless of who owns the rights. However, the decision as to whether the bureau or the district holds the rights appears to have been arbitrary in many cases, and the bureau could further facilitate voluntary market transfers of water by clarifying the procedures that govern the transfer of water rights to contractors after repayment for a project is completed.

Willingness to Seek Changes in Legislation.   There appears to be considerable latitude for voluntary water transfers within existing federal law. However, in some circumstances it may be desirable for the bureau to support changes in legislation that currently inhibits what otherwise would be a desirable water exchange for the parties involved. Probably the most common restrictions that changes in legislation could relax pertain to extension of the project service area and permission for end uses of water that may not have been included in the original project authorization. It has been shown, however, that there is some flexibility in existing Reclamation law for such transfers (for example, the Casper-Alcova Irrigation District/city of Casper, Wyoming, transfer). Nevertheless, it would be useful for the Secretary of the Interior to have authority in such circumstances to approve transfers that were agreed upon by the various parties involved, including those where farmers were willing to retire marginal land from production.

The forgoing discussion indicates some other changes in general Reclamation law that the Bureau of Reclamation could support to facilitate transfers. For one, it could permit title to project works to transfer to a district upon completion of the district's repayment obligation. Completion of repayment could be certified by the bureau, without the need for securing congressional approval, contract by contract. Such a legislative provision could also permit the bureau to receive prepayment of capital costs if a district wished to secure title to project facilities in advance of its scheduled payout date. There could also be some benefit to clarifying the status of the beneficial use and appurtenancy requirements of the Reclamation Act. Most western states have abandoned strict appurtenancy requirements, and many have updated their definitions of beneficial use in order to facilitate transfers. It would be appropriate to make parallel modifications in federal law. For example, the appurtenancy provision could be repealed, and the beneficial use provision could be made more consonant with state definitions of beneficial use. Alternatively, beneficial use could be defined in federal law to indicate that transfers of water to other beneficial uses would not jeopardize the existing contracts and rights of the seller, provided that such transfers did not injure the water rights of other water rights holders and other federal contractors.

Consequences of a Policy to Facilitate Transfers

Several water transfers involving federally supplied water have already occurred, and others are under consideration. In various areas of the West, the Bureau of Reclamation is receiving a growing number of requests to facilitate transfers. Clarifying a policy with regard to transfers of federally supplied water would probably lead to more transfers actually being implemented.

Efficiency of Water Use

The principal goal of a policy to facilitate water transfers is to promote efficient water use. Over time, the water demands in any locale change in ways that could not possibly have been foreseen by the original planners of a water resource project. For example, water demands may shift because of changes in demand for certain crops, the citing of new energy facilities, or unforeseen population growth. Therefore, the original allocations of water probably do not result in water being used where it is most needed years later. Voluntary market transfers of water allow the water to be used where present demands are greatest. Adopting a policy to facilitate water transfers would also allow greater flexibility in meeting future needs.

Increased Income to the Trading Parties

A voluntary water transfer can provide increased income to both the buying and selling parties. A prospective purchaser of water would not enter into the transaction unless he could obtain water at a cost cheaper than from other potential sources, such as construction of new facilities, pumping of groundwater, or purchase from another water user. A prospective seller would not enter into the transaction unless he could obtain an income from the sale that at least compensated him for the loss in income from his current water use.

Increased Revenues to the Federal Government

It may appear to many readers that the policy recommendations proposed in this chapter are undesirable because they allow private parties to make "windfalls" on publicly subsidized water. The general taxpayer, so the argument goes, ought to participate in the income gains he or she helped create. There is merit to this argument, and, according to existing law, the taxpayer will, in fact, participate in such income gains as follows. The greatest increase in value will likely result from transfers of water from irrigation to municipal and industrial use. Because municipal and industrial use bears interest charges under Reclamation law, payments for municipal and industrial water would generally be considerably greater than the repayments for irrigation. The change in repayment terms would depend on the interest rate and the repayment terms applicable to a particular project, but the following examples are illustrative. Payments for municipal and industrial water bearing a 3.5 percent rate of interest would be 1.87 times greater than payments for irrigation, assuming a forty-year repayment period. For a 4.0 percent rate of interest, they would be 2 times greater, and for an 8.0 percent rate of interest, they would be 3.35 times greater. These ratios would increase in cases where the irrigators' "ability to pay" had limited irrigation repayment; that is, the subsidy from power users would be removed. The increase in federal revenues from removing the power subsidy could be significant in some cases. This is because the normal practice is for power revenues to be paid to the irrigation account at the end of the irrigation repayment period—forty or fifty years after repayment was initiated. In contrast, the revenues and interest charges for water transferred from irrigation to municipal and industrial use (or to hydropower use) would be payable over a period beginning immediately after the transfer took effect.

It is worthwhile to digress at this point to discuss in more detail the concern over "windfalls." Opposing views have been presented: for example, Joseph Sax (1965), in his article entitled "Selling Reclamation Water Rights, a Case Study in Federal Subsidy Policy," expressed his disapproval of private gain being made from reclamation project water deliveries. Sax's concern was with the resale of irrigation project lands (and the water deliveries associated with such lands) rather than with resale of water to other uses. Much of his discussion was based on his recommended extension of the practice of using "recordable contracts." Under Reclamation law, a farmer using federal water must sign a recordable contract agreeing to sell any of his lands that exceed the acreage limitation within a specified number of years and at a price that does not reflect the additional value of the project water supply (see chapter 4). Sax reasoned that the same concept should be extended to nonexcess lands as well. His view was that the increases in the value of nonexcess project lands should accrue either to the federal taxpayer or to the irrigation district collectively, but not to individual landholders. The Department of the Interior has refrained from imposing controls on such increases in value on nonexcess lands. Sax stated the department's reasoning as follows:

> First, and most important, Congress does not want (or has prohibited) control of sale of water rights [that is, project lands receiving water]; second, such restrictions are somehow inconsistent with the underlying purposes of Reclamation policy and the private property system in which it operates; and third, even if such controls were permissible and desirable, they are administratively impracticable. (p. 15)

Sax, however, wrote that a different interpretation of Reclamation law was possible and that systems for capturing incremental land values could be administered by using comparable water sales data and other data available in the project area. He did note, however, that "previous attempts to regulate incremental value sales have had little success in finding an easy means for determining that portion of a sale price which is to be designated as a windfall" (p. 40) and that "there are individual differences and market imperfections which make any such process of evaluation speculative and approximate" (p. 43). The review of the administration of acreage limitation in chapter 4 of this book supports the view that regulatory attempts to limit the amount of subsidy through acreage limitation and "full cost" pricing, even as applied to excess lands, have met with little administrative success.

Raymond L. Anderson (1967), in his article entitled "Windfall Gains from Transfer of Water Allotments Within the Colorado–Big Thompson Project," took a view opposite from Sax's:

> The type of concern expressed by Professor Sax which advocates recapture of windfall gains created by public investment is encountered

frequently but it occurs especially frequently in the field of water resource development. Granted, without knowledge of the social rationale involved taxpayers dislike seeing the benefits of tax-developed resources flow to private individuals but it is a widespread phenomenon in our society, ranging all the way from airline subsidies, increased value of land located at interstate highway interchanges, and property benefiting from flood control projects, to grazing rights and other uses of federal lands and even federally-supported research and education at universities throughout the land. Often, however, there is no good way to recapture the benefits stemming from tax-supported resource development without substantial governmental intervention and consequent distortion in the use of the resources and serious inhibitions in the movement of the resources to more economic uses. (p. 265)

In short, Anderson believed that any attempt to recapture some portion of the increased income from water trades would unduly burden the market. Indeed, without some potential for increased income, there simply would be few, if any, transfers.

There are several other factors that militate against the concern for excessive windfalls. For one, as indicated by the subsidy estimates and the estimated increases in land values in chapter 2, current legislation and current water uses already confer substantial "windfalls" on water users (from 1.5 to 51 times their current repayment rates; see table 2-6). If a farmer pays $4 per acre-foot for irrigation water but receives a net agricultural income equivalent to $20 per acre-foot (exclusive of water costs), he receives a $16-per-acre-foot windfall. The Bureau of Reclamation makes no attempt to recapture this income (at least, not below the acreage limits set by Reclamation law). Furthermore, if agricultural income rises from $20 to $40 per acre-foot over time, the additional $20-per-acre-foot increase in value accrues to the water purchaser. The Bureau of Reclamation does not concern itself with recovering this increased income (except in those cases where "ability-to-pay" calculations are used to revise contract water rates).

Additional income arising because water can be transferred to new uses is probably not directly attributable to the original federal subsidy, but rather to population growth or the citing of power plants or other water-using facilities. Privately developed water that can be sold from one use to another also results in an income gain to the owner under such circumstances, but there is no special vehicle for taxing this income gain other than the normal income tax channels. Once one accepts that the value of water in an irrigation use has already resulted in an income gain to the original owner, then there is less basis for distinguishing between federally developed and privately developed water in terms of additional income gains.

Even if the Bureau of Reclamation wanted to tax away some percentage of the additional income deriving from a transfer of federally supplied water, this might be a cumbersome and difficult task. Suppose that the bureau sought to recover 50 percent of the increase in value of water transferred. It would not be easy to determine the current value of water to the seller. One measure, the going market price, would be clearly inappropriate since it would result in a net income gain of zero. Another alternative would be for the bureau to perform a net income analysis of the seller's farm operation, such as is done to measure "ability to pay." This would have several drawbacks. First, it could entail considerable federal expense. Second, however carefully it was done, the results might not reflect the seller's valuation of water, which would depend on expectations of future agricultural prices and costs in a way that an economic study could not easily replicate. Third, the detailed examination of costs and revenues on a particular farm operation or group of operations might be viewed as an undue invasion of privacy. Finally, the analysis itself might involve some considerable delay in the sale and might simply discourage a useful transfer from being initiated.

Other approaches to levying a surcharge on water transfers might be easier to implement but would likely discourage a considerable number of water transfers. For example, a surcharge equal to 50 percent of the difference between the federal contract price and the resale price might at first seem an equitable measure, but it would not accomplish the goal of equally dividing the increased income. For example, suppose a farmer purchases water at a federal contract rate of $4 per acre-foot, derives a net income from water of $20 per acre-foot, and receives an offer of $30 per acre-foot to purchase the water. The transaction, assuming it has no negative impacts external to the trading parties, would be advantageous because it would lead to an economic gain to society of $10 per acre-foot. However, a surcharge of 50 percent of the difference between the original contract price and the sale price would impose a $13-per-acre-foot fee on the transaction. This surcharge would decrease the resale revenue to the seller from $30 per acre-foot to $17 per acre-foot, which is below his current net farm income. Therefore, an otherwise beneficial sale would not take place. The problem with relying on the difference between the original and final contract prices is that this difference fails to take into account that the current value to the seller can be much higher than the original contract price.

A simple flat fee per acre-foot transferred would be another way to avoid having to try to ascertain the value of water to current beneficiaries. The goal of promoting transfers to the most valuable use of water would argue for keeping the fixed fee low, especially since many water exchanges are likely to yield relatively small increases in value. Even a modest $1-per-acre-foot charge for irrigation transfers would, for example, be a 20 percent surcharge on an exchange where irrigation water increased in value from $20 to $25 per acre-foot. The level of any flat fee established would necessarily be arbitrary.

This discussion indicates that direct recovery of income gains in any market is difficult to achieve. This is especially true when increases in value for many transactions will be relatively small, as would probably be the case for transfers between one agricultural user and another. Any method that attempts to estimate the actual income gain is likely to be costly and burdensome to implement. Establishing a fixed fee or percentage would be less so, but could impede market transactions because it would not be based directly on sharing the amount of the efficiency gain. Furthermore, it is not clear that the Bureau of Reclamation would have any statutory basis for levying surcharges on water transfers.

Within any dynamic economy, financial gains and losses are constantly arising from various types of activities. For example, the location of a new highway or urban rail system, or the relocation of a new business, may raise or decrease property values and personal or business income. These financial gains and losses are subject to normal tax treatment through income and capital gains taxation. Income gains attributable to water transfers would also be subject to taxes, either at the level of the water user organization or when the gains are passed on as decreased costs to the individuals in the organization. Finally, those transactions that are likely to involve the greatest income gains—transfers of water from irrigation uses to municipal and industrial use—would be subject to one direct form of surcharge by the Bureau of Reclamation: the payment of interest charges and the removal of "ability-to-pay" limitations.

Effects on Irrigation and Other Water Uses and on Local Economies

Voluntary water exchanges would be beneficial to those irrigation and other water users who were buyers and sellers since they could increase their incomes. National income and income in the region of the transfer could also be expected to increase because water would shift to where it has the highest economic value. However, there are three concerns related to water transfers in general and to shifts of water out of irrigation use to other uses in particular. (1) How would other irrigation water users be protected? (2) How would other water uses, such as for recreation and fish and wildlife habitat, be protected? (3) How would other effects on local economies be taken into account?

One view with respect to the third concern is that the indirect economic effects of a water transfer should not be taken into account by either the trading parties or the state or federal agencies involved in approving the transfer. This view holds that economic transactions of many types are taking place in a changing economy (for instance, companies close or relocate some of their facilities in order to remain efficient and competitive) and that those other sectors of the economy which are affected must adapt to these necessary transitions. Whatever one's perspective on this issue, it is worth examining the types of effects that might be expected.

It is important to consider two types of water transfers or, alternatively, two aspects of a given water transfer. Assume irrigation is the initial water use. In the first type of water transfer, water is conserved and the surplus is sold to a new use, but no decrease in agricultural production occurs. One example of such an exchange is that between the city of Casper and the Casper-Alcova Irrigation District in Wyoming (see chapter 5 for additional detail). The municipality is paying for rehabilitation and betterment work on portions of the canal and lateral system to eliminate seepage. The reduction in seepage will increase the quantities of water available to the municipality while maintaining the same quantity of water delivered to farm crops. In the second type, the water transfer leads to a decrease in agricultural production. An example is the exchange between the irrigation water users in the Emery County Project and the Utah Power and Light Company, where more than 4,600 acres out of a total of 18,755 irrigable acres were designated "not for service" as a result of the water transfer (see chapter 5 for additional detail).

Of course, a single water exchange could exhibit aspects representative of both these cases: namely, some of the water exchanged could represent conserved water, whereas the additional water in the exchange could lead to some decrease in agricultural production. Clearly, in the first case, there is no negative effect on the agricultural sector. Furthermore, there is no negative effect on local industries that sell equipment and supplies to the agricultural sector (such as farm equipment, fertilizer, pesticide, and seed) or on local industries that depend on agricultural output (such as local canneries or trucking services). In fact, the transfer would have beneficial economic effects from a local as well as a national perspective. The conservation methods utilized—canal lining, system automation, better management—might well lead to increased local sales and employment. Furthermore, the conserved water would lead to increased economic activity in the locale of the water purchaser, both by the new purchaser and by activities linked to that purchaser.

In the second case, where some decrease in agricultural production accompanies the water exchange, it is necessary to discuss at greater length how the protection of irrigation water rights of third parties and the protection of other water uses, such as for fish and wildlife and recreation, would be taken into account. This task falls principally to state water law. Transfers of water that involve a change in use or point of diversion have to pass through state approval processes designed to ensure that such changes do not injure other established water uses. Part of this requirement consists of allowing a water user to sell or lease only his consumptive use of water while maintaining the same return flows (for additional discussion, see chapter 5). It is also necessary to take into account changes in the points of diversion before and after the proposed transfer: a transfer downstream would increase instream flow, but a transfer upstream would decrease instream flow between the initial and final points of diversion.

Some additional protection would occur at the federal level as a result of Bureau of Reclamation consultation with other federal agencies (such as the Fish and Wildlife Service) regarding their comments on the draft EIS or draft environmental assessment prepared in accord with the National Environmental Policy Act. Before approving a water transfer, the Secretary of the Interior would need to ensure that the voluntary water exchange did not injure other water users or water districts within a federal project. If one district in a project sold a portion of its water, this could potentially increase the burden of operation and maintenance costs on the remaining water users. Accordingly, the bureau would want to ensure that the district selling the water provided compensation to the remaining water users for any increases in operation and maintenance costs that resulted from the exchange. This payment could be made by the seller or by the purchaser of the water supplies.

If a state became concerned about the extent of water sales from the agricultural sector or about the impact on local economies from extensive water sales, it could find ways to limit such transfers. Most state water authorities are explicitly charged with protecting the public interest. Therefore, transfers considered by the state to be injurious to agricultural development could be disapproved. In some cases, state water engineers operate with the benefit of a state water plan to provide for the orderly development of water resources within the state.

Such a mandate could probably be construed broadly enough to disapprove transfers that state political leadership considered undesirable.

The effects on local agricultural production and other effects on local economies are primarily issues of state and local concern. However, if the Bureau of Reclamation chose to, it could, in cooperation with a state, propose to limit the extent of water transfers involving bureau projects. For example, a specific cumulative limit could be set on the amount of water eligible for transfer, say, 15 or 20 percent of the irrigation water in a project. The exact percentage would necessarily be somewhat arbitrary. However, these percentages are generally representative of the water conservation that could take place without significant decreases in agricultural production (see California Department of Water Resources, 1981; Stavins and Willey, 1983; U.S. Department of the Interior, Bureau of Reclamation and Bureau of Indian Affairs, 1978; U.S Department of the Interior, Bureau of Reclamation, 1983; and Wahl and Davis, 1986) and therefore could imply no decrease in agricultural production in some cases. Any cap on the amount of water eligible for transfer could, of course, limit the economic productivity gains that would be derived from unconstrained transfers.

Even if water exchanges were not explicitly limited by a percentage requirement, decreases in agricultural production within the region of a water transfer would probably be relatively small in most cases and would likely be limited to the least productive agricultural lands. One indication of the overall effect of transfers from the irrigation sector to the municipal and industrial sector is given by looking at the consumptive use figures typical of both. In the western states, irrigation uses typically account for more than 85 percent of consumptive water use, while municipal and industrial uses account for most of the remaining 15 percent. Therefore, if all municipal and industrial uses were to increase by one-third over a twenty-year period, entirely by water exchanges from the agricultural sector, then municipal and industrial use would rise from 15 to 20 percent of total consumptive use. This means that irrigation use would decrease by 5 percent of total water use, which is equivalent to 6 percent of irrigation use. This 6 percent decrease in irrigation water use would translate into less than a 6 percent decrease in agricultural production if water conservation measures were associated with the transfer (this percentage is within the percentage reductions achievable in many locations by conservation measures in agriculture).

Of course, this hypothetical 6 percent decrease represents an average. The percentage of water diverted from agricultural uses could be higher in some locales and lower in others. Table 6-3 presents a

Table 6-3. Consumptive Water Use in Western States by Water Resources Region, 1975

Region	Total consumption Millions of gals/day	Agriculture Millions of gals/day	Agriculture Percent of total	Municipal and industrial Millions of gals/day	Municipal and industrial Percent of total	Public land and other Millions of gals/day	Public land and other Percent of total	Percent decrease in agriculture resulting from 30% increase in municipal and industrial[a]
Missouri	15,469	14,664	94.8	646	4.2	159	1.0	1.3
Arkansas-White-Red	8,064	7,263	90.1	775	9.6	26	0.3	3.2
Texas-Gulf	11,259	9,527	84.6	1,732	15.4	0	0.0	5.5
Rio Grande	4,240	3,924	92.5	294	6.9	22	0.5	2.2
Upper Colorado	2,440	2,221	91.0	116	4.8	103	4.2	1.6
Lower Colorado	4,595	4,073	88.6	503	10.9	19	0.4	3.7
Great Basin	3,779	3,258	86.2	202	5.3	319	8.4	1.9
Pacific Northwest	11,913	11,098	93.2	625	5.2	190	1.6	1.7
California	26,641	24,380	91.5	1,899	7.1	362	1.4	2.3

Source: U.S. Water Resources Council, *The Nation's Water Resources: 1975–2000, Vol. 3: Analytical Data Summary, Second National Water Assessment* (Washington, D.C., Government Printing Office, 1978), table 11-4, pp. 47–51.

[a] Assumes that the entire increase in municipal and industrial water supply comes from a transfer of agricultural use to municipal and industrial use, rather than from water conservation in agriculture.

similar comparison for the nine water regions in the western states. The table shows that for a 30 percent increase in municipal and industrial use obtained entirely from transfers from the agricultural sector, decreases in agricultural use could range from 1.3 percent (in the Missouri region) to 5.5 percent (in the Texas-Gulf region). Again, these are regional totals, and the percentage of water diverted from agriculture could be higher in any specific locale. The reductions in agricultural diversions would translate into smaller decreases in production if water conservation measures were associated with the transfer or if any reductions in production occurred on the most marginal lands.

One concern often expressed about transfers from irrigation use to municipal and industrial use is that urban areas typically can pay so much for water (often hundreds of dollars per acre-foot) that they will simply put agriculture out of production if a market is allowed to work. This is then translated into worry over an adequate level of food production. Such concerns ignore basic relationships between the price of water and the quantity used. As with most any commodity, the quantity consumers are willing to purchase is a decreasing function of price. Although growing municipalities are willing to pay high prices for some additional water, often hundreds of dollars per acre-foot, they would not be willing to pay similar prices for all of the great quantities of water currently used in agricultural production. Also, as cities buy successive quantities of water from farms, the price for obtaining additional amounts will rise. Eventually, a point of equilibrium will be reached at which additional purchases become unattractive. In other words, water has its value in food production also, and, even though some water will be bid away, not all will be.

Conclusions: The Expanding Uses of Water Under Reclamation Law

The rationale for permitting transferability of federally supplied water between different water uses, such as irrigation and municipal and industrial uses, appears to be consistent with the expanding role given to federally constructed water facilities and to federally supplied water under Reclamation law. The Reclamation Act of 1902 limited the water provided by federal construction of dams, reservoirs, and canals to irrigation use. Section 4 of the Town Sites Act of 1906 authorized the delivery of water to towns and cities in the vicinity of irrigation projects, provided the municipality owned the rights to the water to be delivered. Section 5 of the same act authorized the development and lease of surplus power from irrigation projects, provided that the lease did not "impair the efficiency of the irrigation project." The Warren Act of 1911 provided authority to contract out the excess capacity in irrigation project facilities to permit nonfederal water to be delivered to water users, including those outside the federal project. Similar flexibility was provided for project water supplies by the Miscellaneous Purposes Act of February 25, 1920, which authorized the Secretary of the Interior to contract for water from irrigation projects for purposes other than irrigation, provided that he first obtain the permission of the existing water user associations in the project and provided that the delivery of water for these purposes was not "detrimental to the water service for such irrigation project or to the rights of any prior appropriator." The use of reclamation water was expanded still further by the 1935 act authorizing Parker and Grand Coulee dams (49 Stat. 1039; 33 U.S.C. 540), which provided for flood control and navigation as well as for irrigation and hydroelectric power development at these two locations. Section 9(c) of the Reclamation Project Act of 1939 provided general authority for the sale of hydropower and municipal and industrial water in all reclamation projects and contained provisions allowing water formerly designated for irrigation use to be shifted to municipal and industrial use or to hydropower production, so long as the irrigation uses were protected.

This sequence of legislation indicates recognition of the expanding economic value of federally supplied water in terms of both end use and location of use. In this context, it appears that within the general scope of Reclamation law, there is considerable latitude for voluntary water transfers to accommodate new water demands. However, Bureau of Reclamation contracts with water users require the permission of the federal contracting officer to assign rights under the contract. Therefore, the attitude of the bureau and its field personnel is pivotal when it comes to approval of transfer proposals. Accordingly, this chapter has covered a number of recommendations for changes in bureau administrative policy and contracts, as well as in Reclamation law, for the purpose of facilitating the transfer of water.

References

Anderson, Raymond L. 1967. "Windfall Gains from Transfer of Water Allotments Within the Colorado–Big Thompson Project," *Land Economics* vol. 43, pp. 265–273.

Anderson, Terry L. 1983a. *Water Crisis: Ending the Policy Drought* (Washington, D.C., Cato Institute).

———, ed. 1983b. *Water Rights: Scarce Resource Allocation, Bureaucracy, and the Environment* (Cambridge, Mass., Ballinger).

California Assembly Office of Research. 1982. *A Marketing Approach to Water Allocation* (Sacramento, Calif.).

California Department of Water Resources. 1981. *Investigation Under California Water Code Section 275 of Use of Water by Imperial Irrigation District,* Southern District Report (Los Angeles, Calif.).

Environmental Defense Fund. 1983. *Trading Conservation Investments for Water* (Berkeley, Calif.).

Frederick, Kenneth D., with James C. Hanson. 1982. *Water for Western Agriculture* (Washington, D.C., Resources for the Future).

Hartman, L. M., and Don Seastone. 1970. *Water Transfers: Economic Efficiency and Alternative Institutions* (Baltimore, Md., The Johns Hopkins University Press).

Lamb, Berton L. 1986. "Instream Flow Laws and Technology: A Survey." Notes for a presentation at the meeting of the Arkansas, White, Red River Basin Interagency Commission, Sante Fe, N. Mex., October 8–10.

Lamb, Berton L., and Hank Meshorer. 1983 "Comparing Instream Flow Programs: A Report on Current Status," in *Proceedings of the Specialty Conference on Advances in Irrigation and Drainage: Surviving External Pressures* (New York, American Society of Civil Engineers).

Meyers, Charles J., and Richard A. Posner. 1971. "Market Transfers of Water Rights: Toward an Improved Market in Water Resources." Legal Study No. 4 prepared for the U.S. National Water Commission, Washington, D.C. (available from National Technical Information Service, Springfield, Va. NWC-L-71-0-09).

Phelps, Charles E., Nancy Y. Moore, and Morlie H. Graubard. 1978. *Efficient Water Use in California: Water Rights, Water Districts, and Water Transfers* (Santa Monica, Calif., Rand Corporation).

Saliba, Bonnie C., and David B. Bush. 1987. *Water Markets in Theory and Practice: Market Transfers, Water Values, and Public Policy* (Boulder, Colo., Westview Press).

Sax, Joseph. 1965. "Selling Reclamation Water Rights, a Case Study in Federal Subsidy Policy," *Michigan Law Review* vol. 64, no. 13, pp. 13–46 (November).

Stavins, Robert, and Zach Willey. 1983. "Trading Conservation Investments for Water," in *Regional and State Water Resources Planning and Management* (Bethesda, Md., American Water Resources Association), pp. 223–230.

U.S. Department of the Interior. 1979. *Decisions of the United States Department of the Interior, Vol. 85,* edited by Vera E. Burgin and Betty H. Perry (Washington, D.C., Government Printing Office).

U.S. Department of the Interior, Bureau of Reclamation and Bureau of Indian Affairs. 1978. *Report on the Water Conservation Opportunities Study* (Washington, D.C.).

U.S. Department of the Interior, Bureau of Reclamation. 1978. *Special Task Force Report on San Luis Unit, Central Valley Project, California* (Washington, D.C., Government Printing Office).

———. 1983. "Water Conservation Opportunities: Imperial Irrigation District, California." Draft Special Report (Washington, D.C.).

———. 1986. *1985 Summary Statistics. Vol. 1. Water, Land, and Related Data* (Denver, Colo.).

U.S. National Water Commission. 1973. *Water Policies for the Future* (Washington, D.C., Government Printing Office).

Wahl, Richard W., and Robert K. Davis. 1986. "Satisfying Southern California's Thirst for Water: Efficient Alternatives," in Kenneth D. Frederick, ed., *Scarce Water and Institutional Change* (Washington, D.C., Resources for the Future).

Wahl, Richard W., and Benjamin M. Simon. 1988. "Acquiring Title to Bureau of Reclamation Water Facilities," in Steven J. Shupe, ed., *Water Marketing 1988: The Move to Innovation* (Denver, University of Colorado College of Law).

Part III

Case Studies of Potential Water Transfers

7

Water Contamination Problems at Kesterson Reservoir

In 1983 the Fish and Wildlife Service noticed that something had gone terribly wrong at the Kesterson Reservoir in central California's San Joaquin Valley: some of Kesterson's newly hatched waterfowl had crippling deformities. Beaks were grotesquely shaped, wings were missing, legs were twisted, and skulls were unformed; many birds died soon after hatching. The reservoir—ironically, part of the Kesterson National Wildlife Refuge—had become hostile to its inhabitants, and the name "Kesterson" soon became synonymous with environmental disaster.

The cause of this ruin was eventually diagnosed as selenium, a naturally occurring nonmetallic trace element. Selenium was being leached from the soil underlying some portions of the Westlands Water District by agricultural irrigation water. Subsurface drains collected this water and then carried it to the reservoir through the San Luis Drain. Once in Kesterson, the mineral became concentrated in vegetation and small animal life, and the concentrations increased dramatically as selenium moved up the food chain. Selenium in very small amounts is regarded as beneficial to humans, but at higher levels it almost certainly is dangerous. For bird life, the verdict is clear: high concentrations of selenium are fatal.

An earlier draft of this chapter, "Federal Water Pricing, Agricultural Land Values, and Kesterson Reservoir," was presented at the Conference of the Western Economic Association in Anaheim, California, on July 1, 1985. See also Richard W. Wahl, "Cleaning Up Kesterson," *Resources* no. 83, Spring 1986, pp. 11–14 (Washington, D.C., Resources for the Future).

The Kesterson disaster revived long-standing questions about the need for agricultural drainage in the San Joaquin Valley and raised new ones. Who will pay for cleaning up Kesterson and for handling selenium and other trace elements in future drainage water? Should more federal funds support already heavily subsidized agricultural production in the valley? What are the best approaches for determining the appropriate long-term uses of the agricultural lands that require drainage and the federally subsidized water supplies provided to those lands? One way to help answer this last question is to allow farmers with severe drainage problems to sell the associated water supplies at market value in exchange for removing their lands from production. This possibility is explored in this chapter, but first it is important to review the origins of these questions.

History of Drainage Problems in the San Luis Unit

The San Luis Unit, which constitutes a portion of the Central Valley Project, lies on the west side of the San Joaquin Valley (see figure 7-1; for a brief history of the Central Valley Project, see chapter 3). From the earliest plans for irrigation in this unit, subsurface drainage was regarded as necessary for part of the lands served. An impermeable clay layer underlies the soil in parts of the Westlands Water District, which makes up the principal part of the San Luis Unit. Without subsurface drainage, the water applications necessary to leach salt from the soil would eventually raise the water table into the root zones of the crops, reducing productivity and eventually making it impossible to sustain crop production. In the 1956 Feasibility Report for the San Luis Unit (U.S. Department of the Interior, Bureau of Reclamation, 1956), it was estimated that about 96,000 acres of the 458,460 irrigable acres in the unit would eventually need drainage (see also U.S. Department of the Interior, Bureau of Reclamation, 1978, p. 163). The Definite Plan Report, which was completed in 1962, expanded the service area eastward to include a total of 555,000 irrigable acres (see figure 7-1) and estimated that more than 170,000 acres would eventually need drainage (U.S. Department of the Interior, Bureau of Reclamation, 1962). Some 12 percent of the expanded service area consists of class IV lands, which, according to the Definite Plan Report, are "marginal in their suitability for irrigated agriculture . . . because of highly saline, slowly permeable soils with anticipated or present drainage problems" (see U.S. Department of the Interior, Bureau of Reclamation, 1978, p. 163).

The San Luis Authorizing Act of 1960 (74 Stat. 156) required that before the San Luis Unit was constructed, either the Secretary of the Interior would receive satisfactory assurance from the state of Cali-

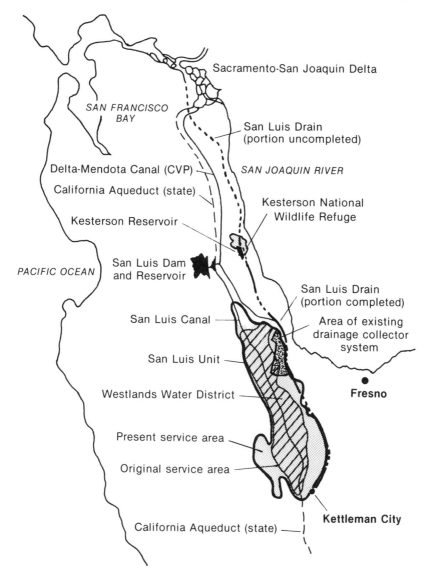

Figure 7-1. Kesterson Reservoir and surrounding areas. *Source:* Bureau of Reclamation, U.S. Department of the Interior, Washington, D.C.

fornia that it would provide a master drain for the entire San Joaquin Valley or the secretary would make provision for constructing an interceptor drain to the Sacramento–San Joaquin Delta sufficient to serve only the San Luis Unit. After the state informed the bureau in 1962 that it would not construct a master drain, the bureau proceeded with its plan for the 188-mile San Luis Drain, extending from Kettle-man City at the southern end of the Westlands Water District to the Delta.

Because of controversy over the potential effects on water quality in the Delta and lack of federal appropriations, only the first 85 miles of the drain were completed. Since 1975, the northern terminus of the drain has been the Kesterson Reservoir (see figure 7-1), originally intended as a regulating facility for the longer drain. The "reservoir" is actually a series of twelve diked ponds, 4.5 feet deep and covering about 1,280 acres. Kesterson Reservoir was made part of the 5,900-acre Kesterson National Wildlife Refuge, established in 1970 by a cooperative agreement between the Bureau of Reclamation and the Fish and Wildlife Service.

Before 1978, surface runoff was the primary source of water dis-charged into the reservoir. In 1978 increasing amounts of subsurface drainage started to flow to Kesterson from the Westlands Water District, and after 1981 this subsurface drainage was the principal constituent in the inflow (California State Water Resources Control Board, 1985). In 1982 the Fish and Wildlife Service first noticed problems at Kesterson Reservoir, including the disappearance of largemouth and striped bass, catfish, and carp. Laboratory analysis of mosquito fish revealed high levels of selenium. In spring 1983, a high incidence of mortality and deformities among newborn coots, grebes, stilts, and ducks was observed. It was hypothesized that selenium from some of the soils in Westlands was being carried to Kesterson in the drainage water and that bioconcentration in the vegetation and other biota was adversely affecting the waterfowl.

As a result of the ensuing public concern, a number of remedial actions were taken. The state Department of Health Services recom-mended that pregnant women and children under the age of ten avoid eating duck from the Kesterson National Wildlife Refuge area and that everyone else limit their intake of duck from the area to one meal a week. A waterfowl "hazing" program was initiated, in which Fish and Wildlife Service employees used propane exploders, fireworks, and scarecrow devices to discourage waterfowl from using the reser-voir. The program appears to have been successful in keeping most ducks and geese from the area, but has been relatively ineffective for removing coots, blackbirds, herons, raptors, and terrestrial mam-mals. The Bureau of Reclamation entered into agreements to deliver supplemental water to areas surrounding Kesterson to provide an attractive substitute wildlife habitat. It also began evaluating the environmental effects of removing vegetation from Kesterson.

On April 27, 1984, Robert James Claus, a landowner in the Grassland Water District, appeared before the California Regional Water Quality Control Board in the Central Valley and requested that it take a number of enforcement actions against the Bureau of Reclamation. The matter was referred to the State Water Resources Control Board (SWRCB) on May 18, 1984. Claus and other landowners in the Grassland Water District had entered into easement agreements with the Fish and Wildlife Service whereby they permanently waived their rights to develop their land for irrigated agriculture or any other purpose inconsistent with the maintenance of waterfowl habitat. Claus alleged that on the approximately 1,000 acres on which he sold the easement, public concerns over the quality of water entering the Grassland District made it impossible for him and his family to continue to earn an income from cattle grazing or from charging fees to duck hunters.

In October and December 1984, SWRCB held evidentiary hearings on Claus's complaint. The board noted concentrations of selenium up to ten times public health standards at the Kesterson Reservoir. In addition, it found that some samples of water stored at Kesterson had levels of other trace elements (hexavalent chromium, cadmium, zinc, mercury, and nickel) that at least modestly exceeded the Environmental Protection Agency's water quality criteria for the protection of freshwater aquatic life or the protection of public health. On February 5, 1985, SWRCB ruled that subsurface drainage water from Westlands was a "hazardous waste" and issued a cleanup and abatement order (California State Water Resources Control Board, 1985). The board ordered the Bureau of Reclamation to submit plans by July 5, 1985, either for upgrading the ponds at Kesterson Reservoir to state standards or for closing the facility. State standards for the ponds would require double lining and installation of a protective leachate collection and removal system. A three-year deadline (February 1988) was set for full implementation of the measures in whatever plan was approved by the state. In its filings with the SWRCB (U.S. Department of the Interior, Bureau of Reclamation, 1984b, 1985a, and 1985b), the bureau noted that for many of the trace elements cited in the board order, the "background" water quality in areas near Kesterson was similar to that in the drainage water (selenium was an exception). The Bureau also emphasized that the cost of meeting the state standards would far exceed what the agricultural lands served by the drain could support and, because federal budgets were limited, adoption of the board might "force 42,000 acres of prime agricultural land out of production."

On March 15, 1985, concerns over possible fines or criminal liabilities for federal officials under the Migratory Bird Treaty Act (44

Stat. 755; 16 U.S.C. 703) led the new Secretary of the Interior, Donald Hodel, to announce his intention to halt the inflow of subsurface drainage to Kesterson and to discontinue the supply of irrigation water to the area served by the drain.[1] On March 28, 1985, the Department of the Interior and Westlands Water District reached an agreement guaranteeing Westlands the continued delivery of irrigation water, to be used anywhere within the district, through 1985 (U.S. Department of the Interior, 1985). However, the district was required to completely halt use of Kesterson Reservoir and of the San Luis Drain north of the district's last disposal point by June 30, 1986. Westlands was required to reduce its deliveries to the drain by increments of 20 percent approximately every two months starting September 30, 1985. Under the agreement, the district assumed responsibility for designing, installing, and operating alternative means for disposal of drain water at its own expense, at least until such time as drainage was provided for the San Luis Unit. Among the available alternative means specifically mentioned in the agreement were evaporation ponds, recycling, and the use of salt-tolerant crops. If Westlands failed to make satisfactory progress toward the June 1986 deadline, the agreement provided that the Secretary of the Interior could plug the necessary portions of the on-district drainage system (to which the United States has title and is assured access by the agreement) "without regard to costs or consequences" and at Westlands's expense. Westlands met the deadline, halting use of the San Luis Drain during the week of June 9, 1986.

The Contribution of Federally Subsidized Water to the Kesterson Reservoir Problem

The availability of federally subsidized irrigation water contributed significantly to the origins of the problems at Kesterson Reservoir. As discussed in chapter 3, the use of long-term fixed-rate contracts in the Central Valley Project and of the rolling repayment concept (under which the repayment period for the entire project is extended whenever a new facility or unit is added) has significantly increased the value of the interest subsidy for irrigation. The practical effect is that repayment for the San Luis Unit, which began in 1968, will, under current proposals, extend to 2030, an interest-free repayment period of sixty-two years. The interest subsidy for the San Luis Unit is about $1,422 per acre out of an actual cost of $1,679 per acre (in 1978

---

[1] The act imposes fines or jail terms on those who kill migratory birds covered by international treaty.

dollars). In other words, water users in the San Luis Unit pay only about 15 percent of their share of project costs (see table 2-3 or U.S. Department of the Interior, Bureau of Reclamation, 1981). Where irrigators pay only a small percentage of costs, one can expect overinvestment in water storage and delivery and the utilization of otherwise marginally productive lands. Similarly, with the prospect of federally subsidized collector drains for the district and a federally subsidized master drain for the valley, local entities had little incentive to implement local and state solutions to drainage problems.

Whatever one's evaluation of the original federal commitment to solve the problems of saline drainage in the San Luis unit, the recent discovery of selenium and other trace elements will undoubtedly influence future federal actions. The need to handle high levels of trace elements was unforeseen in the original water service contracts, and all of the corrective actions known at present are very costly. The secretary's order and the agreement signed with the district effectively gave the district additional incentives to find the most economical interim solution to the drainage problems. As a result, a new set of proposed solutions to the drainage problems of the Westlands Water District and other parts of the San Joaquin Valley began to emerge.

Possible Future Alternatives

Local Recycling of Drainage Water and Local Evaporation Ponds. Recycling of drainage water and evaporation ponds are already being used by necessity in some areas not connected to the San Luis Drain. In some cases, up to one-third of the drainage water is mixed with irrigation water and recirculated. The long-term viability of such recycling is not known.

Some preliminary results from studies by agricultural economists at the University of California, Riverside, indicate that evaporation ponds would require acreage equal to 5 percent of the total farm area provided that optimal management practices were used, but up to 20 percent of the total farm area under current management practices (Knapp, Dinar, and Letey, 1986). The deposits that accumulate in the ponds would need to be disposed of periodically, though perhaps as infrequently as every thirty years. This would require drying out the ponds and removing the deposits by trucking them to a specially constructed disposal site, by transporting them to the ocean for disposal, or by some other means. Even local holding ponds would require double-lining and a leachate detection and recovery system under state standards, which would add to the cost of this alternative. (Of course, it is possible that the state could grant a variance to this standard.) A variation on this idea involves irrigating salt-tolerant grasses with the drainage water and then harvesting and disposing of the crop.

Centralized District Evaporation Ponds.   The amount of water evaporated in ponds is roughly proportional to the acreage of the ponds. Given the cost of collecting and transporting drainage water to centralized facilities, the economies of scale in centralized evaporation ponds may be limited. However, since land values differ substantially within the district, it could be more economical to locate centralized drainage facilities on land that has poor agricultural productivity. The savings in land costs could offset the expenses of operating a collector system. Regardless of whether ponds were on farms or centralized, planners would have to keep in mind that the water was hazardous. Ponds could be designed to not produce vegetation or other conditions attractive to wildlife.

Drainage Charges.   The district may find other techniques such as pricing useful in managing its drainage. At present, all lands in the Westlands Water District are charged $0.50 per acre-foot to pay for collector drains and the San Luis Drain. An increased charge on water deliveries to lands requiring drainage would provide an incentive to reduce water delivered to crops, which in turn would decrease the quantity of drainage. Similarly, an appropriate per-acre-foot charge to farmers connecting to the district's disposal drains would encourage individual irrigators to balance the costs of on-farm evaporation and recycling with the costs of any centralized district facilities. Of course, any system of charges would have to be constructed to take into account the subsurface movement of water to neighboring farms.

Desalting Technologies and Biotechnology.   The Environmental Defense Fund, in cooperation with Westlands, has proposed a study of the application of desalting technologies to drainage water, but these technologies are expensive. One possible means of financing is to substitute the treated water for some portion of current irrigation supplies, which could then be sold elsewhere to municipal and industrial customers. Biological and chemical means of treating contaminated drainage water are also being considered.

Voluntary Sales of Water at Market Value.   Farmers who did not find it economical to bear the expense of some combination of recycling, local evaporation ponds, centralized evaporation facilities, desalting, and biological treatment could sell at market value the water supplies from land with severe drainage problems, rather than irrigate the land. One of the most likely purchasers of such water is the

Metropolitan Water District of Southern California, which could take delivery through the State Water Project.

It is not the purpose of this chapter to explore the economics of all these options. Indeed, one of the advantages of local responsibility is that it provides incentives to the directly interested parties to seek out the most efficient solutions. Those with the greatest knowledge of special local circumstances are those most closely connected with farming production in the district: the farm operators and district managers. This chapter does, however, discuss the voluntary sale of water in some detail to highlight the fact that this alternative would necessarily involve the cooperation of a number of governmental entities.

Governmental Cooperation Required For Voluntary Water Transactions

Various governmental entities would need to cooperate for an exchange possibility to be made available to Westlands farmers. The Bureau of Reclamation would have to agree to allow farmers whose lands were affected with severe drainage problems to sell water at market value to the State Water Project or other potential purchasers. The actual item sold or leased would be contracted water deliveries, not water rights.

The Westlands Water District would also have to enter the agreement, since it, and not the individual landowners, holds the contract for the delivered water. Westlands additionally would have to agree to act as a "broker" in the transaction, assigning farmers an amount of water for sale equivalent to their customary deliveries for irrigation.

Congress would have to authorize delivery of water outside the current service area of the Central Valley Project, since the primary demands on the State Water Project are located in southern California. The rationale for the legislation would be the unusual and unforeseen circumstances arising with regard to selenium in the agricultural drainage water, as well as the desire to promote beneficial long-term use of the water resource. Prepayment of the full federal municipal and industrial costs of the water would provide an additional rationale for forgoing the original agricultural purpose of the subsidized water supply.

The State Water Resources Control Board would need to approve a change in the location of water use. Alternatively, the State Water Project could purchase the water and deliver it to its own contractors in the San Joaquin Valley, freeing up an equivalent amount of project water to be transported to the southern part of the state. The acreage limitations in federal Reclamation law would apply to the state agricultural deliveries.

The 1982 state referendum defeating construction of the Peripheral Canal is evidence of the opposition to moving additional water from northern California to southern California. However, water sold from the San Luis service area would be water that is currently already transported south of the Delta. Transporting the Westlands water farther south would not affect water quality in the Delta since there are virtually no return flows from Westlands to the San Joaquin River. Furthermore, there would be no major third-party water rights needing protection. The Grassland Water District receives a small amount of surface runoff from Westlands, which it mixes with freshwater and reuses; however, Grassland has no established rights to these return flows that could serve as the basis for a legal challenge to the sale of water currently being delivered to Westlands.

Estimated Increase in Income from Voluntary Sales of Water

Maximum Purchase Price

For a number of years, the State Water Project has sought to purchase water from the Central Valley Project. The Coordinated Operation Agreement (COA) between the State Water Project and the Central Valley Project, signed in November 1986 (and authorized by Congress in October 1986 through P.L. 99-546; 100 Stat. 3050), allows some water to be sold on a temporary basis to the state. The main purpose of the COA is to establish the amount of water from the state project and the federal project to be used to maintain water quality in the Sacramento–San Joaquin Delta and to otherwise specify how the use of the state and federal facilities can be coordinated to the benefit of each. The increased operational efficiencies made possible by this agreement, together with the resolution of the amounts of water needed to meet water quality standards, are expected to result in the availability of about 1 million additional acre-feet of water from the Central Valley Project for future contracting.

Article 10(h) of the COA calls for the initiation of contract negotiations that would allow the State Water Project (SWP) to purchase water from the Central Valley Project (CVP) at the same rates available to CVP contractors. This would be an inexpensive source of water for the state, since the water rates would reflect the average-cost-pricing practices used in the Central Valley Project, rather than the cost of new or recent construction (refer to chapter 3 for additional discussion of CVP pricing). This water would be less expensive than water purchased from Westlands farmers, which would also need to include compensation to farmers, as well as CVP charges. (In either case, the prices paid by SWP contractors would include the state project's own delivery and capital costs.) However, water purchased under the COA would be subject to curtailment since the COA stipulates that "when the CVP water sold to the State is needed by existing or new long-term CVP contractors, it shall be reclaimed by the United States for such contractors." The Bureau of Reclamation has requests for up to 4 million acre-feet of additional CVP water and considers about 2 million acre-feet of this amount to represent firm desires to contract for water. Therefore, water purchased by the state under the COA would be an inexpensive supply, but also an uncertain and interim supply.

These considerations indicate that contractors in the state project might find water made available from Westlands attractive because it could be obtainable on a long-term basis. One indication of the highest price that the State Water Project would be willing to pay for such water is the cost of forgoing construction of its next planned facility. The least expensive of the proposed SWP facilities on a per-acre-foot basis is the Cottonwood Creek Project, with a cost of approximately $212 per acre-foot (1982 dollars) for water delivered to the south side of the Delta. This figure is used here as the value of water at that location (refer to table 7-1, which summarizes the values relevant to the voluntary sale of irrigation water from the Westlands Water District).[2]

This value must be adjusted downward because the State Water Project would need to compensate Westlands for certain obligations that Westlands has for repaying the cost of the Central Valley Project. If water were transferred from Westlands at the Delta, then Westlands would no longer incur the corresponding operating costs for conveyance, conveyance pumping, and direct pumping. However, in the absence of any specific agreement to the contrary, the capital costs for these same services would still be payable by Westlands. The major share of SWP water is allocated to municipal and industrial use. In switching CVP water from agricultural use to municipal and industrial use, the capital charges payable would increase because, under Reclamation law, municipal and industrial use bears interest charges, whereas irrigation use does not. The appropriate annual

[2] Still less expensive is the Peripheral Canal, which was designed to transport additional water across the Sacramento–San Joaquin Delta at a cost of approximately $106 per acre-foot in 1982 dollars (see Wahl and Davis, 1986). California voters rejected this alternative by referendum in 1982.

Table 7-1. Estimated Net Income from Voluntary Sales of Irrigation Water from the Westlands Water District, California

(values as of 1982)

	Units	Dollars
Maximum purchase price		
Annual values		
Value at south side of Delta	$/AF-yr	212.00[a]
Less CVP charges for Westlands:		
Capital charges for storage, conveyance, pumping, and direct pumping (for M&I water)	$/AF-yr	−19.28[b]
Distribution system capital costs	$/AF-yr	−10.11[c]
O&M charges for storage (M&I)	$/AF-yr	−0.91
Credit for payments to date	$/AF-yr	0.30[d]
Net CVP charges	$/AF-yr	−30.00
Net value to purchaser	$/AF-yr	182.00
Permanent right per acre-foot	$/AF	1,804.50[e]
Permanent right per acre at 2.5 acre-feet per acre	$/A	4,511.24
Minimum selling price		
Permanent right per acre	$/A	1,360.00[f]
Net income (difference in prices)	$/A	3,151.24

Note: Abbreviations: A, acre; AF, acre-foot; CVP, Central Valley Project; M&I, municipal and industrial; O&M, operation and maintenance.

Sources: Cost of water from the Cottonwood Creek Project is from California Department of Water Resources, *State Water Project—Status of Water Conservation and Water Supply Augmentation Plans,* Bulletin 76-81 (Sacramento, 1981), pp. 30–35, table 3. CVP charges are from U.S. Department of the Interior, Bureau of Reclamation, *CVP Ratesetting Policy Proposal* (April 1984) and *CVP Municipal and Industrial Water Ratesetting Policy Proposal* (October 1984), schedule 1, p. 3, and schedule 8, p. 3.

[a]Based on the cost of the Cottonwood Creek Project. Cost is converted to 1982 dollars using the Gross National Product implicit price deflator.

[b]Annual capital charges for M&I water under the assumption that a purchaser would be held responsible for paying the assigned shares of CVP capital costs for conveyance, conveyance pumping, and direct pumping. For irrigation water, annual capital charges total about $6.073 per acre-foot based on the weighted average of projected contract deliveries from the Delta-Mendota Pool and the San Luis Canal. When water is used for M&I use, interest charges during construction must be added, and the payments must be amortized at the CVP project composite interest rate of 2.6782 percent, which results in an annual capital charge of $19.28 per acre-foot. If paid as a lump sum, the capital balance for M&I water would be $517 per acre-foot, which is approximately $329 per acre-foot higher than the present worth (at a 10 percent discount rate) of the annual payments shown here.

[c]Includes interest charges.

[d]Credit is given for past payments to capital during the period when the water was being used for irrigation purposes.

[e]The annual payment for a permanent right is calculated using an amortization period of fifty years and an interest rate of 10 percent.

[f]Estimated as the difference in market value between irrigated land with field crops ($2,240 per acre) and grazing land ($880 per acre). See table 7-2.

capital charges for conveyance, conveyance pumping, and direct pumping are estimated at $19.28 per acre-foot in table 7-1.[3]

The State Water Project or other purchaser of water from West-lands might be required to assume the district's payments for that part of the federally constructed distribution system that lies on the lands that would no longer receive water. As table 7-1 indicates, this annual charge would amount to an estimated $10.11 per acre-foot. Any water transferred to the project at the Delta would incur the Bureau of Reclamation's annual operation and maintenance charge for CVP storage ($0.91 per acre-foot). A credit could be allowed against these various CVP obligations for payments made toward capital to date by the current irrigation water users ($0.30 per acre-foot per year). As the table indicates, the net annual value of the water to the purchaser after these charges and credits is $182 per acre-foot.

The present worth of an annual water right is the value of a permanent water right. With a 10 percent discount rate and a fifty-year amortization period, the value of a permanent right to water that could substitute for Cottonwood Creek supplies is $1,804 per acre-foot. Water supply in the Westlands area averages around 2.5 acre-feet per acre, which means that the State Water Project might be willing to pay up to $4,511 per acre (in 1982 dollars) to obtain the associated water supplies.

Minimum Selling Price

The value of the permanent right per acre can be compared to the estimated minimum value for which Westlands farmers might be willing to sell their water voluntarily. This can be estimated as the difference between the value of irrigated land producing field crops and the value of nonirrigated land used for grazing. Table 7-2 indicates this difference to be about $1,360 per acre ($2,240 per acre for irrigated land producing field crops, less $880 per acre for grazing land). This is based on values for land in the absence of any drainage problems. Land values have decreased considerably since 1982, so the actual minimum selling price might be lower.

Estimated Increase in Net Income

The difference between the maximum purchase price and the minimum selling price represents the potential income gain from the

---

[3] The charges set forth here are based on the bureau's proposed component rate-setting method (U.S. Department of the Interior, Bureau of Reclamation, 1984a). The actual capital charges for which Westlands would be liable under such an arrangement would depend on the final water rate policy adopted by the Bureau of Reclamation (a final irrigation rate policy was established by the bureau in 1988).

Table 7-2.   Land Values of Field Crop and Grazing Land Acreage, Westlands Water District, California, 1974-1983

(1982 dollars)

Year	Field crops (dollars/acre)	Grazing land (dollars/acre)	Difference (dollars/acre)
1974	2,226	787	1,439
1975	2,359	1,333	1,026
1976	1,998	n.a.	n.a.
1977	2,047	n.a.	n.a.
1978	3,318	n.a.	n.a.
1979	2,513	n.a.	n.a.
1980	2,447	695	1,752
1981	1,249	n.a.	n.a.
1982	2,366	n.a.	n.a.
1983	2,713	n.a.	n.a.
Annual average	2,324	938	1,386
Weighted average[a]	2,237	879	1,358

Note: n.a. means data not available (no grazing land sales were recorded in these years).

Source: Adapted from a land sales data base prepared by Phillip Gardner, University of California, Riverside.

[a]Weighted by acreage of land sold.

transfer—$3,151 per acre (or $127 per acre-foot per year; see table 7-1). In other words, the highest amount that the State Water Project might be willing to pay for water is about three times the estimated minimum selling price in its current use.

The estimates of the maximum purchase price and the minimum selling price do not, of course, represent what the actual sale price would be; it would lie somewhere in between the two values. For example, the state might pay some amount less for water than the cost of its next planned facility. Reciprocally, the Westlands landowners affected by drainage problems might demand an amount for water that exceeds their expected agricultural net income before they would be willing to put their land to another use. They might also be unwilling to give up their water supplies unless they were paid an amount sufficient to cover their relocation expenses and their remaining debts on immobile farm assets with little resale value. The Westlands Water District would probably demand that certain district assessments be prepaid before the water could be sold for uses outside the district. In any event, the increase in net income from a voluntary water transfer would be divided among the parties involved in accord with the financial terms of the transaction.

Table 7-3 indicates the additional income that would be available to growers in Westlands for different sale prices of water, both on a per-

Table 7-3. Additional Income That Would Accrue to a Westlands Farmer at Different Sale Prices for Water

Sale price of water at the Delta less adjustments for CVP charges			Additional income to farmer above minimum selling price[a]	
At Delta ($/AF-yr)	Adjustments ($/AF-yr)	Net to farmer ($/AF-yr)	Per AF/yr ($/AF-yr)	Per acre ($/acre)
212	30	182	127	3,151
200	30	170	115	2,854
175	30	145	90	2,234
150	30	120	65	1,614
125	30	95	40	995
100	30	70	15	375
85	30	55	0	0

Note: Abbreviations: CVP, Central Valley Project; AF-yr, acre-foot per year.
Source: Tables 7-1 and 7-2.
[a]Estimated minimum selling price from tables 7-1 and 7-2 is $55 per acre-foot per year or $1,360 per acre.

acre basis and a per-acre-foot basis. For example, if water sold for $125 per acre-foot at the Delta, a farmer would receive about $40 per acre-foot above his usual agricultural income. This amounts to a one-time payment of $995 per acre above the sale price of the land. The table indicates that sale prices at the Delta ranging from $212 down to $85 per acre-foot would give the farmer some increased income. The floor price of $85 per acre-foot at the Delta would yield a payment of $55 per acre-foot to the farmer, which would leave him with no additional income beyond that currently attainable in irrigation use on land with no drainage problems.

Increase in Federal Revenues

For its part, the federal government would triple its annual revenue for all water shifting from irrigation in Westlands to municipal and industrial use. Since municipal and industrial use bears interest, capital charges would increase by about $13 per acre-foot (from about $6 to $19 per acre-foot—see table 7-1, note b). If water were eventually sold from 40,000 acres (approximately the area currently provided with collector drains, though five times the 8,000 acres currently drained), then the total quantity of water would be about 100,000 acre-feet (recall that water supply in Westlands averages 2.5 acre-feet per acre). If all of the water were sold for municipal and industrial purposes, this would mean an annual increase in federal revenues of $1.3 million per year.

Although the federal government, as a matter of administrative policy and custom, does not make a profit on its water,[4] it could reasonably expect to further enhance its revenue recovery in exchange for allowing water to be sold at market value. For example, it could accelerate its revenue recovery by demanding prepayment of capital costs. This would yield about $517 per acre-foot—$329 per acre-foot more than the present worth of the annual payments set out in table 7-1. This increase occurs because the project interest rate applied to municipal and industrial water in the CVP—2.68 percent—is far below the current costs of government borrowing (refer to table 7-1, note b). At 2.5 acre-feet per acre, this would mean that the federal government would receive an additional $822 per acre of the increased net income from the water transfer, leaving $2,329 per acre to be divided among the other parties to the transaction.

It is also possible that the federal government could use some portion of the market value of water to help finance the cleanup of Kesterson Reservoir. For example, if the government levied a surcharge of $700 per acre (equivalent to an annual charge of approximately $28 per acre-foot), then 40,000 acres of water sales would yield additional revenues of $28 million. This could go some distance toward financing the cleanup of Kesterson.[5] In establishing any accelerated assessments or additional charges to assist in financing the Kesterson cleanup, it would be important for the government and the district not to set the charges so high that the financial incentives for the water sales were negated.

Potential Use of Water by State Water Project Contractors

The sale of water allocated to 40,000 acres in Westlands would yield about 100,000 acre-feet of water. This amount is probably well within the amount that could be sold, particularly to cities in southern California. Table 7-4 shows the annual entitlements for water from the State Water Project by region for the years 1985 and 2000. These total 3.1 and 4.2 million acre-feet, respectively. However, the current firm yield from the State Water Project is only 1.2 million–1.5 million acre-feet. The available yield is divided among the SWP contractors in proportion to their entitlements. As the last row of table 7-4

---

[4] For further discussion of the legislative basis for water charges on reclamation projects, as well as administrative practice, see chapters 2, 3, and 4.

[5] On March 19, 1987, the state ordered the department to proceed with an on-site disposal plan. The department agreed to voluntarily comply in most respects with the state order. However, in light of new studies at the site, this order was modified on July 5, 1988. Estimates are that the revised cleanup will cost $37 million.

Table 7-4.   Annual Water Entitlements from the State Water
Project, California, for the Years 1985 and 2000

	1985		2000		Deliverable entitlement in 1985[a]
	Acre-feet	Percent	Acre-feet	Percent	Acre-feet
North Bay	950	0.0	55,050	1.3	459
South Bay	145,800	4.7	188,000	4.5	70,483
Central Coast	21,138	0.7	70,486	1.7	10,219
San Joaquin Valley[b]	1,079,100	34.8	1,355,000	32.2	521,658
Southern California	1,852,149	59.7	2,497,500	59.4	895,364
MWD only[c]	(1,558,700)	(50.2)	(2,011,500)	(47.8)	(753,506)
Feather River	3,760	0.1	38,610	0.9	1,818
Total	3,102,897	100.0	4,204,646	100.0	1,500,000

Source: California Department of Water Resources, *Management of the California State Water Project,* Bulletin 132-84, September 1984, pp. 178–181, table B-4.

[a]Based on 1.5 million acre-feet of total deliverable water and the 1985 percentages of total deliveries. Total does not add because of rounding. (For actual deliveries, see *Management of the California State Water Project,* Bulletin 132-84, pp. 190–193, table B-5B.)

[b]Includes more than 900,000 acre-feet for the Kern County Water Agency.

[c]MWD means Metropolitan Water District of Southern California. The numbers in parentheses are for "MWD only." Those amounts are included in the Southern California entitlements in the row above.

indicates, the Metropolitan Water District of Southern California (MWD) is a major purchaser of water from the State Water Project, with entitlements running at about 50 percent of project totals. MWD, which serves major metropolitan areas on the coastal plain (including Los Angeles, Anaheim, and San Diego), is also the contractor with the greatest demands for additional water. Under the set of priorities for use of Colorado River water, MWD will lose about 400,000 acre-feet of water per year as the Central Arizona Project increases deliveries. Under these conditions, MWD projects an annual deficit of 140,000 acre-feet during normal years by the year 2000 and annual deficits ranging from 600,000 to 1.2 million acre-feet during periods of drought (Metropolitan Water District of Southern California, 1983; see also Wahl and Davis, 1986). These quantities probably represent the upper limits on the amount that might be purchased for use in metropolitan areas in southern California.

Some of this additional demand could be met by water transfers from the Imperial Irrigation District (see chapter 5 and Wahl and Davis, 1986). A study by Vaux and Howitt (1984) indicates that another portion of the additional MWD demand could be met from sources in the San Joaquin Valley. Vaux and Howitt simulated market trades of water in California, using five demand regions and nine supply sources. Their study suggests that a transfer of 1 million acre-feet of water to southern California municipal and industrial uses from the Imperial and Coachella irrigation districts and a transfer of 300,000 acre-feet from agricultural users in the San Joaquin Valley would bring the market to equilibrium. Water exports from the San Joaquin Valley to southern California are limited in the market simulation both by the demand for municipal and industrial water in southern California and by the costs of transporting the water.

Cost of Water to State Contractors

State Water Project water charges vary depending on the contractor's location in the project. As noted, MWD is the State Water Project contractor most likely to be interested in purchasing additional water. In the following analysis, SWP charges for water delivered along the East Branch Canal in the MWD service area are used because MWD demands are growing most rapidly in this area. The cost of water purchased from the Central Valley Project would be added to the SWP "Delta water charge." According to the rules governing the State Water Project, both the additional water and the additional costs would be divided among existing contractors on the basis of their water entitlements; the result is equivalent to charging each contractor $30 per acre-foot for the additional water (see the first entry in table 7-5). Those project contractors who use pumping energy also have to pay a charge based on the increased energy costs; this was $60 per acre-foot for MWD in 1986. Therefore, the total cost is $90 per acre-foot for SWP charges.[6]

This subtotal includes the amount needed to compensate Westlands for its CVP charges but not the amount paid to Westlands farmers to forgo use of the water. This amount is unknown, but table 7-3 indicates that it would be at least $55 per acre-foot. Using $95 per acre-foot as an illustrative value in table 7-5 for the payments made to Westlands farmers, equivalent to an increased net income of $40 per acre-foot (see table 7-3), the total delivered cost of the water would be $185 per acre-foot. This is cheaper than the 1986 cost paid by MWD for water from the State Water Project, which was about $232 per acre-foot (California Department of Water Resources, 1984, p. 262, table B-23).

---

[6] The other rate components shown in table 7-5 (capital; operation, maintenance, and replacement; and capital charges for power) would not increase because they are paid on the basis of full project entitlements rather than actual deliveries.

Table 7-5. Estimated Increases in State Water Project Charges for Central Valley Project Water Purchased from Westlands Water District, California

State Water Project rate components	Southern California[a]	
	Existing contractor (dollars/acre-foot)	New contractor[b] (dollars/acre-foot)
Increases in total charges at Delta[c]	30.00	14.89[d]
Capital	e	93.44
Operation, maintenance, and replacement	e	49.76
Power		
Capital	e	48.13
Variable	60.05[f]	62.96
Subtotal	90.05	269.18
Payments to forgo production—example	95.00	95.00
Total	185.05	364.18

Note: Values in this table are based on the purchase of 100,000 acre-feet at a net CVP cost of $30 per acre-foot per year (see table 7-1 in this chapter). A different quantity of water would yield a different average increase in the Delta water charge for a new contractor.

Source: Based on California Department of Water Resources, *Management of the California State Water Project,* Bulletin 132-84, September 1984.

[a]Southern California rates are for water delivered to the southern end of the East Branch Canal (reach 28-J).

[b]Southern California rates for new contractors are from *Management of the California State Water Project,* Bulletin 132-84, p. 265, table B-24, unless otherwise indicated.

[c]The increase in the Delta water rate would be $0.742 per acre-foot, levied on each contractor's *full* water entitlement (see note d). Under the operating rule in the State Water Project that newly available water is distributed in proportion to the entitlements, the increase in total Delta water charges associated with purchased CVP water is equivalent to charging the incremental cost ($30 per acre-foot) on just the additional acre-feet purchased.

[d]The Delta water rate charged to a new SWP contractor would consist of the current long-term rate of $14.15 per acre-foot (*Management of the California State Water Project,* Bulletin 132-84, p. 255, table B-20B) plus the increase in the Delta water rate resulting from the purchase of CVP water and assessable to all contractors ($0.74). The latter value is computed as follows (see *Management of the California State Water Project,* Bulletin 132-84, p. 254, table B-20A). Using an interest rate of 4.736 percent, the present worth of 100,000 acre-feet of deliveries at $30 per acre-foot annually for the years 1985–2035 is $57.363 million. Dividing by the present worth of water entitlements, 77.26 million acre-feet, yields $0.74 per acre-foot.

[e]These rate components would not increase because they are paid on the basis of full project entitlements rather than actual deliveries.

[f]Cumulative unit charge for canal reach 26-A from *Management of the California State Water Project,* Bulletin 132-84, p. 242, table B-17.

These costs can be compared to those that MWD would have to pay for water conserved by the Imperial Irrigation District. In 1985 MWD offered Imperial $100 per acre-foot for the first 100,000 acre-feet of conserved water and in fall 1988 reached an agreement with Imperial to make a series of payments with a total value somewhat greater than this amount. When pumping costs are added in, the delivered costs exceed $172 per acre-foot. Water from the Colorado River has a higher salinity content than water from the Central Valley Project, which makes CVP water more attractive (see Wahl and Davis, 1986). Additional water conserved in Imperial (beyond 100,000 acre-feet) could range up to $272 per acre-foot in total delivered cost to MWD. Therefore, it is possible that MWD would find a transaction with Westlands desirable.

The State Water Project has a provision by which noncontractors can purchase conveyance services for water if they pay rate components for all project features. Under this provision, a new contractor could presumably purchase water for the contractor's exclusive use, rather than having to divide it proportionally with other SWP contractors. This type of arrangement might be applicable, for example, to San Diego County as purchaser on its own, rather than as a member of MWD.[7] The last column of table 7-5 reveals that, under the existing rate structure, such an exclusive arrangement would carry the high price of $269 per acre-foot for use in southern California, even before compensation was paid to Westlands farmers for forgoing crop production. The total cost, $364 per acre-foot in the example (see table 7-5), would be considerably higher than the MWD rate to San Diego—$197 per acre-foot.[8] San Diego would have to consider whether this price was attractive given its relatively low priority for water from MWD under drought conditions (refer to chapter 10). An existing contractor, such as MWD, would probably not be allowed to elect to purchase CVP water from Westlands on a new contractor basis. In any event, one conclusion from table 7-5 is that purchase by an existing contractor would be considerably more attractive than purchase by a new contractor.

---

[7] The San Diego County Water Authority indicated its willingness to enter into agreements apart from MWD when it signed an option agreement with the Galloway Group in Colorado (this is discussed in more detail in chapter 10). Under the proposed agreement, the successful implementation of which is highly speculative, San Diego would pay up to 90 percent of MWD rates for 300,000–500,000 acre-feet of water.

[8] MWD's price to its contractors ($197 per acre-foot for noninterruptible untreated water for 1984) is considerably below the cost of water delivered to MWD from the State Water Project because MWD blends relatively inexpensive Colorado River water with water from the State Water Project and bases its price on average cost.

Conclusions About Long-Term Resource Use

According to a recent assessment (California Assembly Office of Research, 1985), the 42,000 acres currently served by the drainage collector system in Westlands contain 165 ownerships and 53 farming operations, eight of which exceed 1,280 acres. In 1984, 57 percent of the area was planted to cotton (and 8.8 percent to tomatoes, 4.9 percent to alfalfa seed, and 4.6 percent to wheat). Current Department of Agriculture policy is to discourage cotton production in order to benefit growers through higher prices, which indicates that there would be little or no national impact from removal of these lands from production.

Considering the entire San Joaquin Valley, the Bureau of Reclamation estimates that 169,000 acres currently need drainage, that 345,000 acres will need drainage by 2020, and that 493,000 acres will need drainage by 2095. The cost of centralized disposal facilities and the controversy surrounding them may further delay their construction, forcing increased reliance on recycling, local drainage ponds, wastewater treatment, and other local solutions. If, for the purposes of illustration, these options proved to be uneconomical on as much as one-third of the acreage needing drainage, and this acreage was taken out of production ten years after drainage was needed, then some 115,000 acres would be removed from production by the year 2030. This is an average decrease of 25,600 acres per decade over that period.

Even greater rates of decrease in irrigated acreage face the High Plains states overlying the Ogallala aquifer, where a widespread decline in groundwater tables is making continued groundwater pumping uneconomical and large acreages are returning to dryland farming. Irrigated acreage in the area overlying the aquifer is expected to decrease at the rate of 30,000 acres per decade in Colorado between 1977 and 2020, 34,000 acres per decade in New Mexico, 206,000 acres per decade in Kansas, and 240,000 acres per decade in Texas, even if water conservation measures are implemented (High Plains Associates, 1982). While these decreases are substantial, there is time to plan for the necessary transitions in local industries related to agriculture.

Some very difficult decisions face federal, state, and local governments in California regarding the long-term disposition of freshwater supplies, agricultural lands with problem drainage, and the drainage water itself. Reliance on the economic values of the resources and transactions between current users of the resources within the state might prove to be a useful way of making these decisions, consistent with efficient long-term resource use. For example, in the High Plains area, it was of value to the nation to bring irrigated acreage into production for several decades, even though irrigation on a permanent basis proved uneconomical in some areas. Similarly, in the San Joaquin Valley, even though some acreage has severe drainage problems, it may be appropriate to irrigate for as long as possible, consistent with appropriate environmental safeguards. On lands requiring drainage, the option to voluntarily sell water at market value would allow those individuals most directly affected by the drainage problems to participate in decisions affecting their economic future. Furthermore, it would allow both the land and water resources of the state to be used to their greatest economic advantage.

References

California Assembly Office of Research. 1985. *Agricultural Land Ownership and Operations in the 49,000 Acre Drainage Study Area of the Westlands Water District* (Sacramento, Calif.).

California Department of Water Resources. 1984. *Management of the State Water Project.* Bulletin 132-84 (Sacramento, Calif.).

California State Water Resources Control Board. 1985. "Cleanup and Abatement Order in the Matter of the Petition of Robert James Claus (Sacramento, Calif.)."

High Plains Associates. 1982. *Six-State High Plains–Ogallala Aquifer Regional Resources Study.* A report to the U.S. Department of Commerce and the High Plains Study Council. (Washington, D.C., U.S. Department of Commerce).

Knapp, Keith, Ariel Dinar, and John Letey. 1986. "On-Farm Management of Agricultural Drainage Water: An Economic Analysis," *Hilgardia* vol. 54, no. 4, pp. 1–31 (July).

Metropolitan Water District of Southern California. 1983. *Water Supply Available to Metropolitan Water District Prior to Year 2000.* Report No. 948 (Los Angeles, Calif.).

U.S. Department of the Interior. 1985. "Statement by Secretary of the Interior Don Hodel on the Closing of the Kesterson Reservoir" and attachments (March 28).

U.S. Department of the Interior, Bureau of Reclamation. 1956. *San Luis Unit, Central Valley Project, California, Feasibility Report* (Washington, D.C.).

———. 1962. *San Luis Unit, Central Valley Project, California, Definite Plan Report* (Washington, D.C.).

———. 1978. *Special Task Force Report on San Luis Unit, Central Valley Project, California* (Washington, D.C.).

———. 1981. *Acreage Limitation, Draft Environmental Impact Statement and Appendices* (Washington, D.C.).

———. 1984a. *CVP Ratesetting Policy Proposal* (April) (Sacramento, Calif.).

———. 1984b. *Post-Hearing Submission Before the California State Water*

Resources Control Board. File No. A-354 (December 17) (Sacramento, Calif.).

———. 1985a. *Submittal Before the State Water Resources Control Board.* File No. A-354 (January 8) (Sacramento, Calif.).

———. 1985b. *Post-Hearing Submittal Before the State Water Resources Control Board.* File No. A-354 (January 25) (Sacramento, Calif.).

Vaux, H. J., and Richard W. Howitt. 1984. "Managing Water Scarcity: An Evaluation of Interregional Transfers," *Water Resources Research* vol. 20, no. 7, pp. 785–792 (July).

Wahl, Richard W., and Robert K. Davis. 1986. "Satisfying Southern California's Thirst for Water: Efficient Alternatives," in Kenneth D. Frederick, ed., *Scarce Water and Institutional Change* (Washington, D.C., Resources for the Future).

8

Water Transfer Possibilities Involving the Central Arizona Project

The Central Arizona Project (CAP) was designed to carry water from the Colorado River more than 200 miles to the cities of Phoenix and Tucson, as well as to about seventy other municipalities; twenty irrigation districts; and twelve Indian tribes. The Secretary of the Interior, who has general jurisdiction over water allocation on the Colorado River, was given specific responsibility for determining the allocation of CAP water among these entities. Naturally, their water demands are likely to change over time; however, the CAP contracts with the Bureau of Reclamation are poorly suited to transferring allocated water among contractors. This chapter explores the problem and recommends changes in the present contract provisions that would facilitate such water transfers.

History of the Central Arizona Project

Of the 7.5 million acre-feet of Colorado River water allocated to the Lower Basin by the Colorado River Compact, the Boulder Canyon Act of 1928 allocated 2.8 million acre-feet to Arizona, 4.4 million acre-feet to California, and 0.3 million acre-feet to Nevada. However, Arizona had no practical means to divert much of its share except for some diversions to low-lying lands along the Colorado River in the Yuma

This chapter is based on a discussion paper entitled "The Possibility of Voluntary Market Transfer of Central Arizona Project Water," prepared by Robert W. Johnson of the Bureau of Reclamation for the Office of Policy Analysis, U.S. Department of the Interior (August 1986).

Valley before the river enters Mexico, and even in the early 1980s was utilizing only about 1.3 million acre-feet per year from the river. In 1968, the state was able to secure passage of the Colorado River Basin Project Act (82 Stat. 885; 43 U.S.C. 1501), authorizing construction of the Central Arizona Project to divert water from the Colorado River to the state's population centers surrounding the cities of Phoenix and Tucson in the south central part of the state. Arizona's success in securing authorization of the Central Arizona Project did not come cheaply, however; in the process, it had to give priority to Lower Basin diversions to California in times of low flow. This means that as demands on the river increase in the Upper Basin (Colorado, Wyoming, and Utah), Arizona will have to bear the brunt of reduced Lower Basin diversions in order to meet the U.S. obligation for water deliveries to Mexico.[1] The financial cost of the project is also high. As of 1986 about $1.6 billion had been committed to it, and the total cost is expected to run about $3.6 billion.

Water from the project will be delivered for agricultural use and municipal and industrial use in the three Arizona counties—Maricopa, Pinal, and Pima—where most of the state's population is located. It is intended to provide some relief from declining groundwater tables in this area. Prior to construction of the project, approximately 3.8 million acre-feet, or 60 percent, of the total annual water supply for this three-county area came from groundwater supplies. Pumping from these supplies exceeded the sustainable yields of the aquifers by an estimated 2.1 million acre-feet annually. The decline in recorded groundwater levels averaged as much as 300 feet in some of the agricultural areas of Maricopa and Pinal counties. In the Tucson area, which was entirely dependent on groundwater, the levels declined 75 feet to total pumping depths exceeding 300 feet. This led to significant increases in pumping costs. Land subsidence was an associated problem: one area of about 1,000 square miles in Pinal County subsided more than seven feet over the twenty-year period prior to authorization of the project, creating significant earth fissures along the periphery of the affected area (U.S. Department of the Interior, Bureau of Reclamation, 1979, p. 38; McCauley and Gum, 1975). Among the more significant impacts were cracks in highways crossing the periphery and damage to wells within the area of subsidence. Although the economic costs of subsidence were relatively minor in rural areas (McCauley and Gum, 1975), there was concern that subsidence in urban areas could have more costly consequences.

---

[1] For additional discussion of the "Law of the River" and the U.S. obligations to Mexico, see chapters 9 and 10.

The groundwater overdraft problem occurred concurrently with substantial growth in the Phoenix and Tucson metropolitan areas. The population in central Arizona increased from approximately 300,000 in 1940 to 1.4 million at the time of the project's authorization. While some increased demand for water in the Phoenix area was met by the conversion of land with surface irrigation water rights to urban use, much of the growth depended on increased use of groundwater. In recognition of this growing urban demand, the authorizing legislation for the Central Arizona Project specifically provided that non-Indian irrigation water from the project could be used only on those lands with a recent history of irrigation, not for expanding irrigated acreage. In addition, under the expectation that water supplies will need to be converted from agricultural use to municipal and industrial use, the CAP master repayment contract requires the reallocation of irrigation and municipal and industrial costs at seven-year intervals throughout the repayment period.

The principal components of the Central Arizona Project are shown in figure 8-1. Colorado River water is pumped approximately 1,200 feet up from Lake Havasu behind Parker Dam into the Granite Reef Aqueduct. This structure, with a capacity of 3,000 cubic feet per second (cfs), has, since 1985, carried water about 190 miles to an area just northeast of Phoenix near the confluence of the Salt and Verde rivers. The second section of the aqueduct, the Salt-Gila Aqueduct, has a capacity of 2,750 cfs and is designed to transport water an additional 58 miles to agricultural areas near the Gila River in Pinal County. It began providing deliveries in 1987. The final portion of the aqueduct, the Tucson Aqueduct, with a capacity of 1,240 cfs, will lift water an additional 1,700 feet and extend another 60 miles to Tucson and the San Xavier Indian Reservation south of Tucson. Initial deliveries through the Tucson Aqueduct are slated for 1991. The conveyance of water from the Colorado River is planned to operate in conjunction with existing and newly constructed reservoirs on tributaries of the Colorado arising within Arizona, such as the New Waddell Dam on the Agua Fria River and the Modified Roosevelt Dam on the Salt River (see figure 8-1). The Cliff Dam on the Verde River was originally planned to be part of the system, but in December 1987, Congress voted to delete it from the Central Arizona Project and authorized the Secretary of the Interior to purchase up to 30,000 acre-feet of water rights (and any associated lands) to provide an alternative water supply (Energy and Water Department Appropriation Act of 1988).

Pumping of water from the Colorado River and at other points along the CAP aqueduct system will require significant amounts of electri-

Figure 8-1. The Central Arizona Project. *Source:* Based on U.S. Department of the Interior, Bureau of Reclamation, *Project Data* (Washington, D.C., 1981), p. 302.

cal energy, which will be supplied by the Navajo Generating Station, a coal-fired power plant located in north central Arizona (see figure 8-1). The plant is jointly owned and operated by a consortium of southwestern utilities. The United States is entitled to 24.3 percent (346 megawatts) of the capacity and an equal percentage of the energy. Energy in excess of the pumping requirements will be sold commercially to aid in the repayment of project costs.

The left half of table 8-1 indicates the costs of various CAP facilities, including the aqueduct system, the U.S. share of the Navajo power plant, the power transmission facilities, and the Indian and non-Indian irrigation distribution systems. The right half identifies the functions to which CAP facility costs are assigned and, as a result,

Table 8-1. Costs of Facilities in the Central Arizona Project and Functions to Which Costs Are Assigned, as of June 1986
(millions of dollars)

Facility	Cost	Function	Cost	Percent of total
Aqueduct system	1,406	Irrigation	867	24
New Waddell Dam	487	Municipal and industrial water	717	20
Modified Roosevelt Dam	238	supply		
Cliff Dam	390[a]	Commercial power	353	10
Buttes Dam	142	Recreation	150	4
Conner Dam	82	New Mexico water	29	1
Navajo Generating Station	231	Flood control	337	9
Transmission lines	82	Safety of dams	223	6
Miscellaneous facilities	95	Miscellaneous	46	1
Indian distribution system	179	Indian	609	17
Non-Indian distribution system	275[b]	Non-Indian distribution system	275[b]	8
Total	3,606		3,606	100

Source: Records of Bureau of Reclamation, Department of the Interior, Washington, D.C.

[a] Modification of the costs associated with an alternative to Cliff Dam is awaiting completion of studies by the Bureau of Reclamation and selection of a specific alternative.

[b] Does not include 20 percent of costs locally funded.

how reimbursement will be made. Of the $867 million in total project cost allocated to the irrigation function, $53 million will be funded by local entities. The remaining $814 million will be federally funded and is reimbursable (interest-free). Approximately $60 million of the costs shown for the municipal and industrial function will be locally funded. The remaining $657 million will be federally funded and subsequently repaid with interest at the CAP repayment interest rate, established at 3.342 percent, considerably lower than recent costs of government borrowing. Approximately $132 million of the costs allocated to the commercial power function will be funded by local entities, and the remaining $221 million will be reimbursable at the project's 3.342 percent interest rate. One half of the separable costs of recreation ($50 million) are reimbursable with interest. The proportionate share of projected water supply costs assigned to water uses in the state of New Mexico ($29 million) is fully reimbursable with interest at the project's interest rate. Approximately $63 million of the costs allocated to flood control will be funded by local entities, and the remaining $274 million will be federally funded and non-reimbursable. In accordance with the Safety of Dams Act, 15 percent or approximately $34 million of the Safety of Dams costs will be funded by local entities, with the remaining costs being federally funded and nonreimbursable. In general, all reimbursable project costs not fully repaid through water sales will be reimbursed through commercial power sales from the Navajo Generating Station and from the Hoover and Parker-Davis power plants, as well as through ad valorem tax revenues collected in the three-county CAP service area. Costs for Indian facilities include $179 million for distribution systems and about $430 million for their share of the CAP water supply. Consistent with the Leavitt Act, the costs allocated to Indian water used for irrigation on tribal lands will be indefinitely deferred.[2]

The Water Allocation Process

The initial allocation of CAP water among the various water-using entities in Arizona was a long and controversial process extending over a period of six years—a process that involved balancing agricultural demands against urban demands and Indian water claims against non-Indian demands (a chronology is provided in table 8-2). This allocation involved more than seventy municipal and industrial entities, twenty irrigation districts, and twelve Indian tribes. The Central Arizona Water Conservation District (CAWCD) was created in 1971 by the Arizona legislature as an umbrella agency charged with coordinating with the Bureau of Reclamation and operating the completed project. The bureau executed a master repayment contract with CAWCD prior to the start of project construction in 1972 that was subsequently validated in Federal District Court in 1982. In turn, CAWCD is responsible for executing subcontracts with the various individual water entities (the Bureau of Reclamation will also be a party to the subcontracts).

Although the Secretary of the Interior has final authority for allocating CAP water, various secretaries have relied heavily on the state of Arizona to make recommendations on the allocation for non-Indian water users. Secretary of the Interior Stewart Udall asked for such assistance in January 1969, soon after the project was authorized, and the first allocation of CAP water to Indians was made by Secretary of the Interior Thomas Kleppe in October 1976 (U.S. Department of the Interior, Office of the Secretary, 1976). The Indian allocation provided 257,000 acre-feet of water annually to five tribes through the year 2005, after which time the tribes were to receive 20 percent of the project's agricultural water supplies or 10 percent of the total project municipal and industrial (M&I) water supplies, whichever was to their greater advantage (these quantities are listed in the second column of table 8-3).

[2] For an account of the April 1986 cost-sharing agreement regarding construction funding for Cliff Dam, New Waddell Dam, and Modified Roosevelt Dam, see Maxey and Starler (1987).

Table 8-2. Chronology of the Central Arizona Project Water Allocation Process, January 1969 to July 1986

January 1969	Secretary Stewart Udall asks the state of Arizona to assist in deciding on the distribution of CAP water.
July 1971	The Central Arizona Water Conservation District is formed to act as the central contracting authority.
October 1976	Secretary Thomas Kleppe makes the first allocation of CAP water to Indians.
June 1977	Arizona submits its recommended (non-Indian) municipal and industrial allocation.
August 1979	Arizona submits its recommended (non-Indian) agricultural allocation.
December 5, 1980	Secretary Cecil Andrus decides to increase the Indian allocation.
December 10, 1980	Andrus files a final *Federal Register* notice of allocation. Arizona files suit to block the increased Indian allocation and withdraws its previous recommended allocations.
December 11, 1980	Andrus signs contracts with eleven of the twelve Indian tribes receiving allocations based on his increased allocation of December 5, 1980.
December 17, 1980	U.S. District Court issues a preliminary injunction preventing the implementation of the Indian contracts.
December 1981	Parties agree that an environmental impact statement will be prepared on the allocation.
January 1982	Arizona submits a new recommended allocation.
March 1982	Secretary James Watt selects a "final" allocation, and a final environmental impact statement is issued.
March 1983	Watt files a *Federal Register* notice of the "final" allocation.
July 1986	Status: some allocations have been declined, and other subcontracts are pending. Allocation of the unallocated water will follow.

On the basis of this supposedly final allocation of water to Indians, the state of Arizona submitted its recommended (non-Indian) M&I allocations to the Secretary of the Interior in 1977 and its recommended (non-Indian) irrigation allocations in 1979 (see table 8-3).[3] The M&I allocation recommended by the state provided approximately 510,000 acre-feet annually for M&I use in target year 2034. This allocation was based on projected water needs throughout Arizona and included uses for power development, recreation, and municipal and domestic needs of cities. It was determined by multiplying projections of future population by estimated per capita water use,

---

[3] The Indian allocation can be used either for agricultural or for municipal and industrial purposes. However, to facilitate references to the allocations in the remainder of this chapter, the non-Indian irrigation allocation will be referred to simply as the irrigation allocation, and the non-Indian M&I allocation will be referred to as the M&I allocation.

Table 8-3. Quantities of Water in the Allocation of Central Arizona Project Water

Water entity	Secretary Kleppe's Indian allocation with 1977/1979 state recommendations[a]	Secretary Watt's allocation[b]	Current status of contracting[c]
	(acre-feet)	(acre-feet)	
Municipal and industrial			
Apache Junction	4,300	6,000	Signed
Avondale	2,000	4,099	Signed
Casa Grande	10,500	8,884	Signed
Chandler	2,600	3,668	Signed
Chaparral City Water Co.	3,900	6,978	Signed
Clearwater Co.	690	2,849	Signed
Coolidge	2,600	2,000	Signed
Consolidated Water Co.	12,600	3,932	Signed
Cottonwood Water Co.	2,500	1,789	Pending
Crescent Valley Water Co.	1,200	2,697	Pending
Desert Sage Water Co.	6,000	5,933	Pending
Eloy	2,700	2,171	Signed
Florence	1,000	1,641	Signed
Flowing Wells ID	0	4,354	Signed
Gilbert	0	7,235	Signed
Glendale	12,700	14,083	Signed
Globe	2,900	3,480	Pending
Goodyear	740	2,374	Signed
Green Valley Water Co.	2,600	1,900	Signed
Litchfield Park Service Co.	5,900	5,580	Signed

229

McMicken ID	2,500	9,513	Signed
Mesa	15,600	20,129	Signed
Miami-Claypool	2,400	1,829	Declined
Nogales	3,800	3,949	Pending
Palm Springs Water Co.	0	2,919	Signed
Paradise Valley Water Co.	3,400	3,231	Signed
Payson	2,700	4,995	Pending
Peoria	0	15,000	Signed
Phoenix	102,000	113,882	Signed
Prescott	3,500	7,127	Pending
Rio Rico	160	2,683	Pending
Scottsdale	17,600	19,702	Signed
Sun City	23,900	15,835	Signed
Tempe	3,400	4,315	Signed
Tucson	97,800	151,064	Signed
Turner Ranches	1,900	3,932	Signed
Other municipal and industrial entities	11,200	22,990	d
Power plant cooling	100,000	43,218	Pending
Mining	0	60,784	e
Recreation	2,456	989	Pending
State land/Phoenix Memorial Park	37,750	39,090	Pending
Total municipal and industrial	509,496	638,823	

(continued)

Table 8-3 *(continued)*

Water entity	Secretary Kleppe's Indian allocation with 1977/1979 state recommendations[a]	Secretary Watt's allocation[b]	Current status of contracting[c]
	(acre-feet)	(acre-feet)	
Indian tribes			
Ak Chin Indian Community	58,300	58,300	Signed
Camp Verde	0	1,200	Signed
Fort McDowell Indian Community	4,300	4,300	Signed
Gila River Indian Community	173,100	173,100	Pending
Papago-Chuichu	0	8,000	Signed
Papago-San Xavier	8,000	27,000	Signed
Papago-Schuk Toak	0	10,800	Signed
Pasqua Yaqui	0	500	Signed
Salt River Indian Community	13,300	13,300	Signed
San Carlos Apache	0	12,700	Signed
Tonto Apache	0	128	Signed
Yavapai	0	500	Signed
Total Indian	257,000	309,828	
	(percent)	(percent)	
Irrigation			
Arcadia Water Co.	0.14	0.13	Pending
Avra Valley Association	3.68	3.69	Declined
Central Arizona I.D.	19.50	18.01	Signed
Chandler Heights I.D.	0.22	0.28	Signed
Cotaro Morana I.D.	2.97	2.14	Pending
Farmers Investment Co.	1.79	1.39	Pending
Harquahala Valley I.D.	8.39	7.67	Signed
Hohokam I.D.	6.97	6.36	Signed

La Croix	0.05	0.04	Declined
Maricopa-Stanfield I.D.	22.10	20.48	Signed
Marley, Kemper Jr.	0.05	0.04	Declined
Marley, Kemper Sr.	0.01	0.00	n.a.
McMicken I.D.	8.65	7.28	Declined
Maricopa County Municipal Water C.D. No. 1	3.12	4.66	Pending
New Magma I.D.	4.88	4.34	Signed
Queen Creek I.D.	4.82	4.83	Signed
Rood, W. E.	0.05	0.04	Pending
Roosevelt I.D.	0.13	2.61	Declined
Roosevelt Water C.D.	5.64	5.98	Signed
Salt River Project	0.00	2.97	Declined
San Carlos I.D.	4.51	4.09	Pending
San Tan I.D.	0.09	0.77	Signed
Tonapah I.D.	2.24	1.98	Signed
U.S. Forest Service	0.00	0.22	Declined
Total irrigation	100.00	100.00	

Note: Abbreviations: C.D., conservation district; I.D., irrigation district; n.a. means information not available.

Sources: Secretary Kleppe's Indian allocation is from U.S. Department of the Interior, Office of the Secretary, "Central Arizona Project, Arizona; Allocation of Project Water for Indian Irrigation Use," 41 *Federal Register* 45,883–89 (October 18, 1976). Secretary Watt's allocation is from U.S. Department of the Interior, Office of the Secretary, "Central Arizona Project, Arizona; Water Allocations and Water Service Contracting: Record of Decision," 48 *Federal Register* 12,446–52 (March 24, 1983). Other data are from records as of June 1986 of Bureau of Reclamation, U.S. Department of the Interior.

[a]Municipal and industrial and irrigation allocations are for target year 2034. Indian allocation is through year 2005, after which Indians receive 20 percent of irrigation or 10 percent of municipal and industrial supplies, whichever is more advantageous.

[b]Incorporates quantities from Secretary Andrus's 1980 Indian allocation and quantities from Arizona's 1982 recommendations. Secretary Watt's allocation calls for 100,000 acre-feet of water for the Gila tribe to be obtained from treated effluent from Arizona cities. All allocations shown, including Indian allocation, are for target year 2034.

[c]As of July 1986.

[d]Includes thirty-five entities with allocations of less than 2,000 acre-feet. Of these, twenty-two have signed contracts, twelve are pending, and one has declined.

[e]Of nine mines with allocations, two have declined and seven are pending.

with deductions for renewable water supplies available to each entity. The projections assumed substantial reductions in per capita water use to be achieved through water conservation initiatives. The total amount of water recommended by the state was significantly less than the 2.1 million acre-feet requested by the M&I entities. The recommendation was limited by what the state thought was a reasonably reliable long-term supply from the project, which it assumed at the time to be approximately 550,000 acre-feet annually. During shortage conditions after the year 2005, Indian water deliveries would be 10 percent of the municipal and industrial deliveries, placing the total commitments for firm water deliveries only slightly above the 550,000-acre-foot quantity used by the state for planning purposes (table 8-4 indicates the priorities inherent in this and subsequent CAP water allocations).

The irrigation allocation recommended by Arizona did not assign specific quantities of water, but instead established pro rata shares of the remaining CAP supplies, based on the amount of historically irrigated acreage in each district during the ten years prior to the CAP authorization, with deductions for land irrigated with renewable water supplies and for expected future urbanization in each area (see table 8-3). The allocation also recognized the requirement of the authorizing legislation that CAP irrigation water be provided only to those lands with a recent history of irrigation. In essence, specifying the allocations on a pro rata basis delegated a lower priority to non-Indian irrigation water in recognition of the fact that the total CAP supplies from the Colorado River were subject to substantial variability (refer to table 8-4).

On December 5, 1980, Interior Secretary Cecil Andrus made final his decision to increase former Interior Secretary Thomas Kleppe's allocation of CAP water to Indians in terms of the number of tribes to receive water, the total quantity allocated to the tribes, and the priority for Indian use. Andrus increased the allocation from 257,000 acre-feet to approximately 310,000 acre-feet for use on twelve instead of five Indian reservations (refer to the third column of table 8-3). More important, he greatly increased the amount of first-priority water allocated to Indian use. Specifically, in shortage years, nearly all of the Indian allocation would share a first priority to water with municipal and industrial users. As indicated in table 8-4, a portion of Indian water used for agricultural purposes (estimated at 26,000 acre-feet) was excluded from this first priority. In total, however, Andrus increased the Indian allocation of first-priority water from approximately 51,000 acre-feet to an estimated 283,800 acre-feet (see table 8-4). Andrus justified this increased allocation by the need to

Table 8-4. Priorities in the Allocation of Central Arizona Project Water
(acre-feet)

Priority	Secretary Kleppe's Indian allocation (1976) with 1977/1979 state recommendations	Secretary Andrus's Indian allocation (1980) with 1977/1979 state recommendations	Arizona recommendation (1982)	Secretary Watt's allocation (1982) (final)
1 M&I	510,000	510,000	640,000	510,000[a]
Indian	51,000[b] (10% of M&I)	283,800	158,300[c]	258,300[d]
Total of priority 1	561,000	793,800	798,300[c]	768,300
2	Agriculture Indian: 206,000	Indian: 26,000	Indian: 51,500	Indian: 51,500
3		Agriculture	Agriculture	M&I: 130,000[d]
4				Agriculture

Note: M&I refers to non-Indian municipal and industrial use; agriculture refers to non-Indian agricultural use.

Sources: Andrus's Indian allocation is from U.S. Department of the Interior, Office of the Secretary, "Central Arizona Project; Allocations of Project Water to Indian Tribes," 45 *Federal Register* 81,265–73 (December 10, 1980). Sources for other data are the same as for table 8-3.

[a]Could be increased up to 130,000 acre-feet through exchange of treated effluent for Indian CAP water.

[b]Allocation after 2005 is 10 percent of M&I supplies or 20 percent of irrigation supplies, whichever is greater. The allocation based on M&I supplies is used here as more representative of a firm supply because of the higher priority accorded to M&I supplies.

[c]Excludes 100,000 acre-feet of water for the Gila tribe to be obtained from treated effluent from Arizona cities.

[d]Could be decreased up to 130,000 acre-feet through exchange of treated effluent for Indian CAP water.

provide an economic base for development of "tribal homelands" on each reservation. The result was to raise the total amount of first-priority water to 793,800 acre-feet, far above the 550,000 acre-feet of firm supply on which Arizona had based its allocations.

The state of Arizona objected strongly to Andrus's new allocation. On the day Andrus formally announced his allocation in the *Federal Register* (December 10, 1980; U.S. Department of the Interior, Office of the Secretary, 1980), the state and the Central Arizona Water Conservation District filed suit in U.S. District Court to prevent implementation of the new Indian allocation, and the state withdrew its own prior recommendations for the allocation of non-Indian water. The state felt that the new allocation would undermine the project's ability to deliver a relatively reliable supply of water for M&I use. Andrus responded the next day to Arizona's objection by further solidifying his Indian allocation. On December 11, 1980, one month before he was to leave office, Andrus signed contracts with eleven of the twelve tribes receiving allocations. On December 17 the court issued a preliminary injunction enjoining the secretary from implementing the Indian water service contracts or from negotiating or signing additional contracts for CAP water. The United States filed an appeal with the Ninth U.S. Circuit Court of Appeals to overturn the injunction. The injunction was voluntarily dismissed in December 1981 with the stipulation that an environmental impact statement be prepared to publicly disclose the impacts associated with the water allocation.

After discussions with Department of the Interior officials in the incoming Reagan administration, Arizona submitted new recommendations to Secretary James Watt in January 1982 (shown in the third column of table 8-3). The new recommendations for a non-Indian allocation included approximately 640,000 acre-feet of water for M&I use (up from the previous recommendation of 510,000 acre-feet), with the implication that the entire 640,000 acre-feet would be delivered on a priority equal to approximately 258,300 acre-feet of Indian water. Accordingly, the remaining 51,500 acre-feet of Indian water would be delivered on a second-priority basis with all remaining supplies going to non-Indian irrigation on a third-priority basis. The state also requested that at least 100,000 acre-feet of treated sewage effluent from Arizona cities be substituted for CAP water allocated to the Gila River Indian Community, the one Indian reservation that had not yet signed a CAP water service contract. The state believed that the exchange of effluent would provide a suitable water supply for irrigation on the Gila River reservation while freeing up a portion of the CAP Indian supplies for M&I use during times of shortage.[4] This would effectively lower the demands on the CAP to 158,300 acre-feet of first-priority water allocated to Indian tribes (see the third column of numbers in table 8-4). Even with this adjustment, the new state recommendations pushed the total allocation of first-priority water for target year 2034 still higher, to nearly 800,000 acre-feet, some 240,000 acre-feet more than the amount used in the state's first allocation. The state recognized that this would result in a somewhat lower reliability of M&I supplies, but new hydrologic evidence suggested that shortage conditions on the Colorado River would be less severe than earlier studies had indicated.

The state increased its M&I allocation partly because new population projections from the 1980 census were substantially larger than previous projections. The increase also reflected the state's desire to place a larger share of the non-Indian CAP water on a priority equal to that of Indian water. In addition, the state adjusted its allocations among M&I entities as well as among irrigation districts. For example, the allocations to Tucson and Phoenix were increased dramatically (see table 8-3).

In March 1982, with the environmental impact statement completed (U.S. Department of the Interior, Bureau of Reclamation, 1982), Secretary of the Interior James Watt selected a "final" allocation of CAP water that embraced most of the Andrus allocation to Indians, as well as most of the non-Indian recommendations submitted by the state in January 1982. The decision included an effluent exchange provision and the shortage criteria recommended by the state for the Gila River Indian Community, as well as an increased amount of water for M&I use. However, consistent with the prior Andrus allocation, Watt's final allocation placed only 510,000 acre-feet of the M&I water on a first priority with 258,300 acre-feet of highest priority Indian water (see the last column of table 8-4). The secretary believed this limitation on first-priority M&I water use was required by provisions in the Indian contracts already signed. As with Secretary Andrus's allocation, the remaining Indian entitlement (51,500 acre-feet) would retain a second priority. The additional 130,000 acre-feet of M&I water requested by Arizona would have a third priority, leaving non-Indian irrigation water with a fourth priority (see U.S. Department of the Interior, Office of the Secretary, 1983).

---

[4] The state recommendation also requested that the Gila River tribe be required to accept a 25 percent reduction in supplies during shortage conditions rather than the 10 percent reduction that was required of other tribes.

Additional Water Allocation

With the initial water allocation approved, the process of negotiating and executing water service subcontracts with entities receiving allocations of CAP water began (and was still in progress in 1986). The last column of table 8-3 shows the status of contracting as of July 1986 for each of the entities receiving final allocations. As of that date, ten irrigation entities had executed contracts for approximately 71 percent of the non-Indian irrigation supplies, and forty-nine M&I water-using entities had signed contracts for approximately 71 percent of the M&I supplies. Of the remaining entities receiving allocations, seven irrigation and four M&I entities formally declined to execute contracts.

Accordingly, it is expected that when the contracting process is complete, a portion of the water initially allocated will not be under contract. Both the state and the Department of the Interior recognized this possibility when the initial allocations were made and provided a mechanism for reallocating the uncontracted water. The state will accept applications for the uncontracted water from entities that want to increase their allocations or entities that did not receive an initial allocation. The state will then make recommendations to the secretary for the remaining uncontracted water. Assuming the secretary accepts the recommendations, the contracting process for the remaining CAP water supplies will then be complete.

Future Reallocation

Of course, the quantities of water in this initial allocation, when it is complete, may not reflect the ultimate water demands of the entities involved—accurate population and per-capita water use projections over periods extending to 2005 and 2034 are not possible. For example, the state projections and recommendations were adjusted considerably between the 1977/1979 period and 1982, as reflected in table 8-3. Thus, a reallocation, especially among urban entities, will be necessary at some time in the future. This could be done through an administrative allocation procedure similar to the initial CAP allocation. However, the existing signed contracts for CAP water might be an obstacle to the reallocation. These contracts, based on the CAP allocations, run for terms of fifty years, with the right of renewal. Furthermore, any future administrative reallocation process could well last as long as the initial process and be just as controversial. This suggests that another alternative is needed, one that can provide a greater degree of flexibility. Clearly, one possibility would be to allow water entities to trade their initial allocations of CAP water among themselves.

Other Water Transfers In Arizona

There are some precedents for water transfer in Arizona. In fact, the water in the Central Arizona Project itself is considered gradually transferable from irrigation use to municipal and industrial use. The Central Arizona Project was originally conceived of primarily as a source for irrigation water. The Bureau of Reclamation's 1947 planning report for the project contemplated that only about 12,000 acre-feet (or about 1 percent of CAP supplies) would be devoted to municipal and industrial use (see U.S. Department of the Interior, Bureau of Reclamation, 1979). However, there was a growing realization of the importance of the rapid urban growth in central Arizona. By 1962, during a revision of the CAP plan, about one-third of the project's water was assigned to municipal and industrial use. Partly as a result of these experiences in planning, the CAP authorizing legislation (P.L. 90-537) recognizes that water will be transferred from agricultural use to municipal and industrial use over the life of the project:

> Long-term contracts relating to irrigation water supply shall provide that water made available thereunder may be made available by the Secretary for municipal or industrial purposes if and to the extent that such water is not required by the contractor for irrigation purposes. (Section 304(b)(2))

The CAP master repayment contract and water service subcontracts provide specific language to allow up to 1 acre-foot per acre of irrigation water to be converted to M&I use as urbanization occurs.

A second class of water transfers in Arizona—transfer of non-CAP water—was motivated by Arizona's groundwater legislation. The Arizona legislature passed the Groundwater Management Act in 1980, which established three "active management areas" in central Arizona for the purpose of reducing or eventually eliminating groundwater overdraft.[5] Under the authority of the act, the state requires developers and municipalities in the active management areas to demonstrate that they have a firm 100-year water supply before urban or industrial expansion can occur. This has prompted a

[5] Secretary Andrus had threatened to withhold funding for the Central Arizona Project unless Arizona passed groundwater legislation to help ameliorate the problems of declining groundwater tables in some areas of Arizona.

number of cities to purchase additional water supplies from locations both within and outside the active management areas.

Purchases by Tucson

Over the years, Tucson has purchased water for urban purposes, but these transfers have not involved water supplied by the Central Arizona Project. Since 1971, the city has purchased more than 22,000 acres of farmland in the Avra Valley, an adjacent farming area. In 1987 Tucson pumped about 15 percent of its supplies from this area. Although it has used only a limited amount of available groundwater from its Avra Valley purchases in recent years and will receive additional surface water supplies when the Central Arizona Project begins delivering water to this area, the city considers the purchases of Avra Valley water critical to its future growth (*The Arizona Daily Star,* February 29, 1988, p. 9; Saliba and Bush, 1987, pp. 102–103).

Purchase by Scottsdale

In 1984 the city of Scottsdale purchased the Arizona Ranch and Metal Company (the Planet Ranch property), located in western Arizona near the Colorado River. The ranch has approximately 8,300 acres of land irrigated with an existing proven right to approximately 8,000 acre-feet of surface water from the Bill Williams River, a tributary of the Colorado (see figure 8-1). Under the provisions of Arizona water rights law, Scottsdale plans to increase that proven right to approximately 13,000 acre-feet by establishing a firm record of beneficial use over a five- to seven-year period. Then it plans to transfer use of the water from the ranch to the city in order to meet M&I water demands during those future years when low flows on the Colorado River force a reduction in diversions by the Central Arizona Project. This will necessitate the construction of pipeline and storage facilities to transport water from the ranch to the CAP's Granite Reef Aqueduct. Scottsdale will also need permission from the Bureau of Reclamation and CAWCD to utilize surplus capacity in the aqueduct. Since Scottsdale intends to use the water during periods of low flow on the river, the surplus conveyance capacity should be available.

The city paid $12.2 million for the ranch (Saliba and Bush, 1987, p. 105; also see *Arizona Republic,* March 19, 1984). Other significant costs will include (1) construction of the pipeline and storage facilities to transport water from the ranch to the Granite Reef Aqueduct, (2) operation and maintenance of the storage and transport facilities, (3) payment of a wheeling charge to the Bureau of Reclamation for the use of CAP facilities, and (4) absorption of projected losses of $1.5 million in the operation and management of the ranch during the period required to establish additional water rights. The total annual cost of the water is estimated to be somewhere between $250 and $300 per acre-foot.

Purchase by Mesa

In 1985 the city of Mesa purchased approximately 11,000 acres of farmland with the intent to eventually transfer the associated groundwater rights to itself. Mesa purchased the land within two CAP irrigation districts located between the Phoenix and Tucson metropolitan areas in a region where groundwater overdraft has been less severe and where groundwater supplies are expected to be available over the long term. Under the Arizona Groundwater Management Act, the lands have a grandfathered right to pump approximately 3 acre-feet of water per acre. The city plans to relocate the wells for the groundwater in an area near the Salt-Gila Aqueduct and then to pump groundwater into the aqueduct for delivery to the city of Tucson in exchange for equal amounts of Tucson's CAP water.

The city reportedly paid up to $3,000 per acre for the farmland (see Saliba and Bush, 1987, pp. 103–104). Other expenses that will be incurred include (1) the cost of relocating the wells, (2) payment in lieu of taxes to the local county government for the retired farmland, (3) payment of operation and maintenance costs for the well field, (4) payment of a share of local irrigation district costs for construction of CAP water distribution systems, and (5) payment of a wheeling charge for the use of CAP facilities. The total annual cost of purchasing and developing the water by the city of Mesa is estimated to be between $200 and $250 per acre-foot.

Business and community groups in the affected farming area expressed concern over the secondary economic impacts that would likely occur as a result of retiring the farmland from production. An alliance was formed to lobby the Arizona legislature to pass a law requiring measures to offset the impacts on the local nonfarm economy: mandatory payment in lieu of taxes and a requirement that at least 1 acre-foot per acre of the grandfathered water rights be permanently attached to the land for continued irrigation of low-water-use crops. The legislature did not enact the measure, but it did appropriate state funds for further study of the economic impacts of water transfers. Therefore, secondary economic impacts can be expected to be an issue of future debate in the Arizona legislature.

Purchases by the United States

Another recent market transfer of water in Arizona is the purchase by the United States of an entitlement to 50,000 acre-feet of water to be used in partially meeting the requirements of the Ak Chin Water Rights Settlement Act. The United States purchased Colorado River water entitlements from the districts of the Yuma Mesa Division of the federal Gila Project, located in southwestern Arizona along the Colorado River. The water will be diverted upstream at the CAP intake facilities for delivery through the CAP aqueduct to the Ak Chin Indian Reservation south of Phoenix (these deliveries will supplement the tribe's CAP allocation). Although this water was obtained by the legal authority of the Secretary of the Interior over Colorado River allocations, the United States agreed to cancel approximately $8.9 million in irrigation project debt owed by the districts of the Yuma Mesa Division and agreed to pay an additional $10.4 million for rehabilitating the districts' irrigation systems to improve their efficiency. This, together with charges for CAP operation and maintenance and the energy required to transport the water to the Ak Chin Reservation, is estimated to result in an annual average cost of approximately $80 per acre-foot.

Two other proposed settlements—with the Salt River Pima Maricopa Indian Community and the Fort McDowell Indian Community—may involve the purchase and transfer of water. Under these related proposals, about 36,000 acre-feet of Colorado River water would be purchased from the Wellton-Mohawk Irrigation District in Arizona. Of this amount, 12,000 acre-feet would be delivered through CAP facilities directly to the Fort McDowell Indian Reservation (this would be in addition to the tribe's CAP allocation shown in table 8-3). The remaining 24,000 acre-feet would be delivered to Phoenix through CAP facilities. There would be a corresponding reduction in deliveries of about 20,000 acre-feet to Phoenix from Arizona's internal Salt River Project, so that the Salt River Project could deliver 20,000 acre-feet of its water to the Salt River Pima Maricopa Indian Community (this amount would also supplement the tribe's CAP allocation shown in table 8-3).

Possibilities for Voluntary Transfers of CAP Water

Although several of the water sales involve the use of CAP conveyance facilities, none involves allocations of CAP water. Nevertheless, these transfers indicate that significant interest may develop in leasing or selling CAP water. There are several different categories of CAP water that could potentially be involved in voluntary market transfers, such as non-Indian agricultural supplies, non-Indian municipal and industrial supplies, and Indian supplies. A number of federal contractual and other legal provisions currently limit the transferability of the water in each category. But, as discussed in the next subsection, the Bureau of Reclamation appears to have the discretion to modify most, if not all, of these.

Transfers Between Agricultural Users and Between Municipal and Industrial Users

Probably the least complicated transactions that could occur with CAP water are transfers within either the agricultural category or the municipal and industrial category, rather than between the two. Charges for agricultural water must cover operation and maintenance costs and an appropriate share of capital. When the CAP was authorized in 1968, the total agricultural water rate was expected to be about $16 per acre-foot. By 1986 the rate had increased to $57 per acre-foot (a capital cost of $2 per acre-foot plus operation and maintenance costs of $55 per acre-foot). This price may make the water unattractive to some agricultural producers, even though they have already contracted for water (under the terms of the CAP contracts, irrigation districts pay only for the amount of water they use each year). For many irrigation districts, local groundwater may remain a less expensive alternative for a number of years (Bush and Martin, 1986). Although contractors could opt simply not to take delivery, they might also lease agricultural entitlements to other agricultural water users. Possible purchasers would include other producers with a competitive advantage or those who grow perennial or high-value crops—for example, owners of citrus groves or pecan trees. Additional CAP agricultural entitlements would be of at least limited value to some agricultural water users because entitlements are determined on a pro rata basis of available CAP agricultural supplies. Of course, purchasers of CAP agricultural supplies would need to recognize that the purchased supplies would also be subject to reductions during years of low flow. As a result, agricultural CAP water would be expected to carry the lowest market price of all the available categories of CAP water.

Within the municipal and industrial category, the growth of urban demands for CAP water may differ from the projections made before the initial CAP allocations. If so, cities may find it advantageous to trade their existing CAP water supplies among themselves in order to balance demands with available supplies. Such transfers of existing contractual entitlements could be made either on a short-term or long-term basis. The charges for CAP supplies by CAWCD to M&I water entities was $55 per acre-foot for operation and maintenance charges in 1986, plus $5 per acre-foot for capital. The capital charge will increase on a preestablished schedule to $40 per acre-foot by

2024. Unlike the charges for CAP agricultural water, M&I entities must pay the capital charges for their water, whether or not they take delivery. Therefore, cities not needing all of the water they contracted for may be willing to sell or lease water to other cities with greater water demands. Those cities that need to purchase additional supplies would find the total cost of CAP supplies—$60 per acre-foot in 1986 and $95 per acre-foot in 2024—to be considerably less than the prices being paid for privately developed water ($200–$300 per acre-foot). Of course, water from the federal project would be subject to mandatory reductions in times of low flow on the Colorado River because of California's priority among Lower Colorado River Basin water users.

At present, there are certain federal contractual provisions relating to transfers of CAP irrigation or M&I water that would severely limit such transactions. Notable among these are restrictions on the increased income that could be realized by any water entity leasing or selling water. Section 4.3(e) of the CAP water service subcontract with each agricultural water district and M&I entity states that

> Project water scheduled for delivery in any year under this subcontract may be used by the subcontractor or resold or exchanged by the subcontractor pursuant to appropriate agreements approved by the contracting officer [the Bureau of Reclamation] and the contractor [CAWCD]. If said water is resold or exchanged by the subcontractor for an amount in excess of that which the subcontractor is obligated to pay under this subcontract, the excess amount shall be paid forthwith by the subcontractor to the contractor for application against the contractor's repayment obligation to the United States.

While this provision clearly acknowledges that transfers may occur, it severely restricts the financial attractiveness to the selling party. No additional income can be immediately forthcoming from the transaction to be used for, say, financing district conveyance systems, installing conservation measures, reducing the district's charges to its members, or making payments to farmers to retire marginal lands from production. Of course, there would be a limited financial incentive in that additional income from the transfer would accelerate payout of the subcontractor's obligation and therefore move nearer the date after which the subcontractor would no longer have to assess CAP capital charges against its members. Furthermore, if the transfer were of sufficiently long duration, there could be increased income to the selling or leasing party *after* the federal obligation was repaid. But in both cases, there is a significantly reduced financial incentive for transfers. It might be technically possible for a water purchaser to comply with the contract language quoted above by making direct payments to members of an irrigation district (for on-farm improvements or for retiring lands from production) while leaving the payments between the water district and CAWCD unchanged. However, this is a somewhat clumsy approach for providing an economic incentive to water users. Furthermore, because direct payments to farmers might require the district's consent, such transactions might be subject to legal challenge on the basis that additional revenues should go to the United States.

Therefore, in order to facilitate transfers, it would be more suitable for the Bureau of Reclamation and CAWCD to indicate their willingness to amend the language in the CAP subcontracts to allow increased income to subcontractors that sell or lease water. For instance, all of the increased income from a transfer could be allowed to accrue to the entity selling the water, provided that payments to CAWCD and the United States were maintained at their originally scheduled rate of payout and that CAWCD and the United States were reimbursed for any added costs of implementing the exchange. Competition among the CAP sellers in each category (agricultural and M&I) would be likely to eliminate any large economic gains from the transactions.

A second contractual provision contained in the master repayment contract with CAWCD and echoed in each subcontract restricts the service area where water can be transferred:

> Neither the Contractor (CAWCD) nor any subcontractor shall sell or otherwise dispose of or permit the sale or other disposition of any project water, including return flows, for use outside the Contractor's service area.

Although this clause limits transfers of water within the three-county service area of the CAP, this would not be a serious restriction in most cases since the greatest demands for water would also be located there. If there were a transfer possibility in Arizona outside of these three counties, then the bureau could possibly amend this contractual provision provided other CAP water users agreed. Section 301(a) of the Colorado River Basin Storage Act contains only a more general restriction on the service area for water deliveries of the Central Arizona Project: "the water deficient areas of Arizona and western New Mexico through direct diversion or exchange of water."

Transfers Between Agricultural Users and Municipal and Industrial Users

Another category of transfers that might arise if the bureau were willing to amend its contracts is transfers from irrigation to municipal and industrial use. It would generally be expected that cities, as they grow, would be able to sufficiently compensate agricultural users to make water sales attractive, such as in the recent purchases of non-CAP water already discussed. Agricultural contractors might be willing to sell some of their agricultural entitlements for two reasons: (1) the expected CAP agricultural water rates have increased significantly since the project was authorized, and (2) CAP water is often more expensive than groundwater. The CAP authorizing legislation recognized that agricultural water use in the Central Arizona Project would eventually give way to increased urban use. However, urban purchasers of agricultural water would likely be willing to pay a reduced amount for CAP agricultural water because of the possibly lower priority attached to CAP water converted from irrigation use. Purchases of water from other municipal and industrial entities would be more valuable in this regard.

The water service subcontracts with each irrigation entity clearly recognize that water could be transferred from agricultural to urban uses, as evidenced by the following provisions (Section 4.3(i)):

> Subject to the prior approval of the Contracting Officer and the Contractor, which approval shall not be unreasonably withheld, agricultural water made available hereunder for eligible lands may be converted to M&I purposes if and to the extent that such water is no longer required by the subcontractor for irrigation purposes and shall be converted in all cases where eligible lands receiving project agricultural water have been converted to M&I use; provided that the water converted from irrigation to M&I purposes as a result of conversion of eligible lands to M&I uses shall be used only for M&I purposes within the service area of the entity responsible for serving the converted lands. Such conversion of water use for eligible lands shall be at the rate of one acre-foot per acre minus the average annual surface water supply for said acre which was available [from sources other than the CAP] for use during the 1958–1976 period as determined by the Contracting Officer. Conversion of water from agricultural to M&I purposes shall take effect only upon execution or amendment of an appropriate subcontract among the United States, the Contractor, and the M&I user.

This clause appears to consider two types of transfers of irrigation water to M&I use: (1) changes of use resulting from land conversions and (2) other transfers. Under the first category, up to 1 acre-foot per acre of water would be converted to domestic uses when land was converted to urban use. This type of transfer requires that the water be reserved for use in the same service area. Other water transfers appear to be allowable under the provision that water can be transferred if it "is no longer required by the subcontractor for irrigation purposes." It appears that transfers in this category may also be limited by the contract language to 1 acre-foot per acre of eligible land, but the area of use may not be limited to the service area of the irrigation subcontractor.

Of course, M&I purchasers of CAP irrigation supplies would have to pay rates that reflected the interest charges in Reclamation law, rather than agricultural rates. The capital charges for M&I water were $3 per acre-foot higher than those for agricultural water in 1986, or $5 per acre-foot. By 2024, they will be $40 per acre-foot. Still, the total charges for M&I water—$60 per acre-foot in 1986 and $95 per acre-foot in 2024—are considerably less than the costs of alternative supplies, such as the purchases by Scottsdale and Mesa that were discussed earlier in this chapter. The CAP water service subcontracts place an additional requirement on agricultural to urban transfers, namely, "payment of an amount equal to the acre-foot charges previously paid by other subcontractors . . . plus interest." In other words, a lump sum payment is required. Clauses of this type are not uncommon in large municipal water supply districts and are designed to encourage all water-using entities with potential future demands to participate in the initial allocation of the financial burden of the project. Otherwise, a city could understate its expected demands and then later purchase additional water at a lower total cost.

In addition to the restrictions already discussed, there are certain other provisions embodied in the CAP water allocations and contracts that in their current form would complicate transfers from agricultural to urban use. For example, even though agricultural use of CAP water is expected to average about 2 acre-feet per acre, the contract language cited above may place a limit of 1 acre-foot per acre on transfers from agricultural to municipal and industrial use.[6] In effect, the M&I purchaser of water in a market transaction would have to value the water about twice as much as the agricultural seller just on this basis alone (the higher federal charge for M&I water and the possibly lower priority for converted agricultural water would also affect the price paid).

The CAP water allocation also stipulates that subsequent increases in M&I use (such as through land conversion) not increase the total amount of first-priority water shared with Indian tribes:

---

[6] The CAP contract calls for deducting the previous agricultural surface water supplies from other sources, which would be zero in most cases. The remaining agricultural water not transferred (approximately 1 acre-foot per acre) would presumably reenter the pool of available CAP irrigation water and be reallocated to all agricultural users based on the percentages established in the CAP allocation (shown in table 8-1).

For the limited purpose of establishing the relative Indian and non-Indian M&I percentages of the shared priority, non-Indian M&I allocations beyond 510,000 acre-feet, including conversions from agriculture to M&I, will not be permitted to be included in the calculations of the non-Indian portion of the shared priority. (This is not to say that future Secretarial allocations for M&I use, or agricultural conversions to M&I use might not take the total non-Indian allocations to a figure greater than 510,000, but that 510,000 acre-feet is an absolute limit when calculating the shared priority between Indian and M&I use in times of shortage.) (U.S. Department of the Interior, Office of the Secretary, 1980)[7]

In contrast, the CAP subcontracts (all written after 1982) state that project water converted from agricultural to M&I use shall be delivered with the same priority as other project M&I water. This provision appears to conflict with the allocation language cited above, although it is possible to read the two provisions in a consistent manner, illustrated as follows. Under the current allocation of water, 640,000 acre-feet are assigned to M&I use. Of this amount 510,000 acre-feet have first priority and the remaining 130,000 acre-feet are assigned third priority (see table 8-4). Therefore, an entity with an existing M&I allocation of 100,000 acre-feet has approximately 80,000 acre-feet of first-priority M&I water (that is, 510/640 × 100,000 acre-feet) and 20,000 acre-feet of third-priority M&I water. If a voluntary transfer of 50,000 acre-feet of irrigation water to M&I use were to occur, there would then be a total of 690,000 acre-feet of project water with an M&I priority. Therefore, the same M&I entity with 100,000 acre-feet of water would now have only 74,000 acre-feet of first-priority water (510/690 × 100,000 acre-feet)—a reduction of 6,000 acre-feet. This 6,000 acre-feet would be, in effect, shifted to third-priority water, which would increase in quantity to 26,000 acre-feet. Therefore, deliveries to each M&I entity in shortage years would be reduced. In other words, under this interpretation of the provision in the subcontracts, a transfer from agricultural to municipal and industrial use would dilute the priority of the M&I water supplies of all other M&I entities. Because of this anomaly, it could be expected that urban entities generally would oppose any one city's purchase of additional CAP water from irrigation users.

The Bureau of Reclamation, in conjunction with the CAP water contractors, should consider reconstructing its contracts such that this dilution does not occur. For example, water transferred from agricultural to municipal and industrial use could be placed in the

---

[7] Since this portion of the notice is not inconsistent with subsequent *Federal Register* notices, this provision remains in effect.

lower priority for M&I water (the third-priority category in the last column in table 8-4), leaving the allocations in the first priority untouched. This interpretation would be consistent with the allocation decisions as published in the *Federal Register*. Of course, such an interpretation would still mean some dilution of the priorities of other municipalities' water in this lower priority class, but that would be less serious than a dilution of their first-priority water. Under this interpretation, cities desiring an increased allocation of first-priority water would have to purchase some portion of the first-priority water allocated to other municipalities.

Another possibility for restructuring the allocation of water converted from irrigation use to municipal and industrial use would be to place the converted water in a new category, lower in priority than all other M&I water, but ahead of agricultural use. Alternatively, such purchases could retain their agricultural priority, which is subject to proportional reduction in times of shortage. In either case, cities wanting additional quantities of first-priority water would have to purchase it from other cities, with the total pool of first-priority water remaining unchanged.

This discussion suggests amendments that could be made to Bureau of Reclamation contracts with water districts that would facilitate exchanges of water to municipal and industrial use. The most important of these are (1) removal of the current restrictions on profitability and (2) establishment of a clear system for transfers that does not dilute the priorities of municipal and industrial water users who are not direct parties to the exchange.

Indian Water

Indian communities might consider temporarily leasing a portion of their water allocations to non-Indian contractors or to other Indian tribes. Under the final CAP allocations, 258,300 acre-feet of water are allocated among Indian tribes under the first priority, of which 130,000 acre-feet can be made available to cities in exchange for treated sewage effluent. The 258,300-acre-foot quantity represents 34 percent of the first-priority allocation. Because of its high priority and because some of this water may not be fully utilized by the tribes for some time, leasing may be attractive. One fundamental restriction on transfer of Indian water should be noted: Indian water cannot be leased or sold on a permanent basis. The Indian Non-Intercourse Act specifically prohibits the sale or exchange of Indian property without specific authority from Congress. However, this would not necessarily prevent long-term leasing arrangements in which the Indians retained their contractual entitlements.

Leasing of tribal allocations to non-Indian water entities would also require higher federal rates to be charged for the water. The capital costs associated with Indian allocations are normally postponed indefinitely under the Leavitt Act. However, if Indian water were leased to non-Indian contractors, capital costs would be payable to the United States based on the irrigation or municipal end use of the water.

Contracts between each tribe and the secretary provide that the tribes not sell or permit the sale or other disposition of any project water for use outside the tribes' reservations except to change, with the secretary's approval, the times and places of delivery. The contracts with each Indian tribe specify that CAP water may be disposed of when and if the water is credited against the finally determined water rights of each tribe and provided that the determination of those rights allows for such disposition. This language appears to accommodate two possibilities: (1) CAP Indian water that has not been credited as part of a tribe's final determination of water rights can, with the concurrence of the Secretary, be leased on a short-term or long-term basis and delivered to points of use outside the reservation, and (2) CAP Indian water that has been credited toward a tribe's final determination of water rights can be leased or sold, provided those rights so allow.

Final water rights for two of the tribes with allocations of CAP water have been determined through water rights settlement acts. The Ak Chin Settlement Act (P.L. 95-328) does not provide authority for water transfers. In contrast, the Papago Indian Reservation has full authority under Title III of P.L. 97-293 to market its allocated share of CAP water within the local groundwater basin. Other tribes in Arizona are in the process of negotiating the settlement of water rights claims and may or may not gain the authority to dispose of their water through market transfers. For example, the proposed settlement of the claims of the Salt River Pima Maricopa Indian Community may allow the tribe to market its CAP entitlement.

State Review of Transfer Requests

In most western states, water rights are gained by applying to the state and by putting the water to beneficial use. However, because the Secretary of the Interior has control over the allocations of water delivered by the Central Arizona Project, there are no state permits involved and hence no direct vehicle for state control. However, voluntary transfers of CAP water would require approval by CAWCD, as well as the Bureau of Reclamation, since both are party to the CAP contracts with irrigation districts and municipal and industrial entities. Because Secretaries of the Interior have routinely relied on the advice of the Arizona Department of Water Resources for allocating CAP water, it is likely that the department would also seek the advice of the state in approving transfers.

The Arizona Groundwater Management Act of 1980 may be another vehicle for state approval of at least some transfer requests. Among its goals is the reduction or elimination of groundwater overdrafts in the three active management areas in central Arizona. If a large amount of CAP water were transferred from one of these areas, the result could be increased reliance on groundwater in that area. This, in turn, could be seen as frustrating the goals established by the act, thereby leading to a rationale for state intervention in transfer approvals.

Conclusions and Recommendations

The state of Arizona, in conjunction with the Secretary of the Interior, went through a long and arduous process, spanning some six years, to decide on allocations of water from the Central Arizona Project among more than seventy M&I entities, twenty irrigation districts, and twelve Indian tribes. The allocations were based partly on population projections and projections of per capita use. Of course, it is likely that, over time, water demands will vary from those projected because of different patterns of population growth, industrial uses of water concentrated in unforeseen locations, or other factors. Indeed, projections of future use by municipal and industrial entities varied considerably between the state's 1977/1979 recommendations and its 1982 recommendations. Therefore, another round of allocations will almost certainly be necessary at some future date. There is an alternative, however, to administrative reallocation that would provide added flexibility for future water use—namely, market transfers of water between CAP water contractors based on their current contractual entitlements.

The CAP project authorization, the allocation published in the *Federal Register,* and the original master contract with the Central Arizona Water Conservancy District clearly envision water transfers from irrigation use to municipal and industrial use, as do the subcontracts with the member water districts. But there are a number of provisions embodied in these contracts and subcontracts that would hinder the functioning of otherwise viable market exchanges: (1) no increased income or profit is allowed on the transfer above the existing CAP contract rates, (2) transfers from agricultural use to urban use may be limited to 1 acre-foot per acre even though the past application of CAP agricultural water exceeds this amount, and (3) transfers to urban use may dilute the priority of M&I water users, including those who were not direct parties to the exchange.

If the water-using entities, in conjunction with the Central Arizona Water Conservancy District, the Bureau of Reclamation, and the Arizona Department of Water Resources, were to decide that the ability to transfer CAP water was desirable, each of these contractual provisions could be restructured to facilitate transfers: (1) the Bureau and CAWCD could allow retention of increased income to the selling district provided project costs were paid; (2) transfer between agricultural use and M&I use could be made on an acre-foot-per-acre basis, and (3) transfers to M&I use from irrigation use could be structured so as to leave the existing priorities for water intact (that is, the transferred water could either be placed in a priority below other M&I water or it could carry its original agricultural priority). Municipal and industrial entities desiring more first-priority water would have to purchase it from other M&I entities. Transfers would also need to be structured so as to comply with existing Arizona groundwater legislation.

Market transfers of non-CAP water are already taking place in Arizona, so it is not unreasonable to believe that transfers of some categories of federal project water would be seen as advantageous as well. Given the length of advance time needed for water planning, it probably is not too soon to begin thinking about how a future market for CAP water might be structured to the mutual benefit of the water-using entities.

References

Bush, David B., and William E. Martin. 1986. *Potential Costs and Benefits to Arizona Agriculture of the Central Arizona Project,* Technical Bulletin 254, Arizona Agricultural Experiment Station (Tucson, University of Arizona).

Maxey, Kenneth G., and Norman H. Starler. 1987. "Cost Sharing in Transition: The Case of Plan 6, Central Arizona Project," *Water Resources Bulletin* vol. 23, no. 5, pp. 749–759 (October).

McCauley, Charles, and Russell Gum. 1975. "Land Subsidence: An Economic Analysis," *Water Resources Bulletin* vol. 11, no. 1, pp. 148–154 (February).

Saliba, Bonnie C., and David B. Bush. 1987. *Water Markets in Theory and Practice: Market Transfers, Water Values, and Public Policy* (Boulder, Colo., Westview Press).

U.S. Department of the Interior, Bureau of Reclamation. 1979. *Final Envi-*

ronmental Statement, Salt-Gila Aqueduct, Central Arizona Project (Washington, D.C.).

———. 1982. *Final Environmental Impact Statement, Water Allocations and Water Service Contracting, Central Arizona Project* (Washington, D.C., March 19).

U.S. Department of the Interior, Office of the Secretary. 1976. "Central Arizona Project, Ariz.; Allocation of Project Water for Indian Irrigation Use," 41 *Federal Register* 45883–89 (October 18).

———. 1980. "Central Arizona Project; Allocations of Project Water to Indian Tribes," 45 *Federal Register* 81265–73 (December 10).

———. 1983. "Central Arizona Project, Arizona; Water Allocations and Water Service Contracting: Record of Decision," 48 *Federal Register* 12446–52 (March 24).

9

Quality of Water in the Colorado River and the Yuma Desalting Plant

The federal government's activities to maintain deliveries to Mexico of Colorado River water of adequate quantity and quality have been haphazard and costly. Even the need for salinity control measures, such as the Yuma desalting plant, is a result of the government's lack of foresight about the effects that major storage works on the Colorado River and diversions of water from the river would have on the flows left to enter Mexico. As discussed in this chapter, purchase or lease of water from willing sellers would be one way to reduce the cost of operating the desalting plant.

The Colorado River Compact of 1922 recognized that the United States would have some responsibility for delivering water to Mexico, but left the quantity (and quality) unspecified. It did state, however, that in the case of a shortage, the Upper Basin and Lower Basin states would share the responsibility for making up the amount. The lack of a quantified international obligation left the Mexicali Valley in Mexico vulnerable to the depletions caused by water users in the United States (see figure 9-1). Frustration over this condition eventually led to the signing of the Mexican Water Treaty of 1944, which allotted to Mexico an average of 1.5 million acre-feet of water annually. The treaty allowed some flexibility for the variable flow in the river since it specified that the 1.5-million-acre-foot amount had only to be met on average over a ten-year period; in other words, 15 million acre-feet of water had to be delivered every ten years. The treaty did not specify any quality parameters, although Mexico expected to receive water of a quality similar to that provided to Lower Basin users in the United States, such as the Imperial Irrigation District. Two events, however,

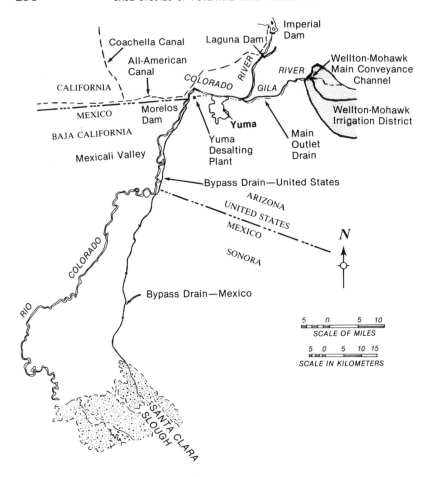

Figure 9-1. Yuma desalting plant and related facilities. *Source:* Adapted from U.S. Department of the Interior, Bureau of Reclamation, *Project Data* (Washington, D.C., 1981), p. 314.

dramatically changed the quality of water entering Mexico: (1) the development of the Wellton-Mohawk Irrigation District and the dumping of its drainage waters into the Colorado River and (2) the filling of Lake Powell behind Glen Canyon Dam.

The Wellton-Mohawk Irrigation District lies along the Gila River in Arizona, to the east of the city of Yuma (see figure 9-1). As one commentator put it (Fradkin, 1981, p. 302), it is

> difficult to imagine an area with a worse record of irrigated agriculture. That crops are still raised on some 65,000 irrigated acres along the Gila

River is a tribute to the persistence of the Reclamation ethos through one disaster after another.

One attempted remedy has succeeded another from the inception of irrigation in the area. Beginning in the 1880s, farmers diverted water for irrigation from the Gila River, but when upstream diversions in Arizona drastically reduced available flows, farmers in the Wellton-Mohawk Valley turned to wells as their source of water. By 1931, about 11,000 acres were irrigated by underground supplies (Fradkin, 1981, p. 302), but wells began to either go dry or turn up water with salinity levels of 6,000 parts per million (ppm) of total dissolved solids (salinity levels above 1,000 ppm begin to have an increasingly detrimental impact on agricultural production). Congress rescued the area by authorizing the Gila Project in 1947 (61 Stat. 195) to divert surface water from the Colorado River, with the first water arriving in 1952. However, surface water irrigation created another problem: the water table soon rose, bringing saline water into contact with the root zone of plants and thereby reducing or eliminating productivity. This prompted the Bureau of Reclamation to drill a number of wells in the district to lower the water table. In addition, saline drainage water was dumped back into the Colorado River by a drainage channel that became operational in 1961. As a result, the salinity levels of water entering Mexico rose dramatically from about 800 ppm to approximately 1,500 ppm, with levels ranging as high as 2,700 ppm in November and December 1961. This increase in the river's salinity was abetted by another factor: the reduced quantity of water flowing into the lower Colorado River because Lake Powell was being filled.

Farmers in the Mexicali Valley, outraged at the increased salinity of the water, marched on the U.S. consulate in Mexicali.[1] President of Mexico Lopez Mateos stated that salinity control was the greatest problem confronting U.S.-Mexican relations. President John Kennedy, in his desire to forge stronger ties with Latin American countries, pledged that the United States would seek a "permanent and effective solution to the salinity problem." Negotiations led to the signing of Minute 218 of the International Boundary and Water Commission in 1965. Under Minute 218, the United States was to construct a channel alongside the Colorado River to carry the Wellton-Mohawk drainage water to a point below Mexico's last diversion point on the Colorado River (at Morelos Dam), but the bypassed

[1] For more detailed histories of the conflicts with Mexico caused by deteriorating water quality in the lower Colorado River, see Fradkin (1981, pp. 300–318) and Hundley (1966, pp. 172–186).

drainage water would still count toward Mexico's 1.5-million-acre-foot allocation. Although the situation for farmers in the Mexicali Valley improved considerably as a result of the bypass, low flows on the Colorado River continued to mean that poor-quality water was being delivered to Mexico.

President Luis Echeverría took office in Mexico in December 1970 and, partly to enhance his own stature in Mexico and among third-world countries, renewed requests to the United States to improve salinity conditions (Fradkin, 1981, pp. 305–306). He also renewed Mexican threats to take the issue to the World Court. He found a sympathetic ear in Henry Kissinger, President Richard Nixon's national security adviser, who "liked Mexico" and "was a close friend of Emilio O. Ratasa, President Echeverría's foreign minister" (Fradkin, 1981, p. 306). Nixon directed the Department of the Interior and the Department of State to reach a new settlement. He appointed Herbert Brownell, Jr., to chair an interagency task force to manage the negotiations with Mexico. During the negotiations, Mexico demanded that its farmers receive water of the same quality as water provided to farmers in the Imperial Valley. Agreement was reached in June 1973 (formalized as Minute 242 of the International Boundary and Water Commission) that the water received by Mexico, while not equal in quality to that received by farmers in Imperial, would be worse by no more than 115 ppm, plus or minus 30 ppm, compared with the water arriving at Imperial Dam. This compromise allowed for the fact that, even excluding the drainage flows from the Wellton-Mohawk Irrigation District, some of the natural flows entering the Colorado River below Imperial Dam were highly saline. How to achieve the salinity levels was left up to the United States.

Congress acted quickly to enable the United States to comply with Minute 242. Title I of the Colorado River Basin Salinity Control Act of 1974 (CRBSCA) (88 Stat. 266; 43 U.S.C. 1571), "Programs Downstream from Imperial Dam," authorized several specific measures. Principal among these was the Yuma desalting plant, designed to raise the quality of drainage water from the Wellton-Mohawk Irrigation District to a level sufficient for it to be returned to the Colorado River. To reduce the load on the desalting plant, the act also authorized the Secretary of the Interior to reduce the irrigable acreage in the district by 10,000 acres, from the 75,000 acres originally authorized in 1947, either by purchase or through eminent domain. Another measure designed to reduce the salt load on the plant was improvement of the irrigation efficiency of the district. The act also authorized the extension of the bypass drainage channel to keep the highly saline wastewater from the desalting plant out of the Colorado River during its entire reach to the ocean. The bypass canal today extends all the way to the Santa Clara Slough, above the Gulf of California (refer to figure 9-1). In addition, the act authorized a number of other measures less directly connected with the desalting plant. Among these were construction of a well-field just north of the Mexican border to supplement the flow of the Colorado River by up to 160,000 acre-feet per year and the lining of the first 49 miles of the Coachella Canal in California (extending north to the Coachella Irrigation District from the All-American Canal) in order to reduce diversions from the Colorado River.

Several years earlier, in the debates over the Central Arizona Project (authorized by the Colorado River Basin Project Act of 1968), Representative Morris Udall of Arizona sought to ensure sufficient supplies for the Lower Basin states by making the provision of water to Mexico a "national obligation." It was Udall's argument that the federal government, because it negotiated the treaty with Mexico, should provide the necessary water supplies, rather than the basin states. Years later, the basin states again pressed the "national obligation" argument as the CRBSCA passed through Congress. Their success is reflected by the fact that the federal expenditures for the Yuma desalting plant and most of the other measures authorized by the CRBSCA are nonreimbursable. The exceptions are the improvements to district irrigation systems and the lining of the Coachella Canal. The CRBSCA further emphasized federal responsibility by making the "replacement of the reject stream from the desalting plant and of any Wellton-Mohawk drainage water bypassed to the Santa Clara Slough . . . a national obligation," except when there is surplus water in the river (Section 101(c)).

Congress sought to relieve pressures on allocation of Colorado River water by other means. Sections 201 and 202 of the Colorado River Basin Project Act of 1968 (CRBPA) (82 Stat. 885; 43 U.S.C. 1501) call for the Secretary of the Interior to develop a comprehensive plan to augment the water supplies of the Colorado River Basin by 2.5 million acre-feet in order to provide sufficient quantities of water to meet basin needs as well as the treaty obligation with Mexico. What Congress had in mind was augmentation through such means as cloud-seeding or importation of water from another river basin. It has been difficult to demonstrate the benefits of cloud-seeding to a sufficient degree to obtain funding for an ongoing program. As for water importation from other river basins, such measures are extremely expensive and politically untenable. For example, out of concern over proposals to divert water from the Columbia River system to the Colorado River Basin, Senator Henry Jackson of Washington secured a provision in the CRBPA that prohibited the United States from even studying such importation for a period of ten years. This prohibition was later extended for another ten years and remains in effect today.

The basin states secured one additional concession from the federal government besides the national obligation language of Title I. Title II of the CRBSCA, "Programs Upstream from Imperial Dam," authorized four salinity control projects designed to enhance water quality for U.S. water users in the Lower Basin, even though no feasibility reports for these projects had been completed by the Bureau of Reclamation. (The four projects were the Paradox Valley Unit in Colorado, the Grand Valley Unit in Colorado, the Las Vegas Wash Unit in Nevada, and the Crystal Geyser Unit in Utah.) In the words of Representative Harold T. Johnson, chairman of the House Subcommittee on Water and Power Resources,

> It is not our intention to try to hold up anything or hold anyone at gunpoint. We would, however, like to have consideration and recognition given to our problems. We will try and perfect you a good title I to take care of the international problems, and we would like to have a title II in the bill that would help give us a little boost on the problems on the American side of the border that are of concern to the basin states. (quoted in Fradkin, 1981, p. 315)

The Paradox Valley and the Grand Valley units are now in the initial stages of construction. The Las Vegas Wash and Crystal Geyser units were found to be of such questionable cost-effectiveness that the bureau suspended plans to complete them (for example, see U.S. Department of the Interior, Bureau of Reclamation, 1983, p. 52).

Title II also authorized the study of twelve other salinity control projects. The measures proposed in these projects include improvement of irrigation efficiency to reduce the leaching of salts and disposal of saline water from natural sources through evaporation, deep well injection, and desalting processes.

The Yuma Desalting Works

The Yuma desalting plant, authorized by Title I of the Colorado River Basin Salinity Control Act, is nearly complete and is about to undergo operational testing. The plant will use a reverse osmosis process to raise a portion of the Wellton-Mohawk drainage water to a level of quality high enough for it to return to the Colorado River before entering Mexico. The drainage water will be pretreated to remove particulate matter that would hasten the clogging of the osmosis membranes. The design specifications of the plant have been modified several times since it was originally devised. Although the plant was authorized in 1974 to treat 129 million gallons of water per day (mgpd), by 1977 this had been scaled down to 108.2 mgpd. Before construction began, the plant capacity was further reduced to 72.4 mgpd, principally because of lower expected levels of drainage water from the Wellton-Mohawk Irrigation District.

For any one given capacity, the plant may be operated in a variety of ways—for example, by mixing different quantities of treated and untreated drainage water. Table 9-1 shows the expected long-term water treatment of the desalting plant, both for the 1986 plant design and, for purposes of comparison, the 1977 design. The 1986 design is based on expectations that the Wellton-Mohawk drainage water will average about 110,000 acre-feet annually with a salinity level of 3,200 ppm of total dissolved solids. The desalting plant will treat about 92 percent of this amount, yielding two products—one highly saline and the other with low salinity content. The 63,000 acre-feet of high-quality water (300 ppm) will be combined with 9,000 acre-feet of untreated drainage water to yield 72,000 acre-feet of water with a

Table 9-1. Quantity and Quality of Water Treated by the Yuma Desalting Plant, Arizona

	1977 plant design[a]		1986 plant design[b]	
	Quantity (acre-feet/year)	Quality[c] (ppm)	Quantity (acre-feet/year)	Quality[c] (ppm)
Flow arriving at Imperial Dam	5,640,000	865	5,600,000	850
Imperial Dam release to Mexico	986,400	845	1,780,000	850
Wellton-Mohawk drainage water	167,000	3,200	110,000	3,200
Water entering the plant	146,100	3,200	101,000	3,200
Treated	102,700	386	63,000	300
Rejected (not returned to river)	43,300	8,874	38,000	7,300
Remaining drain water	20,900	3,200	9,000	3,200
Return blended to river	123,600	854	72,000	660
Inflow below Imperial Dam	250,000	1,578	250,000	1,550
Northern international boundary	1,360,000	980	1,400,000	960
Quality difference, Imperial inflow to northern international boundary		115		110

Source: Data for the 1977 plant design are from the U.S. Department of the Interior, Bureau of Reclamation, *Colorado River Basin Salinity Control Project, Title 1 Division, Desalting Complex Unit, Arizona: Status Report* (Washington, D.C., 1977), p. *g*, table S-1. Data for the 1986 plant design were obtained from the bureau's Yuma Project Office, Yuma, Ariz.

[a]Plant capacity of 108.5 million gallons per day.

[b]Plant capacity of 72.4 million gallons per day.

[c]Total dissolved solids in parts per million.

salinity level averaging 660 ppm for return to the Colorado River. The process will also result in 38,000 acre-feet of high-salinity (7,300 ppm) "reject" water, which, together with surplus or "bypass" Wellton-Mohawk drainage water, will be prevented from reentering the Colorado River and will be placed in the drainage canal that was extended through Mexico to the Santa Clara Slough. The flow remaining in the river at the northernmost point on the international boundary will consist of the blended return from the desalting plant, releases from Imperial Dam, and natural flows entering the Colorado River below Imperial Dam. As table 9-1 shows, the resulting mixture is expected to have a quality of 960 ppm of total dissolved solids, which exceeds the total dissolved solids of the inflow to Imperial Dam by 110 ppm. It is planned that the desalting plant will not operate continuously, but only as needed to meet the obligations to Mexico. The Bureau of Reclamation recently estimated that the plant will operate, on average, six out of every ten years.

The 1977 design would have processed a larger quantity of drainage water (146,000 acre-feet) and would have returned to the river a blend of processed water and drainage water amounting to 123,600 acre-feet with a salinity level of 854 ppm, the approximate level of salinity in the river water entering Imperial Dam. The 1986 plans call for operating the plant under construction to produce a blend of considerably higher quality (660 ppm of total dissolved solids) than the flow entering Imperial Dam. One of the principal reasons for this change is that the quality of water entering Imperial Dam has improved in recent years (from 865 ppm to 850 ppm), necessitating a better quality of water entering Mexico, in accordance with the conditions of Minute 242.[2] Another reason for the improved quality of the blended water shown in table 9-1 for the 1986 plant is the smaller difference in quality between inflows to Imperial Dam and the flow at the northern international boundary (110 ppm instead of 115 ppm). If the salinity of the 1986 plant product blended to the river were increased to 850 ppm (from 660 ppm), the effect would be to increase the salinity at the northern international boundary by about 6 ppm, to 966 ppm. The result would still be a higher quality of water

---

[2] The particular language of the treaty is somewhat problematic in this regard. The recent high flows on the Colorado River have increased the quality of water arriving at Imperial Dam. Further increases in quality at Imperial Dam will make it increasingly difficult to meet the 115 ppm differential specified in the minute, even though the quality of water provided to Mexico is acceptable for agricultural uses. It might have been better for the international agreements to have specified an additional quality criterion at the border beyond which further improvements in salinity were no longer required.

entering Mexico than under the 1977 plan, and the differential compared with the inflow to Imperial Dam would be 116 ppm, still within the Minute 242 standards. In other words, the basic goal of operation of the plant is to return the greatest possible volume of Wellton-Mohawk drainage water to the Colorado River without degrading the quality of the river.

Water will be forced through the plant membranes by powerful electrical pumps. The original plan was to use power from the Navajo Power Plant in northeastern Arizona until such time as it was needed for operation of the Central Arizona Project. However, because current plans are to sell power from the Navajo plant commercially to assist in the repayment of the Central Arizona Project, it may be just as economical to seek power for the desalting plant from another source.

Electricity for plant operation will cost about $72 per acre-foot per year, treatment chemicals will cost another $94 per acre-foot, and replacement of the osmosis membranes will cost $83 per acre-foot (see table 9-2). In addition, the plant will incur operating costs for labor and replacement parts, estimated at $61 per acre-foot. Therefore, operation and maintenance costs will total about $310 per acre-foot per year. As of September 30, 1986, $189 million had been spent on

Table 9-2. **Annual Costs for the Yuma Desalting Plant, Arizona**

	Annual costs (millions of dollars)	Annual costs[a] (dollars/acre-feet)
Capital costs	19.6[b]	273
Operation and maintenance costs		
Electricity	5.2	72
Treatment chemicals	6.8	94
Membrane replacement	6.0[c]	83
Operating and maintenance for labor, replacement parts (other than the membranes), and a test facility	4.4	61
Total operating costs	22.4	310
Total (capital plus operating costs)	42.0	583

Note: Costs are based on a plant capacity of 72.4 million gallons per day.

Source: 1986 budget for Bureau of Reclamation, U.S. Department of the Interior, Washington, D.C.

[a]Based on 72,000 acre-feet of blended water from the desalting plant being returned to the Colorado River.

[b]Based on expenditures of $234 million for the desalting plant, amortized over forty years at 8 percent.

[c]Replacement begins in the third year after initial operation.

the desalting plant and related facilities (excluding the regulatory pumping unit), and total construction costs were estimated to be $234 million. This means that the annual capital costs for 72,000 acre-feet of water produced by the desalting plant will be about $273 per acre-foot, which, when added to the operation and maintenance costs, brings the total cost up to $583 per acre-foot. Since plant construction is nearly complete, the annual operation and maintenance costs are the only costs that could be reduced or avoided by modifying the operation of the desalting plant.

Alternatives to Operation of the Yuma Desalting Plant

There are several less expensive ways than the desalting plant to obtain the same quantity of Colorado River water with a quality comparable to the inflow at Imperial Dam. These are discussed in the following subsections.

Purchase of Additional Lands

The most direct means of reducing the burden on the desalting plant and leaving additional flow in the Colorado River is through purchase of additional lands in the Wellton-Mohawk Irrigation District or purchase of the associated water supplies on an as-needed basis. The Colorado River Basin Salinity Control Act of 1974 provided for the initial purchase by the federal government of 10,000 acres in the Wellton-Mohawk Irrigation District, which was accomplished.[3] However, the act also authorized additional purchase of lands in Wellton-Mohawk:

> The initial reduction in irrigable acreage shall be limited to approximately ten thousand acres. If the Secretary determines that the irrigable acreage of the division must be reduced below sixty-five thousand acres of irrigable lands to carry out the purpose of this section, the Secretary is authorized, with the consent of the district, to acquire additional lands, as may be deemed by him to be appropriate.

Herbert Brownell, Jr., as U.S. representative to the negotiations over Minute 242 to the Mexico-Water Treaty, considered reducing the acreage in the district by an even larger amount or eliminating irrigation in the district altogether. Although the latter alternative would have been the least expensive method of providing the maximum quantities of acceptable-quality water to Mexico, Brownell realized that it would have been politically impossible. For one thing, the effects on the local economy, particularly in Yuma, would have

---

[3] Actually, much of this acreage was not yet in production, so the actual impact on the district was less than a 10,000-acre reduction in production.

prompted opposition. These impacts could be mitigated by purchasing the water, rather than the land, on an as-needed basis, allowing agricultural production to continue during most years. In fact, some additional purchases of water from the Wellton-Mohawk Irrigation District have been under discussion. Although these purchases are for the explicit purpose of satisfying the water claims of the Salt River Pima Maricopa Indian Community and the Fort McDowell Indian Community (see chapter 8), they will also reduce the costs of operating the desalting plant.

Purchase of Water Supplies in Various Parts of the Colorado River Basin

One way to avoid concentration of the economic impacts of purchase of water supplies on the Yuma community is to institute a program to spread these purchases more broadly around the Colorado River Basin. Agricultural water could probably be purchased for $40–$50 per acre-foot in many parts of the basin. For example, both the Bureau of Reclamation and the state of California estimated that conservation investments within the Imperial Irrigation District would cost less than $25 per acre-foot (in 1981 dollars) for a comparable amount of water conserved (see Wahl and Davis, 1986, pp. 121–123). Comparable prices can be found in the Bureau of Reclamation's report on water to replace the reject stream from the desalting plant (U.S. Department of the Interior, Bureau of Reclamation, 1980, p. 7). The report indicates that irrigation districts in the Yuma Mesa division offered to forgo water for prices ranging from $4 to $34 per acre-foot (in 1977 dollars).

The United States could implement a voluntary purchase program in the following manner. It could solicit bids for lease or sale of water to the Bureau of Reclamation. Each bid would specify the quantity of water being made available, the price of the water, and the number of years that the water would be made available. The bureau would then rank these bids from the least to the most expensive, based on the quality of water made available as measured at Imperial Dam. The bureau would accept the lowest-cost bids up to the total quantity needed in any particular year to substitute for or augment the supply of water from the Yuma desalting plant.

Creation of a Voluntary Market in the Resource Inputs to the Desalting Plant

Each of the above alternatives would involve direct federal purchases of water supplies in the basin states, which might be regarded unfavorably by the major water users in the area and by the states themselves. Another alternative is to allow the creation of a voluntary market in the resources needed to operate the desalting plant. This market could function as follows. Any state or water-using entity that agreed to provide the federal government with a replacement for water that would otherwise be produced by the desalting plant would be granted a corresponding share of the electrical energy saved by reduced operation of the plant and would be compensated for the savings in chemicals used in the plant process. Water-using entities entering into the agreement would be free to provide the replacement water from whatever source they chose, as long as it did not adversely affect the quality of water arriving at Imperial Dam.

As table 9-2 indicates, the electrical energy exchanged would be worth at least $72 per acre-foot. If the supplier of the replacement water, such as an irrigation district, were able to obtain water for $40 per acre-foot, then it would realize an income gain of $32 per acre-foot, based on the energy values alone. If the electrical energy could be resold at more than the original cost to the United States, there could be some additional value accruing to the supplier of the replacement water. If the United States were to compensate the supplier for the savings in treatment chemicals as well as in electricity, it should be willing to pay a total of $166 per acre-foot for the replacement water ($94 per acre-foot for the chemicals plus $72 per acre-foot for the electricity; see table 9-2). Alternatively, it could pay the district $94 per acre-foot for the savings in chemical costs and grant it the rights to the power saved. If the supplier of the replacement water were able to obtain the water for $40 per acre-foot, then it would realize an income gain of $126 per acre-foot.

Under these proposals, the United States would realize some cost savings as well—the reduced costs of replacement membranes, other replacement parts, and labor. However, unless a complete substitute supply were made available (72,000 acre-feet), the savings on these costs would likely be less than fully proportional to the replacement water (see table 9-3). For example, if a water district provided 48,000 acre-feet of replacement water (two-thirds of the expected output of the plant), this would reduce energy costs by about 63 percent and chemical costs by 66 percent, but it would reduce the costs of contractor labor by only an estimated 23 percent and the costs of spare parts by only 50 percent. A less-than-proportional reduction in the cost of membrane replacement would be expected as well, because membranes deteriorate with time even when they are not in use. If a single entity or group of entities agreed to supply all of the 72,000 acre-feet of replacement water, then the federal government might be willing to pass along at least some portion of the savings in the costs of

Table 9-3. **Annual Costs of Operating the Yuma Desalting Plant at Full Capacity and One-Third Capacity**

Operating costs	Annual costs at full capacity[a] (millions of dollars)	Annual costs at one-third capacity	
		(millions of dollars)	(percent reduction)
Electricity	5.2	1.9	63
Treatment chemicals	6.8	2.3	66
Membrane replacement	6.0[b]	c	c
Contractor labor	2.6	2.0	23
Government labor	0.4	0.4	0
Spare parts	1.0	0.5	50
Test train[d]			
Electricity	0.29	0.29	0
Treatment chemicals	0.062	0.062	0

Source: U.S. Department of the Interior, Bureau of Reclamation, Yuma Projects Office, Yuma, Ariz.

[a]Plant capacity is 72.4 million gallons per day.

[b]Replacement begins in third year after initial operation.

[c]Unknown; membranes deteriorate with time, so replacement costs will be a function of time as well as of use.

[d]The test train would be operated continuously.

membrane replacement, labor, and replacement parts, as well as in electrical energy and treatment chemicals.[4]

Conclusions

Although federal legislation calls for the Secretary of the Interior to meet the U.S. treaty obligation for water deliveries to Mexico in the least costly manner, the salinity control programs adopted by the Bureau of Reclamation are far from a least-cost method. The Yuma desalting plant, which is designed to increase the quantity of usable water entering Mexico, will actually be a very expensive source. The confused and costly approaches for dealing with these problems have

---

[4] Assuming that such trades are arranged after completion of the desalting plant, no construction costs would be saved. If the replacement water were made available on a schedule that involved shutdown of the plant, followed by operation, then the bureau would incur additional costs that would have to be considered in any agreement. The bureau estimates that the costs of each shutdown/start-up cycle would be about $1 million and that it would cost about $5 million–$7.5 million per year to keep the plant in a state of readiness when it was not in operation.

arisen partly from the conflict between competing interests, as reflected in the federal legislation. What Congress attempted to do in the Colorado River Basin Project Act and the Colorado River Basin Salinity Control Act was to require the federal government to pay for an expensive supply of water for Mexico so far down the Colorado River that it would not harm water uses anywhere in the basin. The rationale offered for this approach was that it was the United States which negotiated the treaty and other agreements with Mexico.[5]

There are two possible interpretations of the national obligation language in this legislation: (1) the United States is responsible for replacing the Wellton-Mohawk drainage water now bypassed to Mexico—an actual quantity of water—and (2) the United States is financially responsible for meeting this obligation. The implication of the first interpretation is that the federal government should locate a source of replacement water that will not reduce water use in any of the basin states. In reality, of course, any replacement water would be from a source that could, in principle, also be tapped by the basin states. Under the second interpretation, the United States would be able to lease or purchase water anywhere in the Colorado River Basin on an as-needed basis to meet the treaty obligations with Mexico (participation in such lease or purchase arrangements would be voluntary).

Even so, a lease or purchase program might be regarded as an infringement on the use of water in the basin states—the very water use that, in the view of the Colorado River Basin states, the agreement was designed to protect. However, the logic of full protection of actual water supplies does not stand up, even within the legislation itself, for several reasons. First, according to the CRBPA, the federal government is supposed to augment the supplies of the basin by such means as water importation. Such methods are so politically untenable that the United States is prevented by legislation from even studying them. Given the stringency of federal expenditures and the desire of water-using areas to maintain supplies arising within their borders, it is unlikely that the federal government will be financing out-of-basin imports. Second, the legislation itself requires that most of the U.S. obligation be met through salvage of water within the basin, namely, by lining a portion of the Coachella Canal and by constructing and operating the desalting plant. Third, the United States is to find a substitute for the saline reject stream from the plant that is bypassed to the Santa Clara Slough. The act indicates that the potential sources of water for the replacement of the reject stream are

---

[5] However, the states, through their representatives in Congress, also approved the treaty.

to be from within the Colorado River Basin states. The Reject Stream Replacement Study prepared by the bureau (U.S. Department of the Interior, Bureau of Reclamation, 1980) includes such alternatives as lining the All-American Canal, lining canals or purchasing lands within the Yuma Mesa Division, and pumping out seepage along the All-American Canal. These are all measures that could be undertaken by states, irrigation districts, or other water-using entities. If the United States is in competition with other water users in performing these salvage measures to meet its obligations, then the argument is less persuasive that it must operate a desalting plant that is more expensive than replacement water available elsewhere in the basin.

In fact, the CRBSCA explicitly provides opportunities for the United States to pursue lower-cost alternatives. For one, the Secretary of the Interior is authorized to acquire additional lands within the Wellton-Mohawk Irrigation District, provided the district consents. More important, the CRBSCA allows the secretary to modify his use of the measures authorized by the act in order to satisfy the treaty obligations at the lowest overall cost, provided sufficient notice is given to Congress and to the governors of the basin states.

The Colorado River Basin Project Act also grants latitude to the United States to pursue alternatives of lesser cost. Section 202 provides that, until augmentation measures are in place and until the secretary has declared that water flows are sufficient to meet the treaty obligations with Mexico, any shortfall in those obligations must be satisfied according to the terms of the Colorado River Compact—that is, divided between the Upper Basin and Lower Basin states on a 50-50 basis. In other words, the states still share the responsibility for meeting the treaty obligations.

Even though construction of the Yuma desalting plant is nearly finished and the plant will soon be ready for operational testing, it may be time to reexamine our approach for controlling salinity on the Colorado River. Since the original analysis of the need for a desalting plant was done, two critical factors have changed that would argue for reexamination. First, the recent high flows on the Colorado River have improved water quality prospects in the Lower Basin. Second, the reservoirs on the Colorado River are now filled, deferring the need for use of reclaimed water from the Wellton-Mohawk Irrigation District to meet the treaty obligation to Mexico. Glen Canyon and Hoover dams store more than 43 million acre-feet of water. Even after accounting for evaporation and conveyance losses, this would be sufficient to ensure supplies of 7.5 million acre-feet to the Lower Basin and 1.5 million acre-feet to Mexico for several years of below-average runoff. The recent unusually high flows on the Colorado River have meant not only that the river reservoirs have been filled, but also that they have had to "spill" surplus water downstream to the Lower Basin and to Mexico. According to the accounting convention adopted by the Lower Basin states and the Bureau of Reclamation, this erases the accumulated obligation of the United States to replace water previously bypassed to the ocean from the Wellton-Mohawk Irrigation District (for example, see U.S. General Accounting Office, 1979, pp. 41, 43). Also, the pace of actual and projected Upper Basin development, as well as associated water depletions, has slowed considerably. Projected oil shale development has not materialized, and several of the Upper Basin reservoirs projected for completion by the bureau in its planning studies have not been initiated. This further defers the need for reclaimed water to meet the treaty obligation with Mexico.

There is now a greater understanding of the fact that the federal government cannot be an unlimited source of funds for expensive water-supply enhancement projects. Accompanying this realization has been a growing appreciation for the benefits of reallocation of water supplies through market trades. Within this context, selective purchase of water by the United States to meet its treaty obligations may be more viable. Such purchases could be made from water users throughout the basin who were willing to forgo water use during years when the United States needed additional supplies. Alternatively, the United States could pay any water user who was willing to leave a substitute source of water supply in the Colorado River for the savings in electrical power and chemical costs resulting from reduced operation of the desalting plant (or, the water users could be granted the use of the electrical energy saved). The United States could also pass along some of its savings in other plant operating costs if a water-using entity were willing to provide the full quantity of water supplied by the plant.

The Yuma desalting plant is widely recognized as an unusually expensive source of water, both from the standpoint of its construction costs and for its high operating costs. As elsewhere in the West, considerable funds are now being spent to mitigate problems of our own making. The question is open as to whether, in planning for the best utilization of the plant, measures and institutional arrangements can be developed that will be more carefully structured than past efforts.

References

Fradkin, Philip L. 1981. *A River No More: The Colorado River and the West* (New York, Alfred A. Knopf).

Hundley, Harris, Jr. 1966. *Dividing the Waters: A Century of Controversy Between the United States and Mexico* (Berkeley, University of California).

U.S. Department of the Interior, Bureau of Reclamation. 1980. *Colorado River Basin Salinity Control Project, Title 1 Division, Reject Stream Replacement Study, California—Arizona: Special Report* (Washington, D.C., June).

————. 1983. *Colorado River Water Quality Improvement Program: Status Report* (Denver, Colorado River Water Quality Office, January).

U.S. General Accounting Office. 1979. *Colorado River Basin Water Problems: How to Reduce Their Impact,* Report No. CED-79-11 (Washington, D.C., May 4).

Wahl, Richard W., and Robert K. Davis. 1986. "Satisfying Southern California's Thirst for Water: Efficient Alternatives," in Kenneth D. Frederick, ed., *Scarce Water and Institutional Change* (Washington, D.C., Resources for the Future).

10

The Prospects for Leasing Compact Rights on the Colorado River

A 1984 proposal by the Galloway Group Limited, a Colorado corporation, to lease water rights in that state to San Diego County in California poses new questions about how Colorado River Compact rights can be utilized. If compact rights can be leased between states, then market trading could increase flexibility in allocating water along the length of the Colorado River and provide revenues to basin states that are not fully utilizing their compact shares. This chapter reviews state allocations under the Colorado River Compact, the details of the Galloway proposal, the principal legal questions that have been raised, and some of the potential advantages of interstate leasing.

Compact Allocations

There have been battles over allocation of Colorado River water since the early 1900s. The various compacts and pieces of legislation pertaining to the river have established the upper limits on water use for each state in the Colorado River Basin. The Colorado River Compact of 1922 states that 7.5 million acre-feet of water must be delivered each year by the Upper Basin to Lee Ferry, the dividing point between the Upper Basin and the Lower Basin. The Upper Basin itself is allocated 7.5 million acre-feet, but, because annual flows of the Colorado River average only around 14 million acre-feet, the obligation to deliver water to Lee Ferry may in effect reduce Upper Basin entitlements to less than 7.5 million acre-feet. This has not been a problem to date because Upper Basin depletions have not exceeded 4 million acre-feet (see table 10-1). The Mexican Water Treaty of 1944 allocates 1.5 million acre-feet of water per year to Mexico, further adding to the oversubscription of entitlements to Colorado River water.

An allocation among the Lower Basin states is specified by the Boulder Canyon Act of 1928 and the Supreme Court's 1963 decision in *Arizona v. California:* 4.4 million acre-feet of Colorado River water to California, 2.8 million acre-feet to Arizona, and 0.3 million acre-feet to Nevada. California and Arizona are each entitled to 50 percent of any surplus flows. However, according to the terms of the Colorado River Basin Project Act of 1968, if there is insufficient water in the river to provide the full Lower Basin allocation of 7.5 million acre-feet, then water use in California has priority over that in Arizona. In 1948 the Upper Basin states agreed to divide their allocation on a percentage basis: 51.75 percent to Colorado, 23 percent to Utah, 14 percent to Wyoming, and 11.25 percent to New Mexico based on net diversions (diversions less return flow) from the Colorado River (Nathanson, 1979).

The various compacts and pieces of legislation and the court decisions based on them are known as the "Law of the River." The water rights stemming from the Law of the River are called compact rights in this chapter, although they in fact involve many agreements other than the Colorado River Compact itself.

The Galloway Proposal

The Galloway Group perceptively made its proposal to lease water rights to San Diego County. This county has the most to lose from a shortage in water available to southern California either from sources within the state or from the Colorado River. The Metropolitan Water District of Southern California (MWD) supplies water to twenty-seven member agencies on the southern California coastal plain. It receives water from the Colorado River through the Colorado River Aqueduct and from northern California through the State Water Project (see Wahl and Davis, 1986). Member agencies are entitled to water based on their percent contribution to total MWD tax revenues. Los Angeles has been the main contributor at about 27 percent, but currently uses only 5 percent of MWD supplies because it relies mainly on water from the Owens Valley and from the Mono Lake area, sources which it developed independently of MWD. Should the Owens Valley and Mono Lake supplies shrink during a California drought, however, Los Angeles would be entitled to substantially increase its utilization of MWD water. In such a case, the San Diego County Water Authority, which currently uses about 30 percent of

Table 10-1. Utilization of Colorado River Water in the Upper and Lower Basins, 1971–1981

(thousands of acre-feet)

	Lower Basin				Upper Basin depletion	Total United States	Mexico	Total
	California	Arizona	Nevada	Total				
Compact or treaty allocation	4,400	2,800	300	7,500	7,500	15,000	1,500	16,500
Utilization								
1971	5,216	1,298	50	6,564	3,413	9,977	1,563	11,539
1972	5,231	1,235	81	6,547	3,266	9,813	1,613	11,426
1973	5,318	1,272	93	6,683	3,423	10,106	1,625	11,731
1974	5,414	1,326	95	6,835	3,819	10,654	1,665	12,319
1975	4,984	1,358	72	6,414	3,479	9,893	1,728	11,621
1976	4,707	1,248	73	6,028	3,776	9,804	1,774	11,578
1977	5,097	1,231	73	6,401	3,433	9,834	1,779	11,613
1978	4,503	1,235	71	5,809	3,906	9,715	1,727	11,442
1979	4,788	1,151	60	5,999	3,658	9,657	3,345	13,002
1980	4,725	1,170	93	5,988	3,788	9,776	7,195	16,971
1981	4,796	1,416	110	6,322	3,840	10,162	2,191	12,353

Note: Values given are net diversions (diversions less measured returns).

Sources: Lower Basin net diversions are from annual reports entitled "Compilation of Records in Accordance with Article V of the Decree of Supreme Court of the United States in Arizona vs. California dated March 9, 1964," U.S. Department of the Interior, Bureau of Reclamation, Boulder City, Nev. Upper Basin depletions and deliveries to Mexico are from *Annual Reports* of the Colorado River Board of California (Los Angeles, Calif.) as reported in Environmental Defense Fund, *Trading Conservation Investments for Water* (Berkeley, Calif., Environmental Defense Fund, 1983), p. 12, table 3.

MWD supplies, would be entitled to only 12 percent.[1] This would be an acute reduction for San Diego County because during years of average precipitation, the county receives about 90 percent of its supplies from MWD and only 10 percent from local sources.

The Galloway Group Limited purchased water rights on the White River in Colorado in expectation of selling them to the developing oil shale industry in the western part of the state. However, the prospects for a robust oil shale industry were largely reversed by moderation of world oil prices and the reduction or elimination of federal programs designed to provide price supports and loan guarantees for the synthetic fuels industry.[2] When the oil shale boom collapsed in western Colorado in 1982, Galloway began searching for other customers for its water. In August 1984 the San Diego County Water Authority signed an option agreement with the Galloway Group and paid a deposit of $10,000. Under the plan proposed by Galloway, San Diego would be leased a minimum of 300,000 acre-feet (up to a maximum of 500,000 acre-feet) of water developed in Colorado and delivered to MWD's pumps on Lake Havasu behind Parker Dam on the lower Colorado River. San Diego would assume responsibility for delivery from that point on, through the Colorado River Aqueduct and other MWD facilities. (Excess conveyance capacity should be available in the Colorado River Aqueduct: when the Central Arizona Project increases its diversions from the river, only about half the aqueduct's capacity will be used by MWD for delivery of its Colorado River allocation of 550,000 acre-feet. San Diego evidently expects to transfer its Galloway water to MWD ownership in exchange for use of MWD's excess conveyance capacity and the guaranteed delivery of a large share of the newly acquired water.)

Under the Galloway proposal, the lease would run for forty years and would provide several intermediate and ultimate protections for Colorado. With five years' notice, sellers of water in Colorado could call back up to 50,000 acre-feet of water each year, so long as San Diego was left with a minimum of 250,000 acre-feet. Therefore, if San Diego were to obtain the maximum entitlement of 500,000 acre-feet, Colorado owners could regain half of the leased amount within ten years. At the twenty-fifth year, under another provision in the agreement, Colorado owners could choose to utilize the full 300,000–500,000 acre-feet leased beginning after the fortieth year, thereby terminating the lease after that date. Alternatively, the Colorado

---

[1] These percentages, based on 1986 data, are from MWD records.

[2] The Synthetic Fuels Corporation, which was established by the federal government in 1980 to subsidize and otherwise encourage production of alternatives to imported oil, was abolished by Congress in 1985.

owners of the water could decide at the twenty-fifth year to continue to lease some amount of water beyond the fortieth year.

The agreement makes clear that San Diego is not to gain any right to continued use of the water after expiration of the lease and even specifies that if a third party were to gain an enforceable interest in the delivered water, San Diego would be responsible for providing a replacement supply to the third party, thereby permitting Colorado to recover full utilization of its compact allocation. As a further protection, the agreement explicitly states that the water transfer is to be undertaken "pursuant to the rules, regulations, laws, treaties, decrees and compacts which govern the allocation of the Colorado River."

The agreement indicates that Galloway intends to supplement its previously acquired rights through construction of additional storage facilities. Although the written agreement with San Diego does not tie the corporation to delivery of water from any specific source, the Galloway Group was considering development of additional reservoir storage on various tributaries of the Colorado River, including the Yampa River and the White River in northwest Colorado (see figure 10-1). Under the agreement, Galloway would charge San Diego a rate

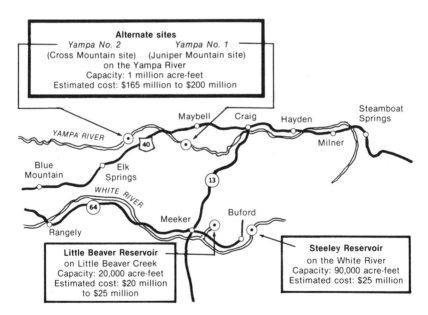

Figure 10-1. Alternative dam sites in northwest Colorado proposed by the Galloway Group. *Source:* Redrawn, with permission, from *Rocky Mountain News,* January 6, 1986, p. 18.

sufficient to recover its costs plus "a reasonable return" on its investment, provided that the charge, plus the MWD conveyance cost, does not exceed 90 percent of the MWD's charge for water delivered to San Diego. Once Galloway pays off its investment, the agreement entitles the corporation to charge a rate equal to 50 percent of the previously amortized capital charge (including interest), as well as the then-current operation and maintenance costs.

The Larger Question: Leasing of Compact Rights

The legality of the specific proposal put forth by the Galloway Group is hotly contested, but, even if the proposal never results in the delivery of water to San Diego, it has raised a number of interesting questions regarding utilization of Colorado River water. For example, if the Galloway lease arrangement, or some similar proposal, is ultimately found to be consistent with the Law of the River, then would other Upper Basin water users propose leasing arrangements at prices below the Galloway offer? Could Upper Basin (or Lower Basin) states, as opposed to water users within those states, lease unutilized compact rights to water users in other states? Would Indian tribes in the basin be willing to lease unutilized water to downstream population centers? Would there be other Lower Basin users that would compete with San Diego for purchase of Upper Basin water? More generally, could the Galloway proposal eventually lead to an interstate market for leasing Colorado River Compact rights?

Some existing holders of Colorado River water rights, such as agricultural water users in the Upper and Lower basins, would probably be able to sell their water for a price far below Galloway's price because they would not need to construct new storage facilities. Also, Wyoming holds a share of the unused water in the existing Flaming Gorge Reservoir, and there has been discussion of assigning the Ute Indians a share of this water, some of which they might be willing to lease to other Colorado River Basin users. The state of Colorado regulates the beneficial use of water for its citizens. Therefore, in principle, the state itself might be able to lease its rights under the Colorado River Compact to San Diego, avoiding the substantial cost of constructing a reservoir.[3] This would be a much cheaper means of delivering the same water to San Diego (or some other Lower Basin water user) because the existing reservoirs on the main-stem Colorado provide a high level of regulation of the river.

[3] For example, Landry (1985) argues that Colorado might be able to legitimately deny Galloway's application for a water right.

The additional 1.1 million acre-feet of storage on the Yampa River proposed by Galloway is likely to do little to raise the overall storage capacity on the river for water to be delivered to Lower Basin states. The only exception would be during years such as 1981 and 1982, when, for the first time, the bureau had to spill water from Glen Canyon Dam. Additional storage would also result in some increased evaporative losses. Therefore, in the overall accounting for water in the river, the reservoirs proposed by Galloway would add only a fraction of their 300,000- to 500,000-acre-foot annual yield to the yield of the Colorado River system. Seen in this light, the main purpose of the proposed reservoirs would not be to increase river yields, but to establish property rights to Upper Basin water for the Galloway Group under Colorado state water law.

Galloway proposes to use the reservoirs for the production of hydropower in order to establish beneficial use of the water under Colorado law. The hydropower revenues would certainly enhance the economic viability of the project. It is not clear, however, that the use of the water for hydroelectric power would guarantee a quantity of water for export. The right for hydroelectric use is normally specified only by the flows of water (and their timing) at the reservoir site, and possibly by some small amount of consumptive use. Once the flow of water from hydroelectric generation is returned to the river, it would be subject to appropriation by other water users. In other words, unlike the private agricultural rights purchased by Galloway, there would be no significant amounts of consumptive use to be claimed by Galloway and leased to San Diego (for additional discussion, see Landry, 1985, p. 967 ff.).

The more general question is whether a competitive interstate market could develop along the Colorado River that would be consistent with the existing Law of the River and that would recognize the Colorado River Compact and other agreements as the basis of the property rights to be traded. It is with the larger question of water rights leasing in mind, as well as the specifics of the Galloway proposal, that we examine whether interstate leases of water might eventually be legally achievable and politically acceptable.

Would a Market Be Legally Permitted?

Reactions to the Galloway Group proposal have ranged from outright opposition by MWD and the State Engineer's Office of Arizona to moderate interest on the part of some Upper Basin states and Indian tribes. MWD has flatly stated that the Galloway proposal is contrary to the Law of the River and, in fact, provided more than thirty pages of arguments to support its conclusion soon after the proposal was announced. At the root of MWD's opposition is a financial consideration: MWD does not want to have to pay fees for surplus water flowing from the Upper Basin states—water that it now receives at no charge. Table 10-1 shows the utilization of Colorado River water from 1971 to 1981. During those years, California used considerably more water than its 4.4-million-acre-foot allocation; in fact, it used more than 5.2 million acre-feet in four of the eleven years shown in the table. This was possible both because Arizona was not utilizing its full share (pending completion of the Central Arizona Project) and because the Upper Basin states were not utilizing their full shares. The Colorado River Board of California also registered its opposition to the Galloway proposal. On October 10, 1984, it voted to oppose "any attempt to amend the 'Law of the River' in order to utilize Upper Colorado River Basin water rights which would try to circumvent the agreements heretofore made and relied upon by the Basin states for their water supplies."

Other Lower Basin states were quick to register their opposition. Arizona's reaction to the Galloway proposal was expressed by Governor Bruce Babbitt, who wrote the San Diego County Water Authority that "any decision by the Authority to contract with the Galloway Group would be immediately countered by a lawsuit by the State of Arizona." Authorization of the Central Arizona Project was premised partly on Arizona's use of surplus Colorado River water for the years preceding buildup in Upper Basin depletions, but the Galloway proposal would divert some of this surplus to California. The Colorado River Commission of Nevada voted a resolution on November 9, 1984, taking "strong opposition" to the sale of Upper Basin water to San Diego.

In the Upper Basin, opinions about the Galloway proposal ranged from opposition to some interest. David Getches, director of the Colorado Department of Natural Resources, indicated that "this particular plan may collapse because of all the complications, but such ideas increasingly should be looked at" (*Wall Street Journal,* November 19, 1984). Warren White, natural resources adviser to Wyoming's Governor Ed Herschler, was skeptical about the proposal but also indicated that the Wyoming attorney general was studying the matter (*San Diego Union,* August 31, 1984). Governor Scott Matheson of Utah called the Galloway concept "attractive" but did not initially indicate a willingness to cooperate in the proposal because of unresolved legal problems (*San Diego Union,* August 31, 1984). Matheson subsequently called for a meeting of Utah water resource leaders to consider the merits of the proposal (*Utah Waterline,* September 12, 1984).

On the basis of these various viewpoints and the collective nature of the agreements surrounding use of Colorado River water (both the Colorado River Compact and the Colorado River Basin Project Act of 1958 represent compromises among the various states along the river), it appears that any leasing proposal will prove viable only if it is found to be consistent with the existing Law of the River through litigation or if a consensus develops that such a proposal would ultimately benefit all parties concerned. Although a number of legal questions concerning the Galloway proposal have been raised by both Upper Basin and Lower Basin interests, they coalesce into the three categories of legal issues discussed next: (1) the security of Upper Basin water rights, (2) the definition of surplus water, and (3) whether beneficial use includes leasing for use outside the state.

Security of Upper Basin Water Rights

The principal concern of the Upper Basin states is whether they could be assured renewed use of leased water at the end of the lease term. In their view, rights to this water are closely tied to the potential for future economic development. As table 10-1 indicates, Upper Basin depletions have been far below those in the Lower Basin, and much of the surplus flow from the Upper Basin has either flowed to Mexico or has been stored in the main-stem Colorado River reservoirs. Full utilization of Upper Basin shares may be contingent on substantial new reservoir construction or such major new industrial development as the synthetic fuels industry represented. Therefore, the date for full utilization of Upper Basin shares is speculative and may lie well beyond the year 2000. However, temporary leasing is not likely to be undertaken if there is any potential for permanent loss of water.

Two factors point to security for the Upper Basin under leasing arrangements such as the Galloway proposal. First is the long-standing nature of existing Colorado River agreements allocating water. Second are the explicit terms of the Galloway option agreement, which acknowledge the governing nature of the Colorado River Compact and the Law of the River and which clearly specify schedules for relinquishment of use by Lower Basin users and even require San Diego to replace any Upper Basin water to which Lower Basin interests might gain a legal claim.

It is an accepted principle of the equitable apportionment doctrine applicable to the river and dating from the 1922 Colorado River Compact that the use of water is not necessary to protect compact rights. For example, the temporary use by California of some of Arizona's share of Lower Basin water before completion of the Central Arizona Project has not resulted in California gaining permanent rights to the water, and the expected relinquishment by California is proceeding without legal or legislative challenge by that state. Another example is the "temporary" contract with Utah International, Inc. (refer to table 6-1), for water from the Navajo Reservoir, part of the Colorado River Storage Project. The term of this contract is forty years, and it is expected to push New Mexico over its Upper Basin allocation between the years 2000 and 2030. The contract is conditioned on a current finding by the Secretary of the Interior that enough surplus Upper Basin water is currently available to accommodate the contract.

Definition of Surplus Water

The Lower Basin states contend that, according to the Law of the River, they have rights to water unused by the Upper Basin states and that any sale or lease of such water by the Upper Basin would be a confiscation of these rights. This is not altogether clear. The Colorado River Compact apportioned "in perpetuity to the Upper Basin and to the Lower Basin, respectively, the exclusive beneficial consumptive use of 7.5 million acre-feet of water per annum." The compact also provided that if the United States afterwards engaged in a treaty with Mexico to supply water from the Colorado River system, then "such waters shall be supplied first from the waters which are surplus" over and above the quantities previously specified and that if such surplus proved insufficient for the purpose, then the burden of the deficiency would be borne equally by the Upper Basin and Lower Basin. This suggests that the Upper Basin states have rights to up to 7.5 million acre-feet of water and that a compact surplus does not occur except under those precipitation conditions where the 7.5-million-acre-foot claims of both the Upper and Lower basins are satisfied, as well as the Mexican treaty obligation of 1.5 million acre-feet.[4] Under this interpretation, most of the water currently released by the Upper Basin would not be surplus. Furthermore, if "exclusive beneficial consumptive use" by the Upper Basin is interpreted to include leasing of water to the Lower Basin (which would benefit the Upper Basin), then leasing proposals would be allowable.

An alternative interpretation of surplus is any water in excess of Upper Basin consumption, the Lower Basin allocation, and the treaty obligation to Mexico. In short, any releases below Lee Ferry that exceeded the Lower Basin allocation and the treaty entitlements of Mexico would be regarded as surplus water that could be divided

---

[4] The 7.5 million acre-feet of water allotted to the Upper Basin is in terms of net diversions or consumptive use, rather than gross diversions.

equally between Arizona and California and utilized without payment of any charges to the Upper Basin.

These two interpretations point out that the concept of surplus is dependent on whether "exclusive beneficial consumptive use" for the Upper Basin encompasses lease for beneficial use in the Lower Basin (this is discussed further in the next subsection).

Whatever the legal merits of these alternative interpretations of law, it is certainly true that in recent years Lower Basin states have come to expect that growth in Upper Basin consumption will not significantly reduce their use until well into the next century (a case in point being the plans by Central Arizona Project water users to utilize surplus flows from the Upper Basin during an interim period). If Upper Basin states do in fact have the right to sell consumptive use to Lower Basin states, then Arizona water users, to achieve the same expected level of water deliveries, will have to bid for upstream rights. This interpretation does not require, as MWD and other Lower Basin critics claim, a wholesale revision of the Law of the River, but rather revised expectations of when and in what form Upper Basin states might exercise their rights to consumptive use.

Within the larger historical context, a more accelerated timetable for upstream water use may not be an improper or startling move. The original political compromise that resulted in funding for the Central Arizona Project also provided for the construction of five upstream dams for Upper Basin development, dams that were to be completed when the Central Arizona Project began delivering water. Only two of these five projects, Dallas Creek and Dolores, are actually under construction (see table 10-2). Animas–La Plata is at the stage of final preconstruction planning, after being authorized for construction in August 1988. Two others, West Divide and San Miguel, have proved economically infeasible when evaluated under current federal water project discount rates. As table 10-2 shows, the net depletions from the three unstarted projects total 227,000 acre-feet, a quantity of water that, coincidentally, is close to the minimum 300,000-acre-foot yield offered for lease by the Galloway Group. Therefore, allowing the Upper Basin states to lease their undeveloped water may be one way of making good on the political promise to guarantee Upper Basin states an income from their Colorado River water entitlement by a date close to the first deliveries of water from the Central Arizona Project.

Does Beneficial Use Include Leasing for Use Outside the State?

One key legal question is whether transfers between states, or between entities in one state and those in another, would be recognized

Table 10-2. Authorized Upper Basin Reservoirs in Colorado

	Water supply (acre-feet)	Net deple- tions (acre-feet)	Percent complete[a]	Increased salt load at Imperial Dam (milligrams/liter)
Dallas Creek	39,400	17,100	83	2.7
Dolores	126,600	80,900	63	11.1
Animas–La Plata	198,200	154,800	0	17.9
West Divide	64,200	38,200	b, c	5.6
San Miguel	56,270[d]	34,000[e]	b, f	g
Total		325,000		
Total for unstarted		227,000		
Total for economically infeasible		72,200		

Sources: Diversions, net depletions, and increased salt load are from U.S. Department of the Interior, Bureau of Reclamation, *Dallas Creek Project, Colorado: Definite Plan Report,* 1976, p. 2; U.S. Department of the Interior, Bureau of Reclamation, *Dolores Project, Colorado: Definite Plan Report,* 1977, p. 3; U.S. Department of the Interior, Bureau of Reclamation, *Animas–La Plata Project, Colorado-New Mexico: Definite Plan Report,* 1979, p. 2; U.S. Department of the Interior, Bureau of Reclamation, *A Report on the West Divide Project, Colorado,* 1980, p. 2; U.S. Department of the Interior, Bureau of Reclamation, *San Miguel Project, Colorado: Concluding Report, Appendix A,* 1981, p. 20. Percent complete data are from records of Bureau of Reclamation, U.S. Department of the Interior, Washington, D.C.

[a]As of January 1987.
[b]Not economically feasible.
[c]Current benefit–cost ratio is 0.62.
[d]Since no plan was found economically feasible, no alternative was recommended. Water supply and net depletions shown are for the optimal municipal and industrial water plan. Water supplies for the other alternatives range from 0 to 58,000 acre-feet.
[e]Estimated at 60 percent of water supply.
[f]Benefit–cost ratios for the plan alternatives ranged from 0.04 to 0.94.
[g]Data not available.

as legitimate uses of compact water under the Law of the River. The Colorado River Compact provides that "the states of the upper division shall not withhold water, and the states of the lower division shall not require the delivery of water that cannot reasonably be applied to domestic and agricultural purposes." The compact does not explicitly rule out the possibility of an Upper Basin state allowing water to be used for domestic and agricultural purposes in the Lower Basin, although it is likely that the framers of the compact did not envision such an arrangement. One interpretation of the compact is that it provides for an allocation of consumptive use of the river for Upper Basin and Lower Basin states as each sees fit, including the production of income from interstate leasing.

The recent *Sporhase v. Nebraska* decision (458 U.S. 941) has given impetus to interstate leasing. It struck down a Nebraska statute that prohibited export of water to a state (in this case Colorado) that did not itself permit out-of-state exports of water. The decision recognized water as a legitimate article of interstate commerce. Colorado law now permits exports of water upon approval by the state water engineer, groundwater commission, or water judge. The export is to be approved if it meets three criteria: (1) the proposed use of water outside the state must not impair the ability of the state to comply with any judicial decree or interstate compact, (2) the proposed use of water must not be inconsistent with the reasonable conservation of water resources of the state, and (3) the proposed use of water must not deprive the citizens of the state of the beneficial use of water apportioned to Colorado by interstate compact or judicial decree. The first condition is met so long as the interstate leasing proposal is consistent with the Law of the River. The second and third conditions are satisfied if the lease of water to water users in another state is considered a beneficial use, provided that the leasing arrangement does not impair future growth in consumptive uses by Colorado (for further discussion of Colorado's export statute, see Landry, 1985, pp. 978–982, and Gross, 1985, p. 944).

Allocation Within California

Several other legal questions have been raised about the Galloway proposal, one of which concerns priority within California. The 1931 Seven-Party Water Agreement established priorities for use of Colorado River water among seven California water contractors (see Wahl and Davis, 1986, p. 110). The first four priorities total 4.4 million acre-feet, which exhausts California's allocation under the Law of the River.[5] MWD argues that any additional water going to California from an interstate leasing agreement must be allocated according to the Seven-Party Agreement. If so, then the additional supply will fall under the fifth priority and most of it will go to MWD, because the fifth priority is shared by MWD (an additional 550,000 acre-feet) and San Diego (112,000 acre-feet). MWD's argument does not seem to carry much weight, however, since the Seven-Party Agreement is designed to allocate California's compact share within the state, whereas the Galloway proposal is a trade of a portion of Colorado's share. The consequences for reallocation within California are fur-

---

[5] In the first four priorities, water is allocated to the Palo Verde Irrigation District, the Yuma Project, the Imperial Irrigation District, the Coachella Valley Water District, and MWD.

ther diminished because San Diego has announced its intention to assign the water to MWD, thereby largely sidestepping the question of in-state priority.

Potential Advantages of Leasing Proposals

Absent any definitive legal ruling allowing leasing, the viability of marketing proposals along the Colorado River will depend on whether market transactions are perceived as beneficial to the various parties. There are several reasons why interstate trading may eventually be accepted.

First, in-state market transactions have become increasingly recognized as a means of solving water allocation problems in the West. Several states have revised their water laws to facilitate water trading. More generally, market transactions are useful where two parties can benefit from a reallocation of resources. At present, the population growth in the Lower Basin states has placed demands on the Colorado River greater than demands from the Upper Basin states. Therefore, some interim reallocation of the endowments of water rights provided by the Colorado River Compact through market transactions would be useful. Market trades would be a more flexible and acceptable method of meeting changed expectations than revision of the original compact allocations.

One question that naturally arises about leasing arrangements is how the lessee will find a replacement for the leased water. In the context of the Galloway proposal, of what value would a temporary water supply be to San Diego County? Would the county not be faced with a water crisis at the end of the forty-year lease term? And, in such a case, would the Upper Basin states not have reason to fear that Lower Basin water users could sufficiently influence Congress to reallocate Upper Basin water to the Lower Basin at that time? As already noted, this latter scenario is unlikely, given the long-standing nature of the Colorado River Compact and the force of the Supreme Court decrees in *Arizona v. California*. The principal value of a temporary leasing arrangement is that it lowers the cost of obtaining water during the lease period and postpones the time when expenses must be incurred for securing additional supplies (such as through the construction of additional storage facilities). Temporary supplies of water to southern California before buildup of diversions by the Central Arizona Project have been seen by California water users as advantageous simply because they postponed having to turn to more expensive sources.

There are several indications that the Lower Basin states could find substitutes for leased water by the end of the lease term. Completion of California's State Water Project as originally envisioned was postponed by Proposition 9 in 1982, when California voters rejected completion of the Peripheral Canal across the Sacramento–San Joaquin Delta. Leasing of water from the Upper Basin could provide an interim period for developing consensus within the state on the form that cross-Delta transfer of water should take. Alternatively, a 1988 agreement between the Imperial Irrigation District and MWD will allow MWD to use water conserved in the Imperial Irrigation District through investment in conservation measures, indicating that it may be possible to conserve substantial quantities of water and to divert them to urban use within California without reducing agricultural production (refer to chapter 5 and Wahl and Davis, 1986). MWD is also exploring other leasing and transfer arrangements with the Palo Verde Irrigation District and the Arvin-Edison Water Storage District in California.

Other types of management measures are available to MWD as a means of balancing supply and demand. As the price of water to final consumers rises, these customers use somewhat less water—about 0.4 percent for each 1 percent increase in price in the MWD service area.[6] Recent estimates indicate that if the twenty-seven member agencies of MWD were to bring the price of water to final consumers more in line with the long-run marginal costs of supply, then the quantity of water demanded would fall by 300,000–400,000 acre-feet per year (see Wahl and Davis, 1986, p. 117), resulting in a considerable savings in MWD supplies. Leasing an interim supply would give the many agencies involved several years to reach a consensus on how to implement a more efficient pricing structure within the MWD service area. In other words, there appear to be several supply and management alternatives available to MWD for finding substitutes for the leased water by the end of the lease term. Essential to the ability to shift to these substitute sources are the provisions for fifteen years' advance notice of nonrenewal and the gradual phase-down provisions of the Galloway proposal.

The principal advantage of a leasing arrangement would be that during the lease term, leased water could be less expensive than other supplies. Additions to the State Water Project, which would require new construction, might run as high as $210 per acre-foot if the

[6] See Wahl and Davis (1986, p. 116). For a range of estimates of the price elasticity of demand for water in southern California, see Conley (1967); Gershon (1960); and Schelhorse and coauthors (1974).

Peripheral Canal were built or $310 per acre-foot (in 1981 dollars) if it were not built (see Wahl and Davis, 1986, p. 114). As the demand for water grows in the Upper Basin states, the price demanded by Upper Basin users for their water could eventually make investments in the California State Water Project more attractive than leasing water from Colorado.

The main objection of downstream states to leasing is that they would have to pay for water that they receive at no charge. While this is true in the short term, certain longer-term advantages might outweigh the short-term losses. For instance, long-term leasing would provide greater certainty of supply to particular downstream users with low priorities for water, such as San Diego County and the state of Arizona. Under the present institutional arrangements, these supplies are subject to elimination over a prolonged dry period. Also, the timetable for development of Upper Basin water is uncertain. Renewed federal financing of Upper Basin water projects (the August 1988 legislation authorizing construction of the Animas–La Plata project is one example) or a sudden development of synthetic fuels there could accelerate upstream depletion. Long-term leases would ensure that Lower Basin users would receive specified minimum supplies for defined periods of time.

Perhaps most important, if upstream users were receiving an income from water flowing to Lower Basin uses, then they might be willing to postpone the development of certain Upper Basin uses. Under the current arrangement, for example, there is no price signal to upstream agricultural water users about the value of water to downstream users. Colorado irrigators can develop farming operations that value water at $15–$20 per acre-foot, with no knowledge that Lower Basin water users would be willing to pay $100 per acre-foot or more for the water. The threat that low-income-producing uses of water by Upper Basin states could displace more highly valued uses in the Lower Basin is all the more plausible because plans for federally subsidized projects in the Upper Basin have already been completed. If at some future dates these projects were to be funded, in much the same way as the Animas–La Plata project is now being initiated, then Upper Basin water users would be able, for a fraction of the cost, to put water to uses that would preempt higher-income-producing uses downstream. The existence of a zero price for unused Upper Basin water may currently be an advantage to downstream users, but it will not continue to be so if upstream development becomes imminent. There are also some additional benefits associated with increased water flow to the Lower Basin states, such as reduced salinity of Colorado River water (see table 10-2) and increased power production at Colorado River facilities.

The benefits of leasing arrangements may be more readily apparent for upstream states, which would receive income for water not currently put to use within the state. Lease revenues would serve as a substitute for the income lost by not developing the Upper Basin projects contemplated under the Colorado River Basin Project Act. Lease revenues could be used by these states for a variety of purposes, including financing of their own water resources development. Development might take place as part of a leasing arrangement, such as in the Galloway proposal, or it might occur at some later date or at different locations within the state.

Conclusions and the Importance of Clarifying Compact Rights

Whatever the allocation of initial water rights, there are almost certainly potential gains from trade. What is lacking at present, however, is legal clarification of what these rights are on the Colorado River in the context of interstate leasing proposals. Two principal legal outcomes are possible.

The first is that out-of-basin leasing of compact rights would simply not be allowable under the Law of the River. In this case, low-value uses in state A could preempt higher-value uses in state B, and there would be no potential for water users in state B to compensate state A for forgoing some of its marginal uses. Under this legal outcome, potential gains from interstate lease or sale of water would simply be prohibited, and Upper Basin states would have a strong incentive to seek federally subsidized water projects as one means of obtaining benefits from their allocations.

The second possible outcome is that out-of-basin leasing would be ruled as allowable under the Law of the River and that Upper Basin states could lease up to their full entitlements under the compact, defined either as 7.5 million acre-feet or as whatever water is left after ensuring delivery of a ten-year average of 7.5 million acre-feet per year to the Lower Basin at Lee Ferry, plus 1.5 million acre-feet to Mexico. One major consequence of this outcome would be that Arizona and California would have to pay Upper Basin states (or water users in those states) for water that they currently receive free of charge. In that event, all of the Upper Basin states would be expected to enter the market with their unused water. This increased quantity of water would likely result in a price for water considerably below that specified to San Diego in the Galloway proposal. The revenues from such interstate leasing would probably postpone lower-value uses of the water in the Upper Basin as well as attempts by Upper Basin states to seek federally subsidized storage facilities.

If leases to Lower Basin states were to be recognized as legitimate Upper Basin consumptive uses, then an increased total allocation of water use on the river would increase the frequency of shortage conditions. This would mean that in years of shortage Arizona would absorb all of the reductions allocated to the Lower Basin. Arizona could maintain an equivalent quantity of delivered water only to the degree that it purchased some portion of Upper Basin leases. This would renew an old battle between Arizona and California over allocation of Colorado River water. More specifically, any lease of Upper Basin water by water users in California would have two effects. First, the frequency of surpluses to the Lower Basin would decrease—surpluses to which Arizona has a 50 percent share.[7] Second, the frequency of shortages to the Lower Basin would increase—shortages that must be borne entirely by Arizona. In effect, California would be allowed to buy away some portion of Arizona's expected water use by making payments to water users in Colorado, but with no compensation to Arizona.

One view is that this would be entirely appropriate: a more rapid pace of Upper Basin development, such as was envisioned by the Colorado River Basin Project Act, would reduce Arizona's share by a similar amount. Alternatively, the basin states could adopt a working agreement that would protect Arizona's entitlement. One possible agreement would function as follows. For any leases or sales of water that had been put to beneficial use in the past, no other special rules would apply, since a reallocation of this water to another location would not affect the water supplies otherwise available to Arizona and California.[8] However, for leases or sales of water that had not yet been put to beneficial use in the Upper Basin, Arizona and California would receive equal quantities from any lease from an Upper Basin user to the Lower Basin during conditions of surplus on the river (this corresponds to the 50 percent division of surplus water in the compact). Arizona could either take delivery of its 50 percent share or resell it. Assuming the greater demand for the water was in California (such as from San Diego County), 100 percent of the water could be sold to California, provided that Arizona was sufficiently compensated financially to allow the transaction to occur.

[7] However, Arizona may not utilize its full 50 percent share even with operation of the Central Arizona Project.

[8] Any sale or lease of water between states on the Colorado River would also have to take into account the evaporation losses for water as it moves downstream.

During conditions of "intermediate shortage" on the river, the entire sale quantity would revert to Arizona. An "intermediate shortage" would be defined hydrologically as a shortage that occurs because of the lease of Upper Basin rights to the Lower Basin; it would not occur in the absence of such leases. Again, Arizona could strike an agreement with a California user either that Arizona would take actual delivery of some portion of the water during periods of shortage or that it would forgo that right for compensation. Finally, in "normal shortage" conditions, defined as those that would occur in the absence of interstate leasing agreements, the leased water would revert to use by California in keeping with the Supreme Court's decision in *Arizona v. California*. The point is that whatever the initial allocation of Colorado River water provided by the compact, there would be potential gains from trade. It may be possible to define an institutional setting for trades that is sufficiently close to current expectations that it would be acceptable to the parties to the compact.

The Bureau of Reclamation would also play a key role in any interstate leasing of water because of the Secretary of the Interior's jurisdiction over management of interstate allocation on the Colorado River. The bureau would need to keep track of the amount of leased water as it passed through the system of main-stem reservoirs, accounting for evaporation losses while at the same time protecting the previously established allocations of other Colorado River contractors.

The current opposition by a number of states and major water interests to the Galloway proposal should not be taken as opposition to the possibility for market trades on the Colorado River. Rather, most of the controversy concerning the Galloway proposal has been over the nature of compact rights. Market trading will probably not be possible until such property rights are clear to the states and water users involved. Lower Basin states that currently receive surplus water are unlikely to agree to purchase rights to water that they believe may be legally theirs at no cost, at least not until such time as Upper Basin development threatens the continued use of the water. Upper Basin states will be unwilling to undertake leasing if they believe it threatens the long-term nature of their water entitlement. Regardless of the current legal squabbles over the Galloway proposal, the broader question concerns sound public policy for managing Colorado River water. This perspective indicates that leasing arrangements could provide greater flexibility of water use. It would be economically wasteful for Upper Basin states to fully execute their rights through construction of expensive storage facilities before interstate leasing could take place.

References

Conley, Brian C. 1967. "Price Elasticity of the Demand for Water in Southern California," *Annals of Regional Science* vol. 1, pp. 180–189.

Gershon, Sam I. 1960. *Unit Water Use Model for the South Coastal Area* (Los Angeles, California Department of Water Resources, Southern District).

Gross, Sharon P. 1985. "The Galloway Project and the Colorado River Compacts: Will the Compacts Bar Transbasin Water Diversions?" *Natural Resources Journal* vol. 25, no. 4, pp. 935–960.

Landry, Stephanie. 1985. "The Galloway Proposal and Colorado Water Law: The Limits of the Doctrine of Prior Appropriation," *Natural Resources Journal* vol. 25, no. 4, pp. 961–983.

Nathanson, Milton N., ed. 1979. *Updating the Hoover Dam Documents*. Prepared for the U.S. Department of the Interior, Bureau of Reclamation (Washington, D.C., Government Printing Office).

Schelhorse, Larry D., Peggy Zimmerman, Jerome W. Milliman, David L. Shapiro, and Louis F. Weschler. 1974. *The Market Structure of the Southern California Water Industry*. Prepared for the U.S. Department of the Interior, Office of Water Resources Research (La Jolla, Calif., Copley International Corporation).

Wahl, Richard W., and Robert K. Davis. 1986. "Satisfying Southern California's Thirst for Water: Efficient Alternatives," in Kenneth D. Frederick, ed., *Scarce Water and Institutional Change* (Washington, D.C., Resources for the Future).

Part IV

Concluding Reflections

11

Concluding Reflections

No doubt some readers may disagree with or be dismayed by many of the observations and conclusions made in this book. They may be concerned about the degree to which the goals and financial terms of the 1902 reclamation program have been stretched to accommodate the interests of irrigation water users at the expense of the general taxpayer. Indeed, a good deal of post-1902 reclamation legislation can be seen as an attempt to support the de facto practices of project water users and the existing administrative policies of the Bureau of Reclamation. And modifications to the program are not limited to adjustments made in the first decades of the program or hardships incurred during the depression: they are as recent as the compromises made during passage of the Reclamation Reform Act of 1982 and the writing of the April 1987 acreage limitation regulations. Today, a nonresident investor in land served by a reclamation project, or even a foreign investor, may receive far more federal assistance than an early settler on a reclamation project. Certainly, tougher-minded administrators of the reclamation program could have molded federal policies in a different direction, and the public could demand more of current officials. More fundamentally, however, the results raise questions over whether an enterprise of long-term financial assistance for water supply can be appropriately structured as a federal program.

Even though the Bureau of Reclamation has acknowledged through its *Assessment '87* report that the era of large-scale new construction has drawn to a close, the program's financial incentives suggest otherwise. The repayment terms set by the Bureau of Reclamation for irrigation are more favorable to water users today than at any other time in the history of the program, with the exception of the high-inflation periods of the 1970s and early 1980s. Both the Carter and Reagan administrations sought to modify the repayment terms by requiring higher levels of cost-sharing from water users before initiating project construction. But under the Reagan administration, the Bureau of Reclamation, bowing to pressure from western senators, indicated that cost-sharing terms would be negotiated on a case-by-case basis, leaving open the possibility of only modest changes from past practice. Even if the pace of construction slows or no major new projects are initiated, federal financial assistance to keep current projects in operation through the dam safety and salinity control programs could someday easily outweigh the original construction cost subsidy.

As long as such favorable financial terms are embodied in federal legislation, there will be a good deal of pressure to use them. Water users argue that certain projects were promised long ago (such as those on the west slope of Colorado or the Garrison project in North Dakota[1]) and that the federal government should repair damage attributable to projects in which it participated (an argument applied in various forms to the dam safety and salinity control programs and the cleanup of Kesterson Reservoir). Of course, an equally strong case could be made that the federal government has already provided considerable financial assistance in constructing projects and that existing projects should only remain viable in our current economic environment if water users and states, as prime beneficiaries, accept responsibility for maintaining them.

Some readers are likely to feel that the financial terms of the reclamation program ought to require higher levels of cost-sharing and higher prices for water. These prescriptions are particularly appropriate for future federal construction, whether for new projects or for repairs or additions to existing projects, although past practice indicates the difficulty of achieving such goals. However, these pre-

---

[1] The Garrison project was authorized in 1965 to provide irrigation water to about 1 million acres in North Dakota, as well as municipal and industrial water supplies. The project was supported by North Dakota as compensation to that state for farmlands that were flooded by federal dams on the Missouri River. The first stage, irrigation of 250,000 acres, was opposed by Canada because of its adverse effects on streams flowing into that country. The project was also opposed by environmental groups principally because of its effect on wetlands and disruption of existing farmland. A stalemate ensued with no substantial funding for the project, but a compromise was sought by the Garrison Diversion Unit Commission in 1984. The commission's recommendations led to congressional authorization of a scaled-down project for irrigating about 131,000 acres. As of early 1989 the project was about 25 percent complete.

scriptions would do little to increase the efficiency of water use on the investment in current projects. Indeed, it is argued in this book that raising the prices for water on existing projects is in most cases impossible because existing contracts have fixed financial terms. These contracts confer certain property interests in water on the project beneficiaries, and these interests are vigorously defended.

Therefore, an alternative means must be sought to make the best use of the considerable resources that are in place—the dams and canals and the water resources that they deliver—to meet the future demands of the West. We may be tempted, as was John Wesley Powell, to want some federal authority to systematize the use of western water. However, we should consider that voluntary transfers of water—as long as they are overseen by local water entities and by state and federal water authorities to protect third-party water users and instream and other public uses of water—may actually serve us better.

Appendix

U.S. Department of the Interior's "Principles Governing Voluntary Water Transactions"

INTRODUCTORY NOTE

The following set of principles was issued by the U.S. Department of the Interior on December 16, 1988. These principles, approved by Assistant Secretary for Water and Science James Ziglar, are designed to guide Bureau of Reclamation review and approval of water transfer requests involving Bureau of Reclamation facilities. The principles embody, in part, the changes in administrative policies recommended in chapter 6 of this volume.

—R.W.W.

U.S. Department of the Interior
Washington, D.C.
December 16, 1988
"Principles Governing Voluntary Water Transactions
That Involve or Affect Facilities Owned or
Operated by the Department of the Interior"

PREAMBLE:

Transactions that involve water rights and supplies are occurring pursuant to State law with increasing frequency in the Nation, particularly in the Western United States. Such transactions include direct sale of water rights; lease of water rights; dry-year options on water rights; sale of land with associated water rights; and conservation investments with subsequent assignment of conserved water.

The Federal Government, as owner of a significant portion of the Nation's water storage and conveyance facilities, can assist State, Tribal, and local authorities in meeting local or regional water needs by improving or facilitating the improvement of management practices with respect to existing water supplies. Exchanges in type, location or priority of use that are accomplished according to State law can allow water to be used more efficiently to meet changing water demands, and also can protect and enhance the Federal investment in existing facilities. In addition, water exchanges can serve to improve many local and Indian reservation economies.

DOI's [the Department of the Interior's] interest in voluntary water transactions proposed by others derives from an expectation that, to an increasing degree, DOI will be asked to approve, facilitate, or otherwise accommodate such transactions that involve or affect facilities owned or operated by its agencies. The DOI also wishes to be responsive to the July 7, 1987, resolution of the Western Governors' Association, which was reaffirmed at the Association's July 12, 1988, meeting, that the DOI "develop and issue a policy to facilitate water transfers which involve water and/or facilities provided by the Bureau of Reclamation."

The following principles are intended to afford maximum flexibility to State, Tribal, and local entities to arrive at mutually agreeable solutions to their water resource problems and demands. At the same time, these principles are intended to be clear as to the legal, contractual, and regulatory concerns that DOI must consider in its evaluation of proposed transactions.

For the purpose of this statement of principles, all proposed transactions must be between willing parties to the transaction and must be in accordance with applicable State and Federal law. Presentation of a proposal by one party, seeking Federal support or action against other parties, will not be considered in the absence of substantial support for the proposal among affected non-Federal parties.

Voluntary Water Transaction Principles

1. Primacy in water allocation and management decisions rests principally with the States. Voluntary water transactions under this policy must be in accordance with applicable State and Federal laws.

2. The Department of the Interior (DOI) will become involved in facilitating a proposed voluntary water transaction only when it can be accomplished without diminution of service to those parties otherwise being served by such Federal resources, and when:

   (a) there is an existing Federal contractual or other legal obligation associated with the water supply; or

   (b) there is an existing water right held by the Federal government that may be affected by the transaction; or

   (c) it is proposed to use Federally-owned storage or conveyance capacity to facilitate the transaction; or

   (d) the proposed transaction will affect Federal project operations; and

   (e) the appropriate State, Tribal, or other non-Federal political authorities or subdivisions request DOI's active involvement.

3. DOI will participate in or approve transactions when there are no adverse third-party consequences, or when such third-party consequences will be heard and adjudicated in appropriate State forums, or when such consequences will be mitigated to the satisfaction of the affected parties.

4. As a general rule, DOI's role will be to facilitate transactions that are in accordance with applicable State and Federal law and proposed by others. In doing so, DOI will consider the positions of the affected State, Tribal, and local authorities. DOI will not suggest a specific transaction except when it is part of an Indian water rights settlement, a solution to a water rights controversy, or when it may provide a dependable water supply the provision of which otherwise would involve the expenditure of Federal funds. Such a suggestion would not be carried out without the concurrence of all affected non-Federal parties.

5. The fact that the transaction may involve the use of water supplies developed by Federal water resource projects shall not be considered during evaluation of a proposed transaction.

6. One of DOI's objectives will be to ensure that the Federal government is in an acceptable financial, operational, and contractual position following accomplishment of a transaction under this policy. Unless required explicitly by existing law, contracts, or regulations, DOI will refrain from burdening the transaction with additional costs, fees or charges, except for those costs actually incurred by DOI in performance of its functions in a particular transaction.

7. DOI will consider, in cooperation with appropriate State, Tribal and local authorities, necessary measures that may be required to mitigate any adverse environmental effects that may arise as a result of the proposed transaction.

Index